PLAS

PITT
LATIN
AMERICAN
SERIES

Intervention,
Revolution, and
Politics in Cuba,
1913-1921

Intervention, Revolution, and Politics in Cuba, 1913-1921

Louis A. Pérez, Jr.

University of Pittsburgh Press

Published by the University of Pittsburgh Press, Pittsburgh, Pa. 15260
Feffer and Simons, Inc., London
Manufactured in the United States of America

Library of Congress Cataloging in Publication Data

Pérez, Louis A   1943-
  Intervention, revolution, and politics in Cuba,
1913-1921.

  (Pitt Latin American series)
  Bibliography: p. 185
  Includes index.
   1.   Cuba—Politics and government—1909-1933.
2.   United States—Foreign relations—Cuba.   3.   Cuba—
Foreign relations—United States.   4.   Platt Amendment.
I.   Title
F1787.P42   320.9'7291'062   78-53601
ISBN O-8229-3386-1

To Susan

Contents

Acknowledgments

The completion of this study is in no small measure the result of the interest and support I have received in the last several years from a number of institutions and individuals. I am especially sensible of the unvarying courtesy of the staffs of the National Archives and the Library of Congress in Washington, D.C. Judith A. Schiff, of the Sterling Memorial Library, Yale University; Nancy C. Prewitt, of the Western Historical Manuscript Collection, University of Missouri; and Allen H. Stokes, of the South Caroliniana Library, University of South Carolina, provided invaluable assistance in the course of my research at these institutions. I also received unfailing cooperation from the staffs of the Historical Branch of the United States Marine Corps, Washington, D.C., the Franklin D. Roosevelt Library, the Robert Frost Library at Amherst College, and the Alderman Library at the University of Virginia.

During the final stages of writing I had the good fortune to conduct a seminar on twentieth-century Cuba at the University of South Florida. The students in this class assisted me in more ways than I can recount. Their questions and discussions forced me to crystallize my thoughts and formulate my approaches to the subject of interventionism in Plattist Cuba. They provided gratifying response to, and stimulation for, many of the ideas developed in the following pages.

This study, further, is in no small way the result of the unfailing cooperation and assistance of the staff at the University of South Florida Library. Florence Jandreau and James Vastine reduced to the commonplace feats of extraordinary magnitude through an otherwise cumbersome interlibrary loan system. Donna Asbell, by her assistance with public documents, saved me hours of what, in many cases, would have been fruitless searching. I owe a particular debt to William L. and Claudia C. Stewart, who, while with the University of South Florida Library, shared my interests in the Caribbean generally and Cuba specifically and embarked on an acquisitions program for the library that gave this study its initial impetus. The University of South Florida system of released time relieved me of my teaching responsibilities for one term and provided me the opportunity to complete the research.

Certain persons contributed to specific aspects of the study. The assistance of Wanda Bradley Morris was essential for the completion of various sections of the study. I am especially obligated to José Keselman. Hours of conversation with him during which we ranged over Cuba's nineteenth- and twentieth-century experiences allowed my understanding of the dimensions of the Cuban past to become sharper. He saved me from egregious errors, but contributed even more to my thinking through disagreement with particular formulations and explanations. A special debt is owed to Steven F. Lawson, who listened patiently and responded critically as my approaches to the issues of early twentieth-century Cuba assumed final form. Over the years, an occasional "¿qué es la vida?" kindled the warmth, humor, and affection that provided the moral subsidy necessary to counteract those moments of solitary confrontations with the past. I am grateful to Robert P. Ingalls and Harry E. Vanden, both of whom provided support and encouragement throughout the course of this undertaking. To James W. Silver, a very special person, a very special thanks for sharing with me in generous dosages his cynicism and sensitivity toward both the past and the present. I am also especially grateful to Nelson Alba, who shared with me important rare materials dealing with the Menocal years. It is not likely that these materials exist anywhere outside of Cuba; they proved central to various portions of this study. My debt to Peggy Cornett is not repaid here — it is simply acknowledged. If it were only the hours of proofreading drafts too many to count, or the helpful suggestions at various stages of this study, the task would be relatively simple. The obligation goes beyond that, however, and involves a deeply felt appreciation for the years of support and assistance. We all owe her a bit more than we dare admit. Most of all, to Susan, for unremitting support and an inexhaustible fund of forbearance for one hopelessly lost in the Cuban past. Amara and Maya remain an important source of comfort and support. And to all those whom, for one reason or another, it is impossible to acknowledge here individually — my gratitude. I share gratefully whatever merit this study may have with all the aforementioned persons and institutions. The shortcomings are wholly mine.

Introduction

The insertion of the Platt Amendment into the center of Cuban national processes in 1901 had an unsettling influence on the Republic. Very quickly, the institutionalized presence of the specter of American intervention made that intervention inevitable; indeed, intervention was as much a cause of instability as it was the result. A national political culture emerged in Cuba organized around Havana's accommodation to, and often manipulation of, the requirements of American policy. Cuba's treaty relationship to the United States generated in the republic a system in which national authorities were held accountable to legitimizing agencies abroad. Under the Platt Amendment, Washington emerged as the center of Cuban politics; increasingly, the Cuban political drama was played for the benefit of an American audience. With foreknowledge of the American commitment to intervene to protect "life, property and individual liberty," Cuban leaders organized a political system around the treaty presence of the United States. By the second decade of the Plattist regimen, American policy had become an integral part of Cuban politics and was one of the most active components of the national system.

United States intervention in Plattist Cuba functioned in a three dimension politico-diplomatic construct. Far from representing the unilateral impulse of a distant metropolitan officialdom, intervention responded in varying degrees to the requirements of larger policy imperatives, the needs of U.S. economic interests, and the demands of the Cuban national system. Indeed, U.S. policy, in general, was indissolubly linked to the vagaries of Cuban politics. The American presence loomed over the polity, used by all power contenders seeking advantage over national rivals. Fierce internal rivalries and intraelite struggles for national hegemony provided the basis for collaboration between Cuban politicians and American policymakers. Political rivals in search of advantage served as active and faithful collaborators with the interventionist power. This collaboration was vastly facilitated in a system

where political issues rarely transcended personalities. Not infrequent-
ly, the United States emerged the captive of political intriguers in
Havana who, over the years, learned to manipulate the Platt Amendment to their advantage with considerable skill and success.

A distinct logic came to characterize the reciprocal behavior of
Cubans and Americans. Cubans not only accepted the reality of U.S.
hegemony but legitimized American preeminence through complicity
and cooperation and, whenever possible and expedient, manipulated
American preeminence to their own advantage. Cuban collaboration
was at once the necessary cause and the inevitable effect of U.S.
hegemony; the intervenors and the intervened together underwrote the
viability of the client state.

American hegemony, however, generated sufficient contradictions to
limit U.S. influence over, and control of, Cuban national processes. At
best, hegemonic relationships represented a mutually self-serving system, during the periods when the interests of politicians in Havana coincided with the objectives of policymakers in Washington. At other
times, Cuban leaders managed to carve out of the Platt Amendment an
enclave of considerable political autonomy, fully exploiting the limitations and contradictions of American policy.

Between 1913 and 1921, many of the features of the Plattist system
began to assume permanent form. Washington began to appreciate fully
some of the contradictions of a Cuba policy based on a narrow interpretation of the Platt Amendment. This realization spurred Washington to
seek alternative forms through which to preserve and promote hegemonic relationships. During these years, the State Department came to
appreciate the extent to which Cubans manipulated American policy
within the context of prevailing interpretations of the Platt Amendment.
American policymakers showed an increasing disinclination to continue
to intervene militarily, devising in the process alternative controls over
the Cuban national system. During this critical period, the United States
moved gradually from ending political disorders by armed intervention
to preventing disorders by politico-diplomatic intervention. At the same
time, the Cuban political system was experiencing severe dislocations.
Traditional party structures collapsed. The bases of political power nar-
rowed, forcing political contenders to seek new sources of alliances.
American capitalists and the Washington policy officialdom moved to

underwrite the solvency of an increasingly discredited and bankrupt republican elite, thereby prolonging its life for another decade.

Washington's interpretation of the Platt Amendment as narrowly defining American authority to intervene, gave way to a view that the Permanent Treaty of 1903 was a carte blanche justifying interventions of all kinds. The lowering of intervention thresholds necessarily involved major revisions of existing interpretations of the Platt Amendment and, concomitantly, the development of the appropriate politico-diplomatic apparatus to meet the new requirements of policy. That they were ultimately successful reflected the specific needs of Cubans at the moment as well as the policy objectives of the United States. The withdrawal of marines — never again to return — soon after the arrival in Havana of General Enoch H. Crowder in 1921 as the "Special Representative of the President," signaled, in more than just symbolic terms, the qualitative nature of the transformation in U.S.-Cuban relations.

*Intervention,
Revolution, and
Politics in Cuba,
1913-1921*

1.

Politics, Diplomacy, and Reelection: The Cuban Electoral Crisis of 1916

Conservative Politics and American Diplomacy

President Mario G. Menocal approached the end of his first term the benefactor of American good will. In 1915, State Department officials in Washington and Havana could review the preceding three years of Conservative government with considerable satisfaction. In contrast to Mexico and the Caribbean, where political conditions were unsettled, Cuba under Menocal conformed in exemplary fashion to American standards of order, stability, and prosperity. The presidential elections of 1912 had seen Liberal incumbents relinquish national administration to Conservative opponents without complications. To be sure, rumors of a conspiracy among disgruntled officials of the outgoing Liberal government of José Miguel Gómez produced some fear in Havana that dissident *miguelista* partisans planned to block the inauguration of the Conservative president-elect.[1] The transfer of power, however, occurred without incident, inspiring confidence in the United States that Cuba had taken an important step forward in self-government. "This orderly transmission of authority," Woodrow Wilson congratulated Menocal in 1913, "is most gratifying and seems to indicate that the Cuban people have successfully undergone one of the severest tests of republican government."[2]

If American officials derived a certain satisfaction from the orderly conduct of national affairs in Cuba, they greeted the election of Mario G. Menocal in 1912 with particular enthusiasm. The new president was a representative of the nineteenth-century creole families that early anticipated, and ultimately lent support to, American hegemony in Cuba.

3

After living in the United States for some ten years, during which he completed his education at the Maryland College of Agriculture and Cornell University, the future president returned to Cuba to participate in the struggle for independence from Spain. During the American occupation from 1898 to 1902, Menocal served the military government in many capacities, including chief of the Havana police, inspector of public works, and chief of the Lighthouse Board. With the establishment of the republic in 1902, Menocal retired from public life to join the Cuban-American Sugar Corporation as manager of the newly organized Chaparra Sugar Estate in Oriente Province. Within a decade, Menocal had transformed Chaparra into one of the most successful sugar enterprises on the island. By the time of his election in 1912, Menocal's interests in, and devotion to, the United States had earned him the reputation of being "more American than Cuban."[3]

Political relations between Cuba and the United States during Menocal's term more than justified Washington's original optimism. The Cuban president scrupulously honored his preinaugural pledge to work within existing treaty relations to resolve all outstanding issues between the two countries.[4] The Cuban economy prospered. Menocal's first three years overlapped the war in Europe; sugar prices increased steadily. The sugar harvest in the year of Menocal's inauguration sold for 2.15 cents a pound. A year later, the price of sugar rose to 2.75 cents. By 1915, sugar was selling at 3.63 cents a pound, and in the following year, it reached an all-time high of 4.77 cents.[5]

Under the Conservatives, moreover, U.S. control over Cuban sugar production increased. Established American companies reorganized and expanded holdings in the traditional sugar-producing zones; new enterprises, in search of additional land, moved into the virgin territories of Camagüey and Oriente. By the end of the decade, U.S. capital controlled some 50 percent of Cuban sugar production.[6]

The one area of conflict between Havana and Washington involved unsettled financial issues remaining from preceding administrations. Two specific disputes, both involving acts of questionable legality on the part of Menocal's predecessor, troubled U.S.-Cuban relations during the Conservative administration. A paving and sewerage contract awarded to the McGiveny-Rokeby Company during the American provisional government of 1906-1909 had lapsed before completion due to a shortage of funds. Negotiations between Havana and the J. P. Morgan Company for a $15 million loan to resume the project drew protests from Speyer and Company, the financial agents underwriting the original contract. Negotiations with J. P. Morgan, Speyer argued, violated the preferential rights earlier awarded under the Gómez government. Menocal disputed his predecessor's legal authority to grant preferential terms. Disregarding earlier arrangements, Menocal pursued negotiations with Morgan for a new loan.[7]

A second dispute proved more troublesome. In 1913, Menocal revoked a concession granted two years earlier by the Liberals to a newly organized Cuban Ports Company. The original contract, prepared by Norman H. Davis, president of the Trust Company of Cuba, joined British, Spanish, and American capital in the Ports Company to undertake the dredging and improvement of a number of Cuban ports; in return, the company received revenues secured from tonnage and port dues over a period of thirty years.[8] In the first year of his administration, Menocal canceled the concession on the grounds that it had been granted illegally. Menocal subsequently refused to negotiate the outstanding claims of the stockholders.[9] In 1915, after prolonged litigation, the Cuban Supreme Court upheld the president's actions.

In both disputes, foreign capital appealed to the State Department for assistance. Owing in part to prodding from Washington and in part to domestic political considerations, late in his first term Menocal committed his administration in principle to search for a compromise settlement satisfactory to all parties concerned.[10]

The Political Context of Reelection

A full year before the 1916 national elections, Menocal shattered national quiescence with an announcement of his intention to seek a second term of office. Presidential reelection had long been a source of intense national controversy. In 1901 the Cuban Constituent Assembly — after hours of acrimonious debate — in principle approved the juridical validity of reelection.[11] In the arena of practical politics, however, distant from the debates on constitutional theory, reelection served to exacerbate political controversy and intensify partisan struggles. Reelectionism quickly became associated with government fraud, coercion, and violence. Indeed, for those in office, incumbency offered monopoly access to the instruments of state with which to promote reelection; the electoral agencies, the courts, and the armed forces, mobilized in the pursuit of partisan objectives, conferred on the incumbent advantages well beyond the reach of his challenger.[12] A constitutionally legitimate end often involved unconstitutional means.

The passions aroused by reelectionism, however, reflected considerably more than an outcry of injured constitutional sensibilities. Monopolization of national office by one party or one faction of a party threatened to block access to the sinecures of state for others. Insofar as the state served as a major source of employment,[13] elections institutionalized a process among political contenders by which all participants shared, more or less equally, a guaranteed access to government.

The forms of conventional electoral competition in the republic disguised the urgent nonpolitical issues of national elections. The republican elite had experienced a skewed development in the closing decades of the colony. Between 1868 and 1898, the Cuban elite took on its definitive characteristics, organizing not around the acquisition and expansion of control over the means of production, but, rather, around the cause of independence. In the course of thirty years of intermittant warfare, exile, and imprisonment, the creoles' hold over the sources of wealth grew increasingly tenuous; by 1898, much of the island's traditional sources of wealth had been absorbed by non-Cubans. Without the funds with which to revive the estates damaged during the war and make good on loans secured before the insurrection, without the positions from which to aggregate capital, the Cuban *libertadores* came to constitute an elite organized around the quest of political office as a means to economic well-being.

Even before the establishment of the republic, Cuban politics had acquired a particular distributive quality. "We are growing to be a nation of petty office seekers," General Enrique Collazo lamented in early 1899.[14] With so much of the national wealth passing into the hands of foreigners, national office in the republic guaranteed the victorious candidate and his immediate constituency access to the levers of resource and benefit allocation in the only enterprise wholly Cuban — government. Few *libertadores* were able to overcome the economic pressures of the early republic through pursuits other than politics. By 1920, the census inspector of Oriente Province could not find twenty men, "good and true [and] out of politics," to serve as municipal enumerators. "As a matter of fact," Ricardo Navarro complained to his superiors, "this last requisite is a serious handicap for such a selection. In a country in which the limited scope of the Civil Service Law leaves a large number of well paid positions within the reach of those who conquer in political struggles, the different parties have tried, and generally succeeded, in attracting all clever, energetic and active men. Those 'out of politics' are either well-to-do persons to whom the modest salary of an enumerator does not appeal in the least; or the refuse of the community, men unqualified for regular work and not thought worthy of the effort to attract them."[15] Reviewing the state of the republic some ten years after independence, Irene Wright observed:

> We have, then, in Cuba, a country owned by foreigners, the govern-
> ment of which is supported by foreigners, but administered by
> Cubans, after such a fashion, however (foreigners have not the suf-
> frage), that these Cubans in office are not answerable to the real
> source of their salaries for the disbursement of these or other reve-
> nues, paid in by foreigners, nor in any legitimate manner can they be
> obligated to consider the welfare of the country (owned by foreign-
> ers) or of the business conducted (by foreigners) within its bound-
> aries. As at present constituted this is the most expensive government
> on earth, and those who operate it (the Cuban office-holding class)
> have every reason to labor to make it even more so, since its ex-
> travagancies run to salaries, which they receive, and to even more
> outrageous contracts and concessions, on which they get liberal
> "rake-offs."[16]

For the members of the generation·of '95, many of whom had de-
voted the better part of their adulthood to the disinterested pursuit of
Cuban independence, republican politics served as the means of acquir-
ing and expanding personal economic power. Success at the polls offered the candidate, his family and personal supporters, and the party
rank and file in general the security and well-being attending control of
the apparatus of government.[17] Hence, reelection designs in which access of the incumbent to the machinery of state all but formally guaran-

teed him a second term violated the informal intraelite understanding by threatening to withdraw from circulation the sources of economic well-being. By virtue simply of the resources available to the chief executive seeking another term, elections involving the incumbent offered the opposition little more than the opportunity to participate in — and thereby lend legitimacy to — a ritualized sanction of presidential *imposición*. Reelectionism contravened the protocol implicit in the electoral method of circulating public office. The American minister in Havana detected, if only partially, the unstated issues of reelection when he observed that Cuban politicians had a "kind of hysterical sentiment against the reelection of a President."[18] If constitutional means failed in the end to dislodge incumbent authorities according to the prescribed electoral methods, the nature of the stakes required the opposition, alternatively, to resort to force.

After 1905-1906, a resort to arms to protest reelection fraud no longer represented simply a hypothetical response to a theoretical problem. The reelection of President Tomás Estrada Palma — the result, the Liberals charged, of widespread government fraud and abuse — had plunged the island into civil war in 1906.[19] Only American intervention in response to Estrada Palma's appeal for assistance had saved the beleaguered Moderate government from falling to the advancing insurgent armies.

Subsequent inquiry into the conduct of the 1905 elections by the United States upheld Liberal charges of government irregularities and abuse.[20] Elections three years later, supervised by the American provisional government, swept Liberals into national office, further vindicating in the eyes of party leaders the efficacy of the decision to rebel in 1906. Armed protest in 1906, even if thwarted by American intervention, had nonetheless restored to the electoral system the balance jeopardized by reelectionism.

After 1906, political leaders of all parties renounced reelectionism. The experience of a postelection civil war and the compromise of national sovereignty resulting from the American occupation had in principle stigmatized reelectionism. A disclaimer of intent to seek reelection became a necessary, if perfunctory, campaign pledge of all presidential candidates. "The principle of nonreelection," candidate Menocal pronounced solemnly in 1912, "is the firmest support of peace."[21]

Likewise, in the following year, the incumbent Liberals dutifully relinquished national office to the opposition party.[22]

President Menocal's decision in 1915 to seek another term, therefore, struck Cuba with the impact of a thunderbolt. Leaders of both parties received news of Menocal's plans with considerable alarm. Many in the president's own party reacted adversely to renominating Menocal.[23] Insofar as renomination functioned within the party structure in much the same fashion as reelection in the national system, a second term for the incumbent promised to confine public office to the *menocalista* faction of the Conservative party.

Various sectors of the party leadership, including appointed and elected Conservative officials, condemned reelectionist politics. Conservative party chieftain Enrique Loynaz del Castillo, reminding Menocal of his campaign pledge in 1912, appealed to the president to withdraw his candidacy for the best interest of Cuba and the party.[24] Elected Conservatives at both the national and provincial level similarly counseled the president to disavow reelection. Representative Wilfredo Fernández of Pinar del Río emerged as the most outspoken Conservative opponent of Menocal's reelection. Patriotic Cubans, Fernández exhorted, remembered all too well the "unforgettable national calamities" resulting from reelectionist designs ten years earlier; to lead the republic knowingly again to the brink of that political abyss was tantamount to treason.[25] Fernando Freyre de Andrade, the Conservative mayor of Havana and the architect of the abortive Moderate reelection effort in 1905, called the president's attention to Estrada Palma's experience. The events of 1905-1906, Freyre warned, demonstrated the certainty that reelection was impossible, leading inevitably to "violence or failure."[26]

Reelection failed to generate much support within Menocal's own administration. Vice-President Enrique José Varona declined the invitation to stand with Menocal for a second term. Varona opposed reelection unequivocally, declaring his intention "to rebuke through example."[27] "I have always been opposed to reelections," Varona announced, "I was opposed to them before belonging to any party and I have continued doing so within the Conservative party."[28] The Secretary of Sanitation Enrique Núñez joined the growing list of disgruntled Conservatives publicly denouncing Menocal's reelectionist designs.

Secretary of Agriculture, Commerce, and Labor Emilio Núñez, himself the frontrunner to succeed Menocal within the party, submitted his resignation from the cabinet in protest of the president's plan to seek another term.[29]

The dispute among Conservatives over the president's bid for reelection continued unabated throughout 1915. In January 1916, an unsettled Conservative party, hardly more than a collection of hostile factions positioned on the issue of reelection, convened to nominate a presidential candidate. Hours of debate and repeated appeals failed to discourage the *menocalista* bid for a second term. In the end, the sizeable antireelectionist faction of the party proved incapable of blocking the *menocalista* drive. Through a subversion of convention procedures, irregularities that included illegal practices, stuffed ballot boxes, and outright bribery, the reelectionist forces obtained for the president the Conservative party nomination for a second term.[30] The convention proceedings, however, further discredited the reelectionist effort and widened the breach between the newly nominated president and the large antireelectionist sector of the Conservative party. Some Conservative leaders bolted the party; others simply refused to endorse the national ticket. In the end, the successful reelectionist forces could find little comfort in the outcome of the convention. The nomination had come dearly — ultimately at the very cost of party support in the election. Menocal prepared for the 1916 campaign at the head of a demoralized party, without the unanimity of purpose or the organizational cohesion necessary to win the November balloting.

Liberals approached the 1916 elections with even greater misgivings than their Conservative rivals. Certainly the proceedings at the Conservative convention did little to allay Liberal fears. As the party victimized by reelectionist abuses in 1905, the prospect of again campaigning against an incumbent opponent caused Liberals to view Menocal's candidacy with considerable alarm. As early as 1915, Liberal spokesman Raimundo Cabrera warned Conservatives that any effort to retain the presidency through "intimidation and violence" would have serious repercussions.[31] With the nomination of Alfredo Zayas in early 1916, the Liberals proceeded to organize their campaign almost exlusively around the issue of reelection.

The Diplomatic Context of Electoral Politics

Both Conservatives and Liberals approached the national elections in 1916 fully sensitive to the diplomatic context of national politics as well as to domestic political considerations. The conditions imposed on Cuban independence at the end of the American military occupation in 1902 had effectively subjected Cuban sovereignty to U.S. supervision. "The Government of Cuba," Article III of the Platt Amendment stipulated, "consents that the United States may exercise the right to intervene for the preservation of Cuban independence, the maintenance of a government adequate for the protection of life, property and individual liberty, and for discharging the obligations with respect to Cuba imposed by the Treaty of Paris on the United States."[32] Appended originally to the Cuban Constitution of 1901 and drafted two years later into treaty form, the Platt Amendment came to serve as the cornerstone of Cuban-American relations.

By virtue of the Platt Amendment, Washington assumed ultimate responsibility for underwriting the solvency of Cuban national administration. The very conduct of national politics emerged as a source of policy concern in Washington. The American presence in Cuba loomed pervasively, functioning always as the understood coefficient of all political strategies.

In principle, the Platt Amendment tended to invest American support effectively in constituted authorities. "I have consistently given," the American minister wrote in 1910, "all practicable support to the existing administration — because it is *existing* and not because I have any special sympathy with it or its methods."[33] The American commitment to constituted government conferred on incumbent authorities considerable advantage in the arena of national politics. Specifically, the Platt Amendment, as the understood basis of U.S. Cuban policy, encouraged outright an incumbent party, assured of American diplomatic support, to embark on a course of partisan excesses, including reelection through illegal, if ostensibly constitutional, methods. As early as 1912, General Enoch H. Crowder, the U.S. legal advisor in Cuba during the second intervention, cautioned Washington against becoming captive to the political maneuvers of any single faction in Cuba. With a sober understanding of the subtle political crosscurrents of U.S.-Cuban treaty relations, Crowder warned:

> Having once gained the official recognition of this government, and so become "the duly constituted authority," . . . it could by fraudulent practices as was undoubtedly done in the last election for President prior to the intervention in 1906, secure its apparent reelection, and if the protest became too violent to be overcome, such government would only have to notify the President of the United States and request assistance. It would then become the duty of the President to furnish such armed assistance as might be necessary to overcome resistance and to establish the fraudulent government in power. The right of a people to change their rulers, and in fact to change their form of government when it becomes subversive of the principle for which it is instituted and to substitute other securities for their protection, is essential to the preservation of a free government. . . . Provision should be so made that the United States will not be made the blind instrument for fastening an undesirable or fraudulent government upon a people for whom we profess to be preserving a free government.[34]

Crowder's plea went unheeded. On the contrary, within a year, Woodrow Wilson proclaimed constitutionality as the cornerstone of U.S. Latin American policy. In condemning as a matter of principle all changes of government occurring outside prescribed parliamentary norms, Wilson's policy formulations increased the advantages of incumbency and formally extended to much of Latin America what had been vaguely implicit in Cuba under the Platt Amendment. "We are the friends of constitutional govenment in America," Wilson averred. "We are more than its friends, we are its champions."[35]

In Cuba, the renewed U.S. emphasis on constitutionality offered Conservative leaders ideal conditions under which to contemplate another term. Conservative leaders, as well as the leaders of the old Moderate party before them, understood the Platt Amendment to commit American support to the de jure government against all internal challenges.[36] Incumbent politicos, in full command of the constitutional approaches to national office and invested with American support as the duly constituted authorities, could proceed with reelectionist designs and, with utter impunity, defy the opposition to take up arms in protest. "The American people," Wilson informed Menocal in 1913, "are the friends of peace and can have no sympathy with those who seek to seize power of government in order to advance their personal ambitions. There can be no lasting peace in such circumstances."[37] Wilson's explicit condemnation of unconstitutional changes of government, corroborating Havana's general understanding of the Platt Amendment, served further to encourage reelection in Cuba. American policy offered the opposition in the electoral system no sanctioned alternative to "constitutional" usurpation of power other than passive acquiescence. Preoccupied with stability rather than with the quality of constitutionality, Washington took little policy cognizance of constitutional usurpation by incumbent authorities. Indeed, Menocal's decision to seek reelection may have been in large measure inspired by the assumption that Wilson's policy all but formally guaranteed the incumbent a second term.[38]

If the Platt Amendment and Wilsonian policy in principle encouraged Conservative incumbents to hazard the perils inherent in reelection, in practice American diplomacy offered the Liberal opposition sufficient precedents around which to organize an antireelectionist electoral strategy based on a resort to arms. Two compelling factors moved the threat of revolution to a position of central importance in the Liberal election strategy. First, the only leverage available to the Liberal opposition with which to persuade the incumbent administration to restrain partisan excesses lay in raising the specter of revolution by protesting fraud and coercion at the polls. In this sense, the invocation of revolution served notice on national authorities that an unlawful imposition of a second term would not go unchallenged. Secondly, and perhaps ultimately of greater significance, the very construct of U.S. Cuban policy — Washington's general policy protestations under Wilson notwithstanding — had demonstrated to the Liberals the efficacy of the insurrectionary response to constitutional usurpation of power. The successful resort to arms in 1906 had established a compelling political precedent. In raising the specter of revolution, the Liberals effectively converted the conduct of elections from a purely national process to a proceeding with the potential of directly impinging on Cuban-American treaty relations. In effect, Liberal strategy appealed directly to Washington and sought to generate pressure on the State Department to assume a measure of responsibility for honest elections. If, in fact, the consequences of a disputed election threatened "life, property and individual liberty," as the Liberals announced in advance, then the very conduct of elections passed under the purview of the Platt Amendment.[39] In this manner, the Liberal leadership sought to mobilize from extranational sources pressure on national authorities to conduct honest elections — elections they were confident of winning if properly conducted.[40] In late 1915, Raimundo Cabrera made this point particularly clear. Taking advantage of a visit to the United States, Cabrera warned American officials that reelection through fraud and violence "would very seriously jeopardize the future peace of the country."[41]

Liberals did not issue preelection threats of revolution idly or without some measure of credibility. The threatened appeal to arms represented a calculated and deliberate attempt to neutralize some of the outstanding advantages of the president's incumbency. The precedent of 1906, moreover, in which the United States had displaced an incumbent government incapable of restoring order, encouraged Liberals to believe that if, in the end, election irregularities did indeed drive them to arms, revolution would produce minimally the conditions requiring American intervention. Inasmuch as the Platt Amendment committed the United States to maintain "a government adequate for the protection of life, property and individual liberty," the inability of authorities in Havana to suppress political disorders obligated Washington, in fulfillment of its treaty commitments, to arbitrate the dispute. Having fared well once before in a similar situation, the Liberals had every reason to welcome American arbitration. "Once let the Liberals be convinced," the resident Associated Press correspondent in Havana speculated, "that, with all their preponderance of voters, they have no chance of victory and we shall see Cuba on the brink of another revolution. . . . Should they see themselves about to lose the election by reason of military intimidation or by being counted out, they will not hesitate to repeat the tactics of 1906 and take such action as will precipitate an intervention, as something infinitely preferable to the continuance of submission to Conservative rule."[42] Conservative frauds would subsequently be exposed, the

Liberal cause again vindicated, and, presumably, as in 1908, in elections supervised by American authorities, Liberals would return to national office. Expectation among Liberals of U.S. intervention found further corroboration in Wilson's actions in the Dominican Republic in 1915 and in Haiti the following year. Twice in the preceding eighteen months, the United States had responded to Caribbean political disorders with armed intervention; American policy responses elsewhere in the Caribbean served to confirm among Liberal leaders the wisdom of the political strategy contemplated for the election year.

The precedent of 1906 dominated the Liberal campaign. Much of Zayas's politicking consisted of admonitions to the Conservatives to hold fair elections; few opportunities passed without Liberals reminding the administration of the consequences of electoral fraud. The Liberal newspaper *Heraldo de Cuba* reminded Menocal that the 1906 revolution did not protest ''constitutional rights authorizing reelection, but the reelection of a resolute government and the means it used to secure reelection.''[43] Liberal leaders repeatedly invoked the anti-Estrada revolt as a parallel between 1906 and 1916. Liberal Speaker of the House Orestes Ferrara extolled the uprising of 1906 as ''patriotic'' and ''purifying,'' intimating that a repetition of the 1905 election frauds in 1916 would result in similar consequences.[44] ''Either Zayas or revolution,'' campaign tracts warned.[45] ''The reelection of President Menocal,'' Liberals vowed, ''would mean a revolution.''[46]

Most American official observers accepted Liberal threats at face value. In Santiago de Cuba, the American consul reported that reelection through fraud would likely produce ''such a serious condition of affairs'' as to make American intervention in the dispute ''quite probable.''[47] ''There may come some serious trouble,'' the American consul in Antilla predicted, ''should the present administration remain in power.''[48]

By 1916, both candidates prepared for the November elections fully satisfied that their respective approaches reflected most accurately — and to their advantage — the reality of Cuba's treaty relations with the United States. Menocal and Zayas had organized strategies around their understanding of American diplomatic imperatives, each convinced that the position he adopted found support in U.S. policy.

Presidential Politics and U.S. Policy

As political strategists in Cuba prepared to exploit U.S. policy to advance partisan causes, Washington, independently of political issues in Cuba, had already perceived interests of its own vested in the 1916 national elections. By 1916, the State Department had come to support the reelection of President Menocal. In general, Washington understood American interests to be better served by the incumbent Conservative government than by the Liberal opposition. Liberal populism, combined with the flamboyancy of former President José Miguel Gómez, had attracted to the party rank and file a representative cross section of the island's social order. Conservative adherents, on the other hand, tended to represent the white, pro-American wealth on the island.[49] The wartime sugar boom, moreover, and the *menocalista* peace of the Conservatives' first term between 1912 and 1916 combined to enhance Menocal's appeal and win him Washington's support for another term. Assistant Secretary of the Navy Franklin D. Roosevelt reflected official thinking when, after visiting Cuba, he concluded that Menocal represented a "continuation of 'orderly progress' "; a victory for the "radical candidate" Zayas, Roosevelt feared, promised to bring an abrupt end to peace and prosperity in Cuba.[50] Menocal made support of his candidacy even more desirable to Washington by issuing a timely intimation of his willingness to settle outstanding claims relating to the Cuban Ports Company and the sewerage contract.[51]

There remained, however, the difficulty of translating American support of Menocal into a domestic asset for the Conservative campaign in Cuba. All preliminary indications suggested that Menocal would fail to win a second term by a considerable margin. Party enrollments alone gave the Liberal party outright a commanding registered majority. Independent observers tended to corroborate Liberal claims that, in elections properly conducted, Zayas would win without difficulty. One observer reported to the State Department that Menocal could not be elected in a fair election, "as it was apparent that a majority was against him."[52] Diplomatic sources in Cuba similarly predicted that the Liberal majority guaranteed Zayas success on the November 1 balloting.[53]

Menocal's apparent inability to secure a second term unassisted aroused some concern in Washington. "The elections," J. B. Wright of the Latin American Division wrote in late April, "will be hotly contested and Menocal will, I fear, not be as strong as we might wish."[54] A little more than a week later, Secretary of State Robert Lansing carried the State Department's case directly to the White House:

> The presidential elections are approaching and the political situation in Cuba is becoming acute. President Menocal, who is a graduate of an American university and well disposed toward us, appears to lack the personal strength and the political support necessary to assure his reelection.
>
> The opposition is of a different caliber and it is believed that Menocal in a second term, strengthened by the consistent support of this Government can accomplish much for his country and solve at least two of the perplexing questions now pending between Cuba and the United States.[55]

American policy for the duration of the campaign consisted largely of monitoring Liberal activities for the purpose of subduing the government opposition. American electoral intervention in 1916, disguised by the invocation of U.S. treaty responsibilities in Cuba and couched in public diplomacy, advanced Menocal's reelection by undermining the Liberal's political position. As early as October 1914, Minister William E. Gonzales, a Wilson appointee, sought to combat the Liberal electoral strategy.[56] "The prevailing popular idea," Gonzales wrote, "that the United States would take charge here at the outbreak of disorder is encouraging opponents of the administration to inaugurate disorders." Gonzales sought authorization to publicize Wilson's 1913 pledge to support only constitutional authorities to "make for securing peace now and hereafter."[57] A week later, the legation informed Washington of the existence of "some men with power to lead a great body of ignorant people who do not understand the new policy of the United States Government." The opposition recalled, instead, that the revolution against Estrada Palma and the subsequent American intervention had resulted in favorable consideration of the rebels. "This idea of being able to upset an administration, by securing intervention by the United States . . . is leading opponents of the Government to inaugurate disturbances. . . . The best time to stop disorders and to save the resultant loss of life and property,'' Gonzales counseled, ''is, in my opinion, before the disorders occur.''[58]

Political developments in early 1916 convinced Gonzales that the purport of American policy had failed to reach Liberal leaders. In January 1916, soon after Menocal had secured renomination, Liberals reminded the Conservative administration of the importance of fair elections to national peace. ''It is . . . a fact,'' Gonzales lamented, ''that our present attitude has not been driven home to the understanding of the vast majority of Cubans.'' Gonzales asked Washington for a ''timely and positive expression of the present attitude of the United States,'' designed to ''have a most wholesome effect.''[59]

The opportunity for Washington to outline American policy directly to the Cuban polity presented itself in mid-1916. On May 8, only four days after Lansing had appealed to the White House for support of the Cuban president's bid for reelection, Rafael Conte, the editor of the Havana daily *La Lucha*, asked Wilson to contribute a statement to the May 20 commemorative issue of the newspaper. Conte's timely invitation offered Wilson a forum from which to outline publicly American policy requirements during that election year in Cuba. Alluding to the war in Europe, Wilson quickly moved to denounce all who threatened orderly political processes. ''I am sure,'' Wilson asserted, ''that all thoughtful Cubans, along with all thoughtful Americans, will perceive that, not only the interests of Cuba, but the interests of the whole world demand now as never before, perhaps, that constitutional authority be upheld in the republic and law and order be maintained at all costs.''[60]

In reiterating support for ''law and order'' and ''constitutional authority,'' Washington at once aligned American support publicly behind the incumbent Conservatives while attempting to disabuse the Liberals and their supporters of any hope they may have held for U.S. endorsement of their strategy. On both counts, the Liberal electoral position suffered. In exhorting Cubans in general to uphold the constituted government ''at all costs,'' Wilson, in effect, enjoined Liberals to accept passively any means chosen by ''constitutional authority'' to remain in power.

Equally important, Washington undermined the basis of the Liberal campaign strategy. The Liberal threat of revolution remained an effective deterrent to fraud and coercion only insofar as the Conservative administration perceived in the events of 1905-1906 the probable consequences of election irregularities in 1916. Confident in their numerical superiority, Liberals threatened postelection violence primarily as a deterrent to fraud at the polls. In a very real sense, by denouncing political violence, the United States neutralized the deterrent value of the Liberal threat. In warning the Liberals to uphold "constitutional authority," without concomitantly exhorting constituted authority to uphold the constitution, the United States may very well have relieved Havana of the need to concern itself with the diplomatic consequences of a fraudulent election protested by arms.

The Election

Menocal could not have interpreted American policy statements, public and private, in any fashion other than as expressions of unqualified support. By late 1916, he could proceed with his plans for a second term, indifferent to Liberal threats and without much concern for the political repercussions of his actions. Progovernment military supervisors displaced civilian officials not entirely committed to the Conservative cause. Government authorities increased the harassment of opposition candidates and Liberal electors. Violence, shootings, and, occasionally, mysterious murders increased as election day neared.[61]

In the end, the administration's reelection efforts failed to neutralize the preponderance of Liberal voters. Within hours of the closing of the polls, Zayas began to move steadily ahead of his Conservative opponent. On November 2, a day after the election, preliminary returns announced a Liberal sweep of four provinces, assuring Zayas of the presidency. "There seems," the *New York Times* conceded editorially, "to be no doubt of the triumph of the Liberal Party at the polls in Cuba and the election of Dr. Alfredo Zayas to the Presidency."[62] The American legation concurred. In a tersely worded wire, the legation informed Washington: "Alfredo Zayas candidate for President seems to be elected."[63] Liberals across the island rejoiced in public celebrations and partisan rallies; Conservative leaders wired messages of congratulations to the Liberal president-elect, pledging in advance their cooperation and support of the new administration.

Late on November 2, however, Menocal, facing the prospect of defeat at the polls, intervened directly in the tabulation process.[64] Key members of the government, including vice-presidential candidate Emilio Núñez, Secretary of *Gobernación* Aurelio Hevia, and Director of Communications Charles Hernández, met secretly with Menocal in the presidential palace to plot the administration's response to the impending defeat.[65] Within hours, telegraph and telephone communication between local election precincts and the Central Electoral Board in Havana inexplicably ceased operations. Election returns in the custody of government offices were altered.[66] In violation of the electoral code, returns reaching Havana passed first through the highly politicized ministry of *Gobernación* before reaching the Central Electoral Board. When the board protested, returns from the provinces ceased flowing to Havana altogether.[67]

The interruption of returns plunged the island into a political crisis. Amid charges and countercharges of fraud and trickery, outraged Liberals threatened civil war. The American consul in Santiago reported an "undercurrent of unrest sufficient, in fact, to strengthen the probability of serious consequences arising later on in the event of the continued voluntary suppression of information regarding the election returns."[68]

National tensions eased somewhat in mid-November when the national committees of both parties agreed to submit the disputed election to the adjudication of appropriate electoral and judicial agencies. Liberals and Conservatives agreed to accept as binding the decision delivered by national tribunals.

Throughout late November and early December tension mounted anew as the Central Electoral Board deliberated behind closed doors. Finally, in the last week of December, the board ruled in favor of the Liberal party. The electoral tribunal awarded the provinces of Havana and Camagüey to the Liberals; the Conservatives received Pinar del Río and Matanzas. The board also scheduled new partial elections for February 14 and February 20 in disputed precincts to resolve the disposition of Las Villas and Oriente. Victory in either province guaranteed Zayas the presidency. The electoral tribunal, lastly, awarded the Liberals a majority of 1,164 votes in Las Villas. Only six precincts, representing a total of some 1,500 votes, remained in dispute. With neither party claiming preponderant strength in the disputed districts, the boards ruling all but formally ensured a Liberal victory.

The decision of the Central Electoral Board, subsequently upheld in

January by the Supreme Court, ended any reasonable likelihood the administration would secure a second term at the polls. The American minister reported that unless the government overcame the deficit in Las Villas — an unlikely development — "the decision of the court as to Santa Clara assures a national Liberal victory."[69] Leading Conservative officials, including Enrique José Varona and Fernando Freyre de Andrade, conceded outright the election to Zayas.[70] Cosme de la Torriente, former president of the Conservative party, admitted that the administration could not carry the partial elections without resorting to flagrantly improper means, measures resulting inevitably in civil war.[71] Days after the Supreme Court decision, the American minister found Menocal "bitter against the Supreme Court," having a "mental attitude" that led Gonzales to fear that the Conservative president could not be restrained from using every means possible to overcome the Liberal majority in Las Villas Province. "This means employment of force," Gonzales predicted, "killing of liberal managers at the polls, and declaration of palpably fictitious results."[72]

Within days of the Supreme Court decision, government activities confirmed Gonzales's worst fears. Menocal had authorized the distribution of considerable quantities of arms and ammunition among Conservative partisans in precincts scheduled for partial elections.[73] As early as February 1, local Rural Guard units inaugurated a "reign of terror" against registered Liberal electors in an effort to produce mass Liberal abstentions.[74] In Las Villas, Havana unabashedly assigned progovernment army officers to serve as military supervisors; arms from unknown sources appeared in the province. Officials with progovernment sympathies assumed control of precinct posts and telegraph offices.[75] Election booths were enmeshed by barbed wire fences and posted with Rural Guards to oversee the balloting.[76]

For the second time in as many months, Cuba stood at the brink of civil war. Again Liberals threatened to resort to arms. On February 3, former President José Miguel Gómez asked Menocal to replace partisan officials in Las Villas with impartial observers; Menocal rejected the former president's request.[77] By early February, a political impasse had been reached.

2.

"La Chambelona": Insurrection in the Plattist System

The Conspiratorial Impulse

By early 1917, Washington had come to appreciate the dimensions of the political crisis brewing in Cuba. Information from Havana corroborated Liberal charges. Menocal's determination to secure a second term at whatever cost promised to plunge Cuba into civil war. The Conservatives' subversion of partial elections, Gonzales conceded late in January, threatened to provoke a "revolution of much more bitterness and more difficult of solution than that of 1906." While still "personally sympathizing with President Menocal's reelection," Gonzales feared that the administration's fraud and violence at the polls, "even without a revolution, would be an enduring calamity to Cuba."[1]

Without entirely withdrawing its support of Menocal, Washington proceeded in late January 1917, to distribute greater responsibility for order on "constituted authority." On January 26, Secretary of State Robert Lansing instructed the legation to inform Menocal that Washington viewed the political situation "with a great deal of friendly interest" and "deplored the employment of force by either party." Any "action which would cause disturbance in Cuba," Lansing cautioned, "and upsetting of the extremely good economic conditions would be decidedly regrettable."[2]

On February 1, only days after Lansing's veiled admonishment to Conservative authorities, Liberal party leaders convened in Havana to exchange impressions of the political situation. No one within the Liberal directory harbored illusions about Conservative intentions for the upcoming partial elections. Rather, the issue before the Liberal chieftains in early February consisted entirely of party strategy in the face of almost certain government fraud and coercion at the polls. One faction of the party, represented by presidential candidate Alfredo Zayas and Senator Eduardo Guzmán, proposed appealing to the United States to supervise the upcoming elections. Orestes Ferrara and José Miguel Gómez opposed the project.[3] To invite American intermeddling in Cuban political affairs, Ferrara and Gómez contended, opened the party to charges of collaborating with foreigners to compromise national sovereignty. More to the point — it was, indeed, the central issue — open support of U.S. supervision of the elections promised, if unsuccessful, to cause the Liberal party lasting damage nationally without satisfactorily resolving the immediate question of partial elections. In a compromise settlement, party leaders agreed to solicit American assistance publicly only after having received in advance a private commitment from Washington to supervise elections. In early February, Zayas privately communicated the purport of the party compromise to Gonzales, asking the legation to transmit the Liberal request to the State Department.[4] At the same time, the Liberal directory dispatched Orestes Ferrara and Raimundo Cabrera to New York and Washington to organize an information service for the purpose of seeking a "quick remedy to avert a disaster."[5]

At some point during Liberal deliberations in early February, moreover, party leaders also completed arrangements for a second course of action. Final plans for the much threatened Liberal uprising were consummated. Only a disagreement over timing, between the *miguelista* sector advocating a strike before the partial elections, and the Zayas faction, arguing for a postponement until after February 14, separated the party leadership.[6] Liberal chieftains did agree, however, on a plot organized around a far-flung conspiracy with leaders of the army. The plan consisted essentially of a swift seizure of military installations in Havana, seconded by army takeovers of provincial capitals, and the kidnapping of the president.[7]

Hope for a quick transfer of power depended almost entirely on winning the support of the armed forces. Organized less than a decade earlier under the Liberal government of José Miguel Gómez, the national army in 1917 still remained substantially under the command of *miguelista* appointees.[8] The vast preponderance of senior and middle-grade officers in 1917 had secured their ranks and positions between 1909 and 1912. A number of the ranking chieftains of the Liberal directory, moreover, had served the Gómez government in positions of command over the armed forces and counted many of the senior army officers among their closest friends. Gerardo Machado, the Liberal leader of Las Villas Province, had served as inspector general of the army. Liberal party president Faustino "Pino" Guerra had been the army chief of staff during the Gómez administration. In addition, relatives of key Liberal leaders continued to occupy strategic positions in the armed forces. Colonel Julio Morales Coello, son-in-law of José Miguel Gómez, served as chief of the navy. The brother of Liberal vice-presidential candidate Carlos Mendieta commanded the army communications center in Havana.

Nor did army support of the Liberal conspiracy respond entirely to partisan impulses and kinship links. Military leaders, for their part, brought to the Liberal plot a wide range of distinct professional and personal grievances against the incumbent administration. In some instances, officers felt professional standards betrayed by the use to which the Conservative government had employed the armed forces during the November elections. Other officers concluded the Menocal's violation of the constitution provided sufficient justification for the army to withdraw support of the government. Still other army leaders, appointed orginally during the Gómez government and subsequently discriminated against professionally by Conservatives for their Liberal origins, seized the opportunity to participate in the planned Liberal restoration in the hope of advancing their careers.[9]

Enlisting the support of the army command engaged the talents of leading Liberal authorities across the island. In Havana, former President Gómez and ex-army chief Guerra intrigued with the commanders of Camp Columbia and La Cabaña military fortress. Gerardo Machado assumed responsibility for recruiting his former subordinates in the Santa Clara regiment.[10] In the eastern capitals, provincial Liberal leaders in contact with regimental commanders completed local conspiratorial liaisons. The ranking officers in Camagüey, including Colonel Enrique Quiñones, chief of the military district, and Comandante Luis Solano Alvarez, chief of the cavalry, pledged to carry the regiment for the Liberals.[11] In Santiago de Cuba, Comandantes Rigoberto Fernández and Luis Loret de Mola committed the Oriente military district to the conspiracy.[12] In all, the Liberal plotters fully expected some 75 to 85 percent of the regular armed forces to rise against the Conservative government.[13]

Liberal plotters, furthermore, gained the support of key municipal police departments across the island. Colonel Eliseo Figueroa, chief of the police department in Camagüey, joined the conspiracy immediately. The police chief of Marianao, Miguel Parrado, committed the Havana suburb to support the military stroke. Most important, the Liberal conspiracy won support among the officers of the national police in the capital.[14]

The conspiracy also secured the endorsement of party functionaries at both the appointed and elective levels. Several members of the Liberal delegation in the national congress pledged to abandon Havana to join the party leadership in the field. At the provincial and municipal levels, elected Liberal officials ratified the conspiracy. The governor-elect of Camagüey, Enrique Recio Agüero, coordinated party directives in the province. In total, one governor·and some thirty *alcaldes* placed the resources and authority of their offices at the service of the Liberal plot.

So confident, in fact, were the Liberals of the success of the movement that the conspirators conferred on the insurrectionary movement a distinctly festive quality. "La Chambelona," as the revolt was to become known, was seen as something of a musical jamboree, in which street dancing, strolling musicians, and minstrel orchestras would lead the triumphal Liberal advance on Havana. The conspirators planned a swift and bloodless stroke seconded by the armed forces and supported by the rank and file of the party. Liberal leaders planned to kidnap Menocal, force him to resign, and organize a bipartisan caretaker government under Vice-President Varona to complete the electoral process with apropriate guarantees.[15] Swiftness was essential also to present Washington with a *fait accompli,* thereby minimizing the effect in Cuba of the expected American protest. Ferrara and Cabrera no doubt received contingent instructions outlining the appropriate public relations requirements of the planned Liberal enterprise prior to leaving for the United States.[16]

In early February, however, the far-flung conspiracy remained only a well-organized alternative to unsatisfactory policy responses from Washington. Throughout the first week of February 1917, Liberals continued to search for a diplomatic solution to political problems. The arrival of Ferrara and Cabrera in the United States established direct if unofficial communications between the Liberal party and the State Department. Apprised, no doubt, of the conspiracy momentarily abeyant in Cuba, the two-man commission appealed to Washington to comply with the Liberal request for supervision without further delay. A government victory under the conditions prevailing in Cuba, Ferrara and Cabrera warned Lansing with disguised certainty, "implies a forcible revolution." The Liberal envoys urged the State Department to counsel moderation to authorities in Havana. Ferrara and Cabrera repeated the Liberal request for the appointment of a "witness," with the advice and consent of the American legation in Havana, to supervise the elections in Las Villas.[17]

The State Department responded on the same day. On February 10, Lansing instructed Gonzales to deliver to Menocal, and subsequently make public in Cuba, a strongly worded note demanding appropriate electoral guarantees. The United States, Lansing cautioned in the formal text, "is regarding with no small concern the question of new elections in Santa Clara." The United States, the note concluded, remained confident that the "means provided for by the Cuban Constitution and the laws enacted for this very purpose will bring as a logical result a satisfactory and peaceable settlement of the present difficulties." In his final private instructions to Gonzales, Lansing directed the legation to emphasize to Menocal:

> this Government is confident that he will use every means in his power to prevent any disturbance of the present peaceful conditions in Cuba. That this Government is observing with the closest scrutiny every act of each of the parties which might indicate intimidating action by armed forces or illegal pressure exerted by the military or the police at the time of the election.[18]

Lansing's note of February 10, made public in Cuba immediately, responded in spirit if not in detail to the Liberal communiqué the State Department had received the same day. On the central issue of supervision, however, Washington remained silent. More than a week had passed since Zayas had appealed privately to the legation for American supervision. With partial elections only four days off, the most recent

American policy statement offered Liberals little hope of U.S. surveillance of the balloting. More important, however, between February 9 and 10, government authorities had apparently exposed the topmost roots of the Liberal military conspiracy in Havana. On February 10, Secretary of *Gobernación* Aurelio Hevia announced the discovery of a plot in Havana's military installations designed to overthrow the government.[19] After the arrest of key officers associated with the conspiracy in Camp Columbia and La Cabaña and the flight of some forty officers and men, the Liberal plot in the capital collapsed. Facing the prospect of the nation-wide conspiracy's unraveling through disclosures in Havana and despairing of American supervision, the Liberal leadership moved against the Conservative government. Ironically, the Liberals were unaware that only hours later, amid rumors that armed fighting had broken out in Cuba, Lansing was to authorize the legation to dispatch the military attaché to Las Villas province to "observe" the elections.[20]

The Uprising

The Liberal uprising enjoyed complete success in the eastern provinces. In Oriente mutinous army chieftains seized command of the regiment and arrested progovernment officers. The insurgent army command moved on Santiago de Cuba, displacing Conservative government officials and organizing a new Liberal de facto administration under military control. Within hours, the pro-Liberal forces had seized control of the province. To augment the insurgent military force, army leaders distributed some 1,500 rifles seized from the regimental armory among Liberal volunteers. In all, some two thousand persons had immediately taken up arms in Santiago against the government.[21] Army mutinies in smaller interior cities, supported by municipal authorities, resulted in Liberal seizures of Campechuela, Guantánamo, Bayamo, Holguín, Mayarí, and Baracoa.[22] By mid-February, virtually all of Oriente had passed under insurgent authority.

The insurrection in Camagüey enjoyed similar success. The majority of the province's military posts fell to Liberal partisans.[23] In the provincial capital, insurgent officers and troops seized the regiment, arrested progovernment commanders, and ousted civilian provincial and municipal authorities. Some two thousand rifles were distributed to Liberal partisans who were subsequently organized into provincial militia units.[24] By February 14, Camagüey had joined Oriente under Liberal authority. Insurgents immediately cut both provinces off from the rest of the island. Rail movement between the eastern third of the island and the west stopped; all telephone and telegraphic communications were suspended.

The Liberal effort in Las Villas experienced mixed results. Municipal authorities in Abreus, San Juan de las Yeras, Camajuaní, and Corralillo followed the party leadership into rebellion. Military subposts and Rural Guard stations, moreover, defected in sufficient numbers to allow José Miguel Gómez to follow the original plans of establishing in Las Villas the insurgent field headquarters. The regimental command in the provincial capital, however, under a *menocalista* officer, Colonel Wilfredo Ibrahim Consuegra, remained loyal to the government.[25]

The inability of the Liberals to take the city of Santa Clara and its regiment deprived the insurgents of the interior of all but the most tenuous hold on the province. Most immediately, the failure to seize the Santa Clara regiment represented the loss of some thirty-five hundred rifles and more than five hundred thousand rounds of ammunition. In the long run, and more important, Las Villas came to serve the government as a buffer between the insurgent districts of the east and Havana on the west, making a coordinated Liberal advance on the capital virtually impossible.[26] On February 13, government forces destroyed the railroad bridge at Jatibonico in western Camagüey, the main rail artery between the east and Las Villas. This at once prevented the main body of insurgent forces from joining the Liberal field command in Las Villas and isolated the rebel leadership in central Cuba with only a meager force.

The uprising failed in the three western provinces almost as completely as it had succeeded in the east. Alerted to the Liberal conspiracy in Havana, the government moved swiftly against suspected plotters. Outside a scattered number of short-lived mutinies, largely Rural Guard posts, military stations in Pinar del Río, Havana, and Matanzas provinces remained under government authority. By February 12, at which time the eastern third of the island had passed almost entirely under insurgent control, the American legation could report "perfect quiet" in the west.[27]

The stillborn outbreaks in the west had far-reaching repercussions for the Liberals nationally. The failure to capture Camp Columbia and La Cabaña ended all Liberal hopes for a quick seizure of power. The axis of the conspiracy had passed through the capital's military garrisons. Upon the seizure of Camp Columbia and La Cabaña rested the taking of Havana and, ultimately, the seizure of power. Within forty-eight hours, it had become apparent that the Conservative government had survived the initial conspiratorial thrust intact, retaining control over the western two-thirds of the island in varying degrees and seemingly retaining the allegiance of the bulk of the armed forces. The failure to take Havana, moreover, persuaded many Liberal coconspirators, committed to, but not yet compromised by, the conspiracy, to delay active participation pending subsequent developments. Failure in the capital ended for many Liberals all hopes for success; for many of them, events in Havana signaled the collapse of the movement, thereby serving to discourage any further participation by Liberals earlier committed to the revolt. Indeed, this was the argument Colonel Consuegra advanced so effectively in the barracks of the Santa Clara regiment. The failure of the conspiracy in Havana, as Consuegra harangued to the restless regiment, condemned the uprising to failure nationally; why should anyone now risk his life and career to support a movement patently foredoomed to failure?[28]

The politico-military achievements of the insurgent Liberals, however, were not inconsiderable. Within forty-eight hours, the Liberals had established complete mastery over two provinces and partial control over a third; insurgent bands operated throughout the national territory. A quarter of the army had immediately flocked to Liberal banners; the rest of the armed forces, many believed, waited only for a Liberal victory or two before abandoning the government altogether. In all, some thirty thousand men had taken up arms to support the Liberal protest.[29]

3.

Counterrevolutionary Diplomacy: Policy, Politics, and the "February Revolution"

La Chambelona Stalls: "The February Revolution"

Insurgent successes throughout Cuba, however immediately impressive, did not obscure the singular reality of the Liberals' failure. As military lines crystalized and delineated insurgent field positions across the island, it became readily apparent that Liberals had fallen far short of their original objectives.

Within forty-eight hours, an uneasy truce settled between both armed camps. In Havana, the president, uncertain of his army and still unapprised of the full scope of the insurrection, moved haltingly. Officers suspected of Liberal sympathies were relieved immediately of command; old veterans of the army came out of retirement to lead government forces. Hastily organized militia units, composed largely of volunteers between the ages of eighteen and forty-five, prepared for field duty against the Liberal forces.[1]

Behind insurgent lines, the Liberal command took advantage of the mid-February quiescence to adjust political strategies to the new military realities. Considerable effort went, first, into a propaganda campaign to explain at home and abroad the motives behind the uprising. "Under no circumstances," Gómez explained to Minister Gonzales, "is it intended to constitute a revolutionary government, overthrowing one legally constituted; nothing could be further from this." The Liberal party, Gómez insisted, sought only a guarantee of constitutional rights and partial elections free of fraud and violence.[2] In New York, Orestes Ferrara informed the State Department that the Liberal Party was "willing to accept . . . the mediation of the President of the United States, or any high officer of the American Nation.'' The party leadership, Ferrara assured Lansing, was prepared ''to accept the decision of the Government at Washington . . . provided such decision be based on the maintenance of public Cuban liberties and the Independence of the Republic of Cuba.''[3]

Two days after the ill-fated coup in Havana, the Liberal directorate reissued in the United States its original demand for honest elections. In so doing, Liberals acknowledged effectively, if only tacitly, the insolvency of the plot to seize power. The willingness to revive the original, if more modest, objectives, however, did not result entirely from failure. On the contrary, it stemmed from an appreciation of actual successes and, more specifically, the movement's potential. Securely entrenched in the eastern provinces, districts of considerable American investment, the Liberals offered to exchange peace and continued wartime prosperity for honest elections. On February 12, the Liberal envoys in New York informed the State Department of the Party's willingness to discontinue the armed protest and ''put an end to the deplorable state of things which the Liberal Party has been and is still the foremost to wish to avoid.'' A minimum condition for peace in Cuba, Ferrara and Cabrera explained, necessarily included the suspension of the partial elections in Santa Clara and Oriente until some future date when conditions of impartiality could be guaranteed.[4]

The State Department seized the Liberal overtures of February 12 as the basis upon which to pursue an end to the incipient disorders in Cuba. On February 13, Lansing instructed Minister Gonzales to ''exert all your efforts'' to secure a postponement of partial elections in Santa Clara, scheduled for the following day, until such time as ''present disturbances are at an end and quiet through the Republic reestablished.''[5]

Washington's proposal generated little enthusiasm in Havana. The bitterness prevailing among Conservative authorities, many still uncertain about the future, left little desire in Havana for reconciliation with insurgent Liberals. On February 14, as originally scheduled, Menocal proceeded with partial elections in those precincts of Las Villas Province under government authority. To the surprise of few, the Conservatives not only defeated the Liberal ticket in the run-off elections but, in the process, claimed to have overtaken the Liberal majority established during the general elections in sufficient numbers to carry the province:[6]

	Conservative	Liberal
Ranchuela	493	3
Pedro Barba	602	3
Purial	411	3
Yaguarama	425	9

Concurrent with elections in Santa Clara, Havana launched its first military drive against insurgent positions in the east. On the eve of the February 14 balloting, the cruiser *Cuba* left Havana for Camagüey with some seven hundred officers and men abroad. A day later, government forces attacked Liberal strongholds in Santa Clara and western Camagüey.

In observing partial elections as scheduled, Menocal, undeterred by American counsel, indifferent to the existing unsettled political conditions on the island, and simultaneously moving militarily against the insurgent Liberals, committed his government to nothing less than an electoral victory at the polls and a military triumph in the field. The meaning of these maneuvers became apparent immediately. In a single stroke, Menocal had pushed the Liberals irrevocably into full-scale rebellion and, at the same time, secured American support for his — constituted — government. With little hope of securing a politico-diplomatic settlement of the disputed election, insurgent Liberals, pursued militarily in the field by government forces, had little choice after the events of February 14 and 15 other than to surrender or resistance.[7] Thousands had originally joined the protest in the expectation of a quick turnover of governments. Career officers, congressional leaders, and provincial and municipal officials had wagered their careers on the success of the Liberal plot; too many had risked too much to abandon the field only because the ante for victory had risen. Hope for success shifted to the expectation that political disorders would, as in 1906, require the sympathetic attention of the United States.

The United States, too, for its part, found its options reduced by Menocal's politico-military maneuvers. Treaty relations and Wilsonian policy left Washington little immediate choice other than to assist constitutional authorities in Cuba. Indeed, with this foreknowledge, Menocal had little to gain from the compromise settlement proposed earlier by the Liberal leadership and seconded by Washington. When the revolt sputtered, when it became apparent that the Liberals sought in Washington a way out of their predicament in Cuba, the party leadership sought to make the election question again the central issue. As long as honest elections remained the subject of dispute, Menocal could expect — and fear — American attention to Liberal grievances. As early as February 11, in a personal note to Minister Gonzales, Menocal complained that "biased reports" had reached Washington. His "past history and life," the president insisted, entitled him to the "American Government's confidence."[8] Once Havana had maneuvered the Liberals beyond the point of return, however, the issue became clearly one of an illegal attempt to overthrow the constitutional government of Cuba. Unlike the vague electoral controversy, for which Washington had no adequate policy response in either practice or precedent, the issues in Cuba after February 14 had been defined in forms clearly understood by American policymakers.

The Diplomacy of Suppression in the Plattist System

The Liberal decision in mid-February to remain in the field after the stillborn coup in Havana stemmed not so much from any real expectation of defeating *menocalista* forces in battle as from anticipation of a favorable American policy response.[9] Given the binding nature of Cuban-American treaty relations, particularly U.S. responsibility for political stability on the island, the insurgent leadership reasoned, with some justification, that the mere specter of civil war in Cuba perforce involved the United States. Out of this treaty involvement, the Liberals expected to obtain at least a favorable mediation of the dispute. If all else failed, a prolonged insurgency, one designed specifically to activate the intervention clause of the Platt Amendment, offered still another method of overturning the Conservative government.

From the outset, however, the United States shrank from the prospect of another armed occupation in the Caribbean. Washington searched, instead, for the politico-diplomatic means with which to prevent the rise of conditions potentially requiring full-scale armed intervention.[10] The reluctance to intervene in Cuba in 1917 on the scale of 1906 was determined by a variety of circumstances inside and outside of Cuba.

Most immediately, Menocal avoided admitting — as Estrada Palma had in 1906 — the need for American military assistance. On the contrary, Havana consciously and repeatedly assured Washington that it possessed the capacity to suppress the revolt expeditiously, with minimum loss to foreign interests, and without American armed assistance. Menocal deliberately refrained from asking Washington for anything more than "moral support" and "benevolent neutrality."[11] However bleak the future of his administration may have appeared in mid-February — indeed, at one point few in Havana expected the Conservative government to survive the Liberal challenge — Menocal recalled only too well the fate of the Estrada Palma government and never admitted that events in Cuba had developed beyond the control of authorities in the capital.

The Conservative cause, moreover, drew support from the American minister. Personally committed to Menocal, Minister Gonzales presented Havana's case to Washington in the most compelling and favorable manner. For Gonzales, the long-range policy issues raised by the February revolution transcended all immediate considerations. At issue in 1917, Gonzales argued, was the very solvency of republican government in Cuba. The American minister consistently argued that an armed intervention in response to the Liberal protest, however much sanctioned by treaty relations, would only generate future instability and virtually condemn the republic to a cycle of quadrennial insurrections in which, after every election, the losing party would find inspiration for revolution in the past conduct of American diplomacy. Gonzales stressed that in 1917, after some fifteen years of republican government, it behooved the United States to help Cuba establish the permanent foundations upon which constituted authority would in the future base the management of the affairs of state without assistance from abroad. Only by permitting Havana to demonstrate its capacity to meet internal armed challenge unassisted, and thereby conclusively establishing its ability to suppress political disorders without foreign involvement, could future stability in Cuba be guaranteed; otherwise, the political opposition would have available in the record of the republic's past palpable proof of the efficacy of a resort to arms to overthrow constituted authorities. Gonzales detected in the events of 1917 the opportunity to establish policy on the basis of long-range considerations. The legation, in fact, was prepared to accept the destruction of some property and the possible loss of life in order to reach these goals. "However we may deplore the consequences of violence," Gonzales counseled, "the Government should have the opportunity to demonstrate its capacity to suppress uprisings. Only through such a showing of strength will the people respect the Government."[12]

International considerations further tended to weigh in favor of Havana's position. Developments in Europe, perhaps more than any other single factor, precluded the conventional American military response to Caribbean political disorders in February 1917. Deteriorating relations with Germany increased the likelihood of American involvement in Europe. Only a week before the outbreak of fighting in Cuba, the United States had severed diplomatic relations with Germany. As Washington prepared for war in Europe, the American military presence in the circum-Caribbean decreased. United States occupation forces in Haiti and the Dominican Republic were reduced; more and more American occupation officials prepared to transfer some responsibility for order in these countries to newly organized constabularies. During the early months of 1917, volunteers replaced marine regulars in the Caribbean. In another war-related move, Wilson ordered General John Pershing out of Mexico, just days before the Liberal revolt.

Hence the American approach to developments in Cuba rested in large measure on broader policy considerations prompted by the requirements of the European war. Those military authorities charged with the responsibility for organizing contingency plans around European events hoped for a speedy settlement of the political dispute in Cuba, without the need for American armed forces.[13] American military planners projecting the requirements of a possible occupation enterprise in Cuba estimated a minimum need of some five thousand to seven thousand officers and men.[14] "The possibility that we may have to send an army of 10,000 men and some of our ablest officers," the *New York Times* speculated editorially, "as well as warships for which we have other uses, to Cuba at this critical period is naturally disturbing Washington."[15] Other newspapers and periodicals echoed similar concerns. Cuban disorders, the weekly *Independent* feared, "so near our shores would demand the attention of our army and navy when international affairs of far graver import need all our watchfulness."[16]

The ill-timed political disorders in Cuba required Washington to device alternative politico-diplomatic solutions to substitute for a full-scale occupation. Most immediately, the State Department sought to ensure the viability of Conservative rule in Havana. A solvent government in Havana, in full possession of the means to resist the insurgent challenge, offered the United States the minimum necessary guarantees against an armed intervention.

Unwilling to commit armed forces to a full-scale occupation of the island, Washington sought to bolster the badly shaken Menocal government by diplomatic means. The course of the revolt in the first seventy-two hours had left Havana seriously weakened and highly vulnerable to mounting insurgent momentum. Having immediately lost almost half the island to insurgent military and civil authorities, Menocal's ability to survive the Liberal challenge rested almost entirely upon his capacity to contain any further erosion of his support in the western provinces.

Many ostensible supporters of the government in mid-February included persons awaiting only a more propitious moment to defect to rebel forces. The swift suppression of the military conspiracy in Havana allowed many committed but uncompromised pro-Liberal officers to remain in the armed forces undetected. Although several members of the Liberal delegation had joined the party leadership immediately in the field, many more had delayed making a final commitment to arms pending the outcome of early fighting; a defection of any magnitude of the Liberal congressional membership threatened to deprive Congress of a quorum and cripple national legislative processes. Many who were sympathetic to the Liberal cause in various branches of government, and upon whose neutrality the ultimate fate of the Conservative government depended, judiciously avoided making a precipitous commitment until the course of events in February yielded more clues as to the probable outcome of the political dispute. In early February, the full strength of the Liberal challenge remained undetermined. "Much depends," Gonzales speculated, "on whether the people in [the] country who have not responded to local insurgent leaders will rally around Gomez."[17]

Immediate uncertainty centered on the loyalty of the armed forces. Organized and expanded to full strength under Gómez, the army had served at its inception as a major source of patronage for deserving Liberals.[18] The magnitude of the initial army defections in February jolted government leaders. Menocal feared, moreover, that these early defections merely foreshadowed desertions on a mass scale. The government, Gonzales reported on February 13, "is unquestionably uneasy chiefly because [the] extent of disaffection in the army is unknown and on account of so many reserve rifles being captured."[19] Few in the Conservative government believed Menocal capable of retaining the loyalty of the armed forces over any extended period of time. "If Gomez should gain advantage through failure of government's forces to fight loyally," Gonzales predicted, "I believe there would undoubtedly be uprising of Liberals in Habana of sufficient strength to place President and governor in peril."[20] Once assured of the allegiance of the armed forces, however, if only the loyalty of the units that had remained with Havana immediately after the initial defections, many believed the government fully capable of ultimately overcoming the insurrection.[21]

Hence, American policy in mid-February sought at once to raise the morale of progovernment forces and arrest the erosion of the administration's support. Washington hoped through diplomatic support to aggregate for the beleaguered Conservatives the strength they lacked nationally. An expression of American support was vital on several counts. Most immediately, diplomatic support promised to disabuse the insurgent Liberals and would-be rebels of the prevailing supposition that, as in 1906, Washington planned to intervene militarily on the side of the protesters to resolve the dispute. Indeed, no other single belief was as vital to Liberal strategy as the expectation of U.S. intervention. The decision to remain in the field well after the failure of the coup rested almost wholly on the Liberals' confidence in their ability to create the conditions requiring the desired American intervention.

An expression of American support was of crucial importance in still another sense. Once the army had received public assurances that the United States would not abandon the Conservatives, there was no possibility that the progovernment activities of the military in the course of the election campaign would later be subject to the scrutiny of American investigators and the subsequent reprisals of a future Liberal regime — as had happened to the armed forces in 1906. The army command therefore had little inclination to defect to what seemed a cause diplomatically foredoomed to disappointment. Apprised of the gravity of his situation on February 12, and aware that on the ultimate disposition of the armed forces rested the fate of the government, Menocal appealed to Washington for an "expression of moral support from the Government of the United States."[22]

The State Department stepped directly into the Cuban crisis to oversee the survival of the Conservative government. Whatever hopes Washington had for the survival of Menocal depended largely on both containing further defection of government support and persuading insurgent Liberals of the folly and futility of the scheme to provoke intervention. In a series of dramatic moves, Washington chose to publicize select diplomatic notes as the means by which to outline its position in the face of the Cuban political crisis. Insofar as the threat to U.S.-Cuban relations emanated from a disgruntled sector of the citizenry seeking to overturn a government, and not from the acts of properly constituted national authorities to which American diplomatic agents were accredited, the immediate issues confronting American policy involved Washington directly with the the Cuban body politic. A sector of the Cuban electorate — not the Cuban government — had to understand the basis and direction of American policy. For this, the State Department resorted to public diplomacy. The American approach to Cuban disorders turned on publicizing select notes, with the legation serving as a public information center disseminating in Cuba periodic policy bulletins.[23]

In a series of public notes transmitted to the Cuban people through the legation, the United States mounted a major campaign to establish the Conservatives on firm ground nationally. In principle, Secretary of State Lansing sought to reiterate Washington's opposition to all governments founded on force and revolution.[24] More specifically, the State Department condemned the Cuban insurrection directly. On February 13, Lansing expressed "the greatest apprehension" over the news of the revolt in Cuba. "Reports such as these of insurrection against the constituted Government," Lansing warned, "cannot be considered except as of the most serious nature since the Government of the United States has given its confidence and support only to Governments established through legal and constitutional methods." The State Department ordered the February 13 note made public throughout Cuba, particularly in zones that were held by insurgents.[25] In a second note five days later, the State Department reiterated in considerable detail its support of the

Menocal government and its view of the insurgency:

1. The Government of the United States supports and sustains the constitutional Government of the Republic of Cuba.
2. The armed revolt against the Constitutional Government of Cuba is considered by the Government of the United States as a lawless and unconstitutional act and will not be countenanced.
3. The leaders of the revolt will be held responsible for injury to foreign nationals and for destruction of foreign property.
4. The Government of the United States will give careful consideration to future attitude towards those persons connected with and concerned in the present disturbance of peace in the Republic of Cuba.[26]

To give maximum publicity to U.S. condemnation of the revolt, Havana distributed thousands of copies of the notes throughout the island.[27]

The American notes immediately had a far-reaching effect. Indeed, for a movement organized in large part around the expectation of a favorable hearing from the United States, the two notes proved devastating. Many Liberals who had earlier delayed their decision to join Gómez now altogether abandoned their plans to support the movement. Publicity of American support of Menocal, moreover, contributed to arresting the deterioration of the government's position nationally. A considerable number of insurgent Liberal chieftains in the field, now convinced that the American position ended the movement's only remaining hope of success, surrendered to government authorities.[28] Other Liberal leaders, weighing personal political aspirations in the future, pondered the meaning of the fourth clause of the February 18 note; given the nature of U.S. controls over the Cuban national system, few political leaders in the field, thinking into the future, could receive such a warning without pausing to reexamine the wisdom of their position in 1917. Many yielded to the future. Two days later, members of the Liberal congressional delegation caucused under the leadership of Juan Gualberto Gómez and declared themselves "pacifists."[29] The mayor of Camajuani, Pedro Sánchez del Portal, surrendered with his forces. In perhaps the most demoralizing defection of all, the Liberal presidential candidate, Alfredo Zayas, disassociated himself from the rebel leadership and surrendered to Conservative authorities in Havana. Immediately after the February 13 note, Zayas contacted the American legation seeking a safe conduct pass to the capital.[30] Zayas remained in Havana as a repentant insurgent, living in quiet luxury for the duration of the insurrection.

Washington's public diplomacy contributed powerfully to stabilizing Havana's position. The publication of the February 13 note, the legation reported two days later, had had a "beneficial effect in abating [the] ardor of [the] revolutionary party."[31] Both notes contributed to halting further defections in the armed forces. The announcement of American policy had induced many officers who might otherwise have joined the Liberals to remain with the government.[32] "Publication of statement giving position of the United States regarding revolutions," Gonzales wired Washington, "has had most clarifying effect upon public mind and the Government officials deeply grateful."[33] With the publication of the second note on February 18, the American legation expressed confidence that Havana could "completely dominate" the political situation in a matter of weeks.[34] Cuban authorities concurred. The publication of the February 13 note, Foreign Minister Pablo Desvernine informed the Cuban legation in Washington, had produced a "most favorable impression" on the island.[35] Several weeks later, Desvernine acknowledged the strategic importance of the American notes. American policy had decisively disheartened the rebels, the foreign minister proclaimed. "The action of the United States Government," Desvernine announced, "in disapproving, almost rebuking this outbreak, has been the most important factor in the whole situation."[36]

Concurrent with diplomatic measures, Washington rushed military assistance to Havana to help Menocal suppress the insurgency. Menocal's appeal for military supplies received immediate approval. On February 12, Cuba requested some ten thousand rifles and two million cartridges.[37] A week later, the Cuban government announced the acquisition of twenty-eight machine guns and ten million rounds of ammunition. A number of airplanes, in addition, arrived in Havana to assist the Cuban government in reconnaissance and bombing.[38]

Military assistance served two purposes. Most immediately, American weapons enhanced the ability of the Cuban armed forces to end the revolt, compensating the government for the arms and ammunition lost to insurgent forces in the east. The final organization of government militia units, moreover, awaited only the arrival of U.S. supplies. By February 21, the government had organized some forty-five hundred men into militia and irregular forces to assist municipal police departments.[39] Havana's offensive campaign in eastern Cuba could not begin until American arms and supplies had arrived.[40] Lastly, in providing the Conservative government with military equipment, Washington proclaimed in still another fashion its support for the government and contributed generally to an uplifting of morale within the armed forces. Menocal fully appreciated the political implications of military aid, stressing to the legation the "tremendous moral effect" of an early compliance with Havana's request.[41]

The Interventionist Impulse

The inefficacy of full-scale intervention as a viable solution to the national crisis in Cuba did not preclude intervention in response to local situations. Armed landing parties, organized largely from naval units dispatched to Cuban waters in mid-February, contributed significantly to underwriting at the regional level the larger American diplomatic position. United States military involvement in the provinces offered a short-term alternative to the prospect of a prolonged occupation of the entire island. American armed forces, distributed provisionally throughout rebel-held zones in the east, acted at once to support the Cuban government and to protect American lives and property; on occasion, American forces served to mediate an end to the armed protest at the local level. Beleaguered government troops caught behind insurgent lines, moreover, received direct aid from American naval patrols. In Manzanillo, one of the larger cities in Oriente to remain under Conservative control and distant from the center of government operations and surrounded by insurgent forces, *menocalista* authorities received arms and ammunition from American offshore naval units. On February 22, an American landing party disembarked in Manzanillo, transferring to the government commander machine guns, rifles, and ammunition to equip a recently organized militia in the city.[42] Some days later, another American vessel delivered an additional 35,000 rounds of small arms ammunition to the Manzanillo post.[43] Cuban naval units operating off the southeastern coast came to rely on American ammunition and supplies to permit extended periods of operations in Oriente waters.[44] The American task force cooperated fully with government sea and land operations on the southeastern coast.[45] Washington also organized a naval blockade of the coast of rebel-held territories to prevent the landing of filibustering expeditions and block the arrival of additional arms and ammunition from abroad.[46] In specific instances, U.S. landing parties went ashore to assist local *menocalista* army authorities in the protection of American lives and property. Conservative enclaves that survived behind insurgent lines, lacking the means to safeguard property beyond their immediate positions, requested the United States to land troops to protect foreign interests.[47]

Within a month of early Liberal successes in the eastern provinces, American armed forces had taken up key positions in many of the insurgent-dominated zones. Sugar centers in Camagüey and Oriente passed under the protection of marine garrisons. In late February, marine detachments disembarked at Guacanayabo Bay in Camagüey to guard the Francisco Sugar Estate. In Oriente, marine units garrisoned the Río Cauto properties northeast of Manzanillo. On the Atlantic coast, United Fruit Company properties at Preston, Felton, and Banes received a detachment of marine guards. A small marine unit, in addition, established camp on the property of the Manatí Sugar Estate.[48] In early March, a Cuban Expeditionary Battalion, organized out of the American occupation forces in Haiti, arrived in Cuba to garrison positions in the interior inaccessible to naval landing parties. For almost two months, units of the Marine Expeditionary Battalion remained on garrison duty at the Ermita, Guantánamo, and Santa Cecilia estates.[49] By the early spring, American armed forces had extended protection to U.S. mining enterprises in Oriente, including the Cuba Copper Company and the Bethlehem Steel iron mines at Juraguá.[50]

The presence of American armed forces in eastern Cuba undermined many of the premises upon which the Liberals had based their decision to remain in the field. The Liberals, by creating conditions that would reveal Havana as incapable of protecting life and property, had hoped to precipitate full-scale American intervention and thus oust Menocal. To the extent that the United States assumed through the Platt Amendment surrogate sovereignty over Cuba — specifically, responsibility for life and property — constituted authorities in Havana remained always accountable to Washington. Thus Havana's inability to safeguard foreign interests, Liberals expected, promised to provide sufficient cause for an intervention that would displace Menocal in the same fashion as the American intervention a decade earlier had ousted Estrada Palma. Within the context of Cuba's treaty relations, the final measure of Havana's capacity to govern — and thereby retain American support — was the ability of Cuban authorities to guarantee the safety of foreign lives and property; in those instances where Havana proved unequal to treaty requirements, sovereignty was exercised by Washington.

Local American interventions in February and March, however, frustrated Liberal efforts to create the conditions that would have otherwise required Washington to meet in full its treaty obligations. Organized specifically to protect property, American armed landings provided relief and assistance to the Cuban army and, at the same time, directly appropriated responsibility for the safety of foreign interests.

American authorities in Cuba recognized from the outset the military difficulties confronting the Conservative government. Few believed Menocal's armed forces capable of protecting the vast property holdings of foreigners in Cuba while at the same time mounting a successful offensive drive against the insurgent armies.[51] Local intervention met the central politico-diplomatic issues raised by the Liberal insurrection. The arrival of American armed forces released Cuban troops for field duty against the rebel bands. As early as February 25, Gonzales, anticipating an insurgent campaign against property to provoke intervention, warned the State Department that Havana could not hold the towns and guarantee railroad service while pursuing insurgent units in the field. The Cuban government would require "friendly assistance," specifically "physical aid." "The earlier it comes after the need is determined," Gonzales recommended, "the greater its moral influence, and the greater its utility in releasing Cuban troops to suppress bands."[52] Some days later, Gonzales reiterated his fears that a Liberal campaign against property would impede the government war effort and prolong disorders interminably. "Physical aid from the United States," Gonzales urged, "if given, can be best employed in guarding railroad trunk lines and the more central properties, leaving Cuban forces to protect outlying interior properties and pursue bandits.''[53]

The distribution of U.S. armed forces in eastern Cuba conformed to larger policy considerations. In their garrison capacity, American military units served Havana as surrogate rearguard forces. From camps in port cities and sugar estates, marines patrolled outlying interior districts.[54] *Menocalista* commanders relinquished to American armed forces authority over towns and cities to permit the government to evacuate its troops to conduct field operations. Marines often assumed police duties in towns where municipal policemen had been conscripted into local militia detachments. Areas otherwise threatened by Liberal takeovers thus remained securely under progovernment authority.[55]

Local armed intervention also relieved Havana of much of the responsibility for the security of mills, warehouses, railroad junctions, and wharfs. United States troops provided the security for estate labor to return to work and continue the sugar harvest.[56] Railroad lines vital to the transportation and marketing of sugar and essential to the movement of troops remained out of insurgent hands were guarded by American military forces; on several occasions, U.S. Marines prevented insurgent saboteurs from destroying bridges and railroad tracks.[57] Landing parties, additionally, protected vital communications networks, dams, and water works and on occasion repaired telegraph and telephone lines.[58] Inevitably marines clashed head-on with Liberal forces. In one such encounter in Oriente Province, American forces killed some twenty-five insurgents and wounded another forty.[59]

American cooperation with and participation in Havana's field campaign, together with U.S. diplomatic and political support, further contributed to consolidating the Conservative administration in the early weeks of the insurgency. The American presence in Liberal-controlled Oriente and Camagüey, areas inaccessible to government forces, provided a shield behind which Havana advanced eastward, and freed Menocal of the diplomatic liabilities that otherwise would have attended the insurgents' effort to destroy foreign property.

The Mediation Impulse

Concurrent with efforts to guarantee the survival of a national government in Cuba, the State Department continued to press for an immediate political end to the insurrection. By late February, it had identified two central issues raised by the Liberal uprising. The first involved the politico-military survival of Cuban authorities in the face of an internal challenge. This matter was satisfactorily resolved by the end of the month. The second, and still unresolved, question concerned the ability of Cuban authorities to end disorders quickly and without extensive damage to property. The revolt had broken out at the height of the sugar harvest. A movement initially organized around a swift seizure of power by the third week of February had assumed all the qualities of a civil conflagration. "La Chambelona" had developed into a war of positions with hostile armies poised to campaign on battlefields of sugar cane. The Liberals had established themselves securely in districts containing the most important foreign-held sugar enterprises of eastern Cuba; military operations in insurgent-held zones necessarily risked enormous damage to sugar properties. Indeed, the early weeks of the conflict had confirmed the State Department's gravest apprehensions. Isolated skirmishes and the movement of opposing forces through sugar districts, each seeking to secure positions of advantage, had devastated cane fields. Railroad lines and rolling stock vital to sugar production served as strategic objectives for opposing camps; where they could not be controlled to advantage they were destroyed. The destruction of bridges further interrupted transportation. Insurgent and government forces alike seized horses and livestock at will. Labor dispersed and fled the interior for the refuge and safety of the cities; other workers deserted the estates to join either local insurgent units or government militias. Contract labor from Jamaica and Haiti, refusing to work in the interior without adequate protection, fled to the cities for safety. [60] Without an adequate supply of labor, sugar production in eastern Cuba quickly came to a halt.

The prospect of a prolonged conflict in Cuba, one in which foreign property remained constantly subject to the vagaries of civil war, heightened in Washington the urgency to end the dispute. Within a week of the abortive coup in Havana, the Liberals themselves offered Washington one alternative to civil war. The insurgent forces, the Liberals told the State Department, would abandon the field if the United States agreed to mediate the dispute. [61] Many Conservative leaders likewise appealed to Washington to mediate the unresolved electoral dispute before opposing parties plunged the entire island into an interminable civil conflict.[62]

Cuban overtures for mediation attracted the support of American economic interests on the island. Willard King, president of the Columbia Trust Company, an insurance agent of American sugar properties in Cuba, recounted to Colonel Edward M. House the details of recent conversations with insurgent leaders in Oriente. At the request of the Liberal leadership, King urged the White House to dispatch to Cuba a commission to mediate the dispute and arrange for new elections. "They will lay down their arms" King predicted confidently, "and vote peaceably and abide by the result."[63] The American Chamber of Commerce in Santiago de Cuba similarly appealed to the White House for assistance to end the dispute. "If present conditions prevail," the Santiago chamber petitioned President Wilson, "immense damage and loss will surely be caused that can be easily avoided by your timely mediation."[64]

Washington took advantage of appeals for mediation to encourage publicly a negotiated end to the revolt. Intimating a willingness to mediate the dispute, Wilson insisted on February 23 that the insurgents first lay down their arms. The United States, Wilson declared, "cannot hold communication with leaders of this rebellion while they are under arms against the Constitutional Government." Wilson continued:

> No other question except the reestablishment of order throughout the Republic through the return of those in rebellion to faithful allegiance to the Government can be considered under the existing conditions.
>
> The Government of the United States, as has been made known to the people of Cuba, will support only constitutional methods for the settlement of disputes and will exert every means in its power as the friends of the Cuban Republic, to effect such settlement, but, until those persons who have revolted against the Government lay down their arms, declare allegiance to their Government and return to peaceful pursuits, the Government of the United States can take no further step.[65]

Growing daily more absorbed by the crisis in Europe, moreover, the

State Department privately did not rule out the possibility of guaranteeing elections as a way of returning order to Cuba immediately. On March 7, stressing the importance of honest elections to peace in Cuba, Lansing reminded Gonzales confidentially of the "serious international situation."[66] Convinced that the solution of the Cuban problem lay in honest elections, Washington prepared to dispatch to Cuba an American commission to investigate and adjust the electoral dispute.[67]

The very day the State Department informed the legation in Havana of plans to organize an electoral commission, the Cuban government scored its most important military victory over insurgent forces. On March 7, in Caicaje, in the province of Las Villas, government troops defeated one of the main bodies of the insurgent army, taking prisoner some two hundred Liberal soldiers and virtually the entire field command of the revolution, including José Miguel Gómez, his son Miguel Mariano, Colonel Enrique Quiñones, and Enrique Recio Agüero. Only Carlos Mendieta, the Liberal vice-presidential candidate in 1916, and Colonel Eliseo Figueroa escaped government forces.[68]

Morale soared in Havana. Confident that the government had delivered a mortal blow to the insurgency, Menocal stiffened his resistance against U.S. meddling in Cuban affairs through an electoral commission. Such a commission, the Cuban minister in Washington protested, no longer served a useful purpose and could only injure the prestige of the constitutional government.[69] After March 7, the subject of an American electoral commission was never again raised.

The government victory on March 7 also eased American fears of a large-scale involvement in Cuban disorders. Many U.S. officials shared Havana's view that an end to the rebellion was imminent. Caicaje definitively guaranteed the politico-military survival of the Menocal government. "There seems to be," army chief of staff General Hugh L. Scott wrote with some relief after Caicaje, "no prospect of our going into Cuba at the present time."[70]

4.

Gunboat Diplomacy:
Naval Mediations and Liberal
Politics in Oriente Province

Liberal Government in Santiago de Cuba

The policy of supporting Menocal in order to protect American strategic and economic interests and, concomitantly, of denouncing would-be usurpers of constitutional government enjoyed success only insofar as the Conservatives survived the initial insurgent challenge. The Liberal seizure of power in Santiago de Cuba, however, presented Washington with a radically different politico-diplomatic construct. In the second largest city of Cuba, the provincial capital of Oriente, and the commercial and financial hub of the east, insurgent Liberals had overturned local government, arrested Conservative authorities, and established a de facto administration.

The Liberals had executed the coup in Santiago swiftly and without complications. Upon seizing control of the First Military District, insurgent army units under Comandantes Rigoberto Fernández and Luis Loret de Mola displaced *menocalista* commanders and proceeded to occupy the city. Rebel officers assumed direction of provincial and municipal administrative offices; Liberal partisans replaced *menocalista* military and civil authorities. National and provincial funds located in the regional treasury and deposited in local banks, as well as customs receipts, were seized and applied to the payrolls of the regular army, the Liberal militia, and the de facto government.[1] With the news of Liberal setbacks in Havana, insurgent authorities in Oriente immediately prepared Santiago for siege. All normal communication with the western half of the island ended. Liberal military authorities took custody of telephone and telegraph offices; regular railroad service stopped.[2]

Liberal successes in Oriente presented Washington with a new set of policy issues. In defiance of Wilson's pronouncements, insurgent Liberals had illegally ousted constitutional authorities in the provinces and, through the force of arms, established a de facto government. The policy organized to meet specific politico-military requirements of Conservative authorities in Havana had little relevance in Oriente, where constituted authorities had failed to survive the insurgent challenge. The administration of government, and the attendant responsibility for order and the protection of foreign life and property, had passed to the de facto Liberal regime. All inquiries concerning the status of foreign nationals in Oriente, Comandante Luis Loret de Mola announced, were to be directed to the appropriate insurgent authority in Santiago.[3]

In assuming responsibility for order and the safety of foreign interests in Oriente, insurgent Liberals conferred on the de facto government the credentials necessary to enter into direct negotiations with American authorities. United States diplomatic officials in these districts entirely within insurgent-held territory, who were charged with responsibility for the protection of American interests, necessarily adopted perspectives of, and approaches to, the insurrection very much in conflict with the policy maneuvers emanating from such distant points as the legation in Havana and the State Department in Washington. In both Havana and Washington, American policy efforts went toward supporting long-term American interests dependent on the ability of constitutional government to survive the internal challenge; in Santiago de Cuba, where constitutional government had failed to survive, U.S. approaches rested on pragmatic response to local issues immediately at hand. Whereas in Havana and Washington the insurgents represented a remote — and apparently unsuccessful — threat to order and stability, in Santiago de Cuba, Liberals were the guarantors of order and stability.

Within twenty-four hours of the Liberal seizure of Oriente Province, U.S. warships had converged on Santiago. President Wilson's refusal to sanction U.S. mediation notwithstanding, American naval and consular officials in Santiago immediately conferred with rebel officials to explore ways to maintain order. For local American representatives, the Liberal de facto government represented the only authority, however unconstitutional, capable of protecting foreign lives and property. For the duration of the Liberal administration in Santiago, collaboration between American officials and insurgent authorities offered the most efficacious means through which to assure continued protection of U.S. interests. Americans in Santiago de Cuba supported the existing administration simply because it existed — a microcosm of larger policy imperatives.

In Oriente, Havana was responsible for the threat to constituted government and, concomitantly, to the order and safety of lives and property guaranteed by the Liberals in Santiago. Any attempt by the national authorities to retake the province by force necessarily involved large-scale fighting and, consequently, the loss of foreign lives and property.[4] Indeed, immediately following the news of Liberal reversals in the west, the insurgent leadership in Santiago organized defenses to resist the anticipated government advance into the province. Military chieftains distributed some twelve hundred rifles to Liberal sympathizers. To the more than one thousand officers and men of the regular army who had joined the rebellion at the outset, the Liberal government added some two thousand armed partisans organized into militia and regular units. All Liberal resources, Comandante Fernández pledged, would be committed to resist any *menocalista* effort to recapture the province.[5]

Concern for American interests in Santiago required U.S. mediatory intervention from the outset. In early February, the Liberal government ordered Santiago Bay mined and the channel approach to the city blocked with a sunken sea transport. These measures, Fernández announced, were designed to deny Havana access by sea to Santiago and constituted the minimum military requirement necessary to guarantee peace in the province.[6]

American authorities immediately opposed the Liberal project. The contemplated measure, U.S. naval and consular officials protested, quite apart from interrupting mail service and effectively halting passenger service to and from the city, threatened to disrupt domestic and foreign commerce by closing the only link left to Santiago with the outside world.[7]

Insurgent authorities proceeded with defensive preparations undeterred by American protests. To leave the maritime approaches to the city unprotected, Loret de Mola responded, simply invited Menocal to attempt to retake Santiago by sea. Should the government lay siege to the city, Liberals declined to accept further responsibility for the safety of foreign lives and property; without the appropriate defenses in the bay, the city proper would be converted into a site of combat for mastery over the province. And if, in the end, Loret warned, reversals compelled the Liberals to evacuate the city, insurgent authorities were prepared to dynamite entire sections of Santiago.[8]

Liberal authorities offered a counterproposal, however, designed to satisfy both insurgent requirements for security and American concerns for commerce and trade. If the American naval task force assigned to Cuban waters pledged to prevent the entry of hostile ships into Santiago Bay, Loret suggested, Liberal authorities would abandon plans to block the channel and reaffirm earlier pledges for the safety of foreign interests.[9] The senior naval officer present, Admiral D. W. Knox, in consultation with Consul P. Merrill Griffith, accepted the proposed compromise provisionally, pending final authorization from the commander of the Atlantic Fleet, Admiral Henry Mayo. Within twenty-four hours, Mayo repudiated the agreement and ordered Knox to prevent by whatever means necessary any insurgent attempt to interrupt maritime traffic.[10]

In Washington, however, American officials detected in the temporary Santiago compromise a means of bringing the conflict in Oriente to a satisfactory end. On February 17, the State Department reversed Mayo's decision and instructed the American legation to inform Menocal of "the wishes of this Government" that no federal ship attempt to enter Santiago until further notice.[11] A day later, Havana ordered warships en route to Santiago to remain outside the bay.[12] By the end of the first week of the rebellion, a small American flotilla had converged on Santiago to guarantee the enforced truce. In accordance with the terms of the original compromise, American warships established a blockade at the approaches to Santiago Bay to prevent entry of hostile government naval units.[13]

The Santiago Settlement

Once the minimum defense requirements of Santiago had been met, insurgent authorities turned their full attention to national developments. For much of the first two weeks of the revolt, Liberals in Santiago, far from the insurgent command in the west and preoccupied with consolidating their hold in Oriente, remained marginal onlookers to Liberal politico-military reversals on the island and diplomatic setbacks in Washington. By late February, securely in power in eastern Cuba, Liberals went to the assistance of the faltering movement. Most immediately, the Liberal government in Santiago attempted to loosen American ties to Havana by seeking from Washington some measure of recognition of insurgent authority as a preliminary step to negotiations. On February 24, angered by President Wilson's response to the Santiago Chamber of Commerce's petition a day earlier, Fernández ordered all sugar estates in rebel-held territory to suspend all operations immediately under penalty of destruction.[14] The insurgent proclamation, addressed directly to authorities in Washington, sought to demonstrate in dramatic terms that upon Liberal authorities in Santiago — and not, as Menocal claimed, upon the Conservatives in Havana — rested the security and prosperity of American interests in eastern Cuba. The decree, moreover, sought to raise a negotiable issue with American authorities. Three days later, Liberal officials contemplated expanding the work stoppage to include American mining operations in Oriente.[15]

Sugar estates felt the impact of the decree immediately. Already straining under adverse conditions, sugar production throughout Oriente and much of Camagüey ceased altogether. Sugar estates prepared for the grim prospect of losing enormous quantities of harvested cane. Facing an indefinite suspension of activity, mills began to release workers, many contracted at considerable expense from neighboring West Indian islands.[16] One estimate placed the cost of the work stoppage at $80,000 daily.[17] The managers of some twenty-five estates in eastern Cuba, facing total financial losses for the year, urgently appealed to Washington to acknowledge the authority of the Liberal government and mediate an end to the political dispute in Cuba at once.[18]

The supremacy of insurgent authority in eastern Cuba further heightened the necessity for direct negotiations with Liberal officials. Once the initial military operations had delineated the island politically, the war in the east had come to a standstill. Due in part to insurgent strength and in part to the truce imposed by the United States, the conflict had become a war of position. "The territory held by the insurgents," Consul Griffith reported, "which extends from Guantanamo to Camagüey is so large and the sympathy of the people so favorable to the movement in this section, that it appears that the administration of President Menocal cannot control the situation."[19] One former American consular agent in Santiago described a hopelessly deadlocked situation. "It is just as impossible," Otto Reimer wrote, "for the . . . Liberals, in control of the Eastern Provinces of Oriente and Camaguey, to dominate Menocal or Conservative forces in Havana, as it is for the followers of Menocal to dominate this end of the Island."[20] The commander of the American naval squadron in Santiago, Admiral Reginald R. Belknap, concluded that the conflict had reached a stand-off. "There is a deadlock," Belknap wrote, "neither side capable, *unassisted*, of overcoming the other, either soon or late."[21]

In late February, the large-scale fighting hitherto avoided in Oriente appeared imminent. On February 23, a full infantry battalion drawn from Havana arrived in Manzanillo in preparation for a land assault on Santiago. For many observers, the government offensive appeared ill-conceived and doomed to failure, threatening to result only in enormous damage to property without any real possibility of ousting Liberal forces. Insurgent authorities in Santiago possessed sufficient arms and provisions to resist a government siege for several months. Havana, under optimum circumstances and after considerable cost to life and property, could, perhaps, dislodge Liberal forces from the city. A government victory in Santiago, many feared, promised only to drive the insurgents into the surrounding countryside in anticipation of a protracted guerrilla campaign.[22] A renewal of hostilities, Belknap predicted, threatened to destroy property, increase bitterness, and make pacification ultimately more difficult. "The amount these insurgents may do," Belknap warned, "is greatly feared, should they be driven into the interior and begin guerrilla warfare; and even before that, distress and anarchy are feared as a result of stoppage in industry and traffic, shortage of food and funds, conditions which will soon start predatory bands, beyond the power of either party to control."[23]

Impelled by worsening economic conditions and the specter of renewed military operations in Oriente, American consular and naval authorities conferred with Liberal leaders to search for a political solution to the dispute. On February 27, Belknap proposed "friendly mediations" as a step preliminary to a satisfactory resolution of the conflict.[24] A day later, Belknap offered to sponsor a series of conferences among

Liberal authorities, government representatives, and American officials aboard his ship. On February 28, all parties agreed to a five-day truce.

For American authorities in Santiago, the proposed conference offered immediate security to life and property in Oriente. More important, successful mediations promised to yield a long-term political settlement of the conflict.[25] By February 28, insurgent successes in Santiago had accomplished what the movement had failed to secure nationally — a platform upon which Liberals would detail their grievances and seek to mobilize American intercession in their behalf.[26]

In a larger sense, the naval offer to mediate and the Liberals' acceptance of Belknap's invitation was a direct response to Washington's earlier pledge to assist the Cubans settle the conflict. Proposed just days after Wilson's reply to the Santiago Chamber of Commerce, mediations were seen essentially as a way to arrange the details necessary for Washington's *quid pro quo*. On February 28, the first day of the conference, Comandantes Fernández and Loret de Mola, Admiral Belknap, Consul Griffith, together with the commanders of three American warships anchored outside Santiago Bay met aboard the U.S.S. *San Francisco*. A day after the mediations commenced in Santiago, conferences in Guantánamo brought together the local American consular agent, district Liberal leaders, and Colonel José Jané, the *menocalista* commander of government forces.

Throughout the early sessions in Santiago, Liberal officials reiterated the original party position and restated the objectives of the uprising. The armed protest, Fernández and Loret stressed, sought only to thwart a Conservative dictatorship and secure honest elections.

Within forty-eight hours of the opening of the conferences, and after receiving from American representatives reassurances of Washington's commitment to assist in the dispute, Liberal leaders agreed to a tentative settlement. In return, the insurgent authorities requested guarantees of fair elections and amnesty for all army officers and troops involved in the revolt.[27]

Before the proposed Santiago settlement could take effect, however, Liberal negotiators asked Washington to underwrite formally the terms of the accord, specifically, guarantees for honest elections and amnesty.[28] The unsuccessful army revolt, in which thousands of officers and men had violated their military oaths, had raised the issue of amnesty to preeminent importance as a precondition for peace. Within weeks of the outbreak of the uprising, Gonzales discerned that many insurgent leaders sought American intervention to reduce the severity of punishment and eliminate all possibility of reprisals.[29] "When the revolutionaries are told to go home by the U.S. government," one correspondent cautioned the White House, "they must be guaranteed an amnesty. Otherwise there will be a war of endless vendettas."[30] A lasting political settlement depended entirely on the insurgent military leaders' receiving from Havana appropriate guarantees validated by the United States. "Insurgent Liberals," the military attaché conceded, "will never give up their leaders, now in rebellion, for punishment by the present government."[31] Belknap reminded his superiors that the Liberals could not be disarmed by force without first resorting to a prolonged and costly campaign. "They are conscious," Belknap explained, "of their power to do great property damage in a few hours without the remotest possibility of our preventing." Liberal concessions during the mediations had convinced Belknap that the insurgents shared with the United States a desire for a quick end to the dispute. "But to disarm," Belknap pointed out, "is to give up everything, personal as well as their cause, unless they have guarantees."[32]

By March 1, the Santiago settlement was awaiting final approval in Washington. The Navy Department, before sanctioning the accord proposed by naval personnel in Oriente, asked the secretary of state to clarify the meaning of the president's statement of February 23. Without much further elaboration, Lansing repeated that "when the rebels laid down their arms, return to their allegiance and peaceful pursuits, the United States, as a friend of Cuba, would act to effect a settlement of the dispute by constitutional methods."[33] Lansing subsequently reiterated State Department assurances directly to Belknap, thereby endorsing, if only tacitly, the navy-sponsored settlement in Santiago.[34] On March 2, naval authorities informed Liberal leaders that Washington had ratified the proposed settlement.[35]

In early March, U.S. consular and naval officials in Oriente secured within a week the settlement that had eluded Havana and Washington for a month. Liberal leaders in Oriente pledged to persuade insurgent forces operating in Camagüey and districts further west to adhere to the settlement.[36] Colonel José Jané, confident the revolt had ended, asked the American minister in Havana to secure an extension of the five-day armistice to allow representatives of both camps to inform respective field forces of the peace accord.[37]

In Santiago, the settlement had an immediate calming effect. Conditions of normality gradually returned to Oriente. In a good-will gesture to demonstrate the Liberals' confidence in the accord, Fernández lifted the injunction against sugar operations in insurgent territory.[38] On March 3, Liberal authorities agreed to release all military and political prisoners taken in the immediate aftermath of the coup; a day later, Liberal civilian officials replaced military authorities in municipal and provincial government offices. Comandante Fernández was appointed, and recognized by U.S. consular and naval authorities, as the military commandant of the province.[39] In compliance with the last, if only symbolic, requirement, Liberal partisans in the district prepared to pledge allegiance to the national government.[40] "Present arrangements," Consul Griffith reported with some satisfaction, "will maintain order, restore confidence and prevent untold loss [of] life and property. People confident and happy over changed conditions."[41]

Conforming to the spirit of the larger policy construct outlined earlier by the White House and negotiated with the approval of the State Department, the Santiago accord offered Washington an immediate end to Cuban disorders. Lansing was overjoyed. It only remained now to persuade Havana to endorse the settlement negotiated in Santiago. Within hours of the eastern accord, Lansing instructed the legation to obtain Menocal's ratification of the peace. Extending to Menocal nominal congratulations for government successes against the insurgents, Lansing passed quickly to the substantive issues at hand. "Any further fighting," the secretary of state cautioned, "would result only in needless loss of life and destruction of an immense amount of property of both Cuban and foreign owners." Lansing urged Menocal to "make clear to the people of Cuba and to the rest of the world his position as the patriotic advocate of constitutional methods for the settlement of electoral disputes" by issuing a proclamation declaring that "coincident with the laying down of arms by the insurgents and the return of their allegiance, elections will be called in Santa Clara and Oriente and an amnesty granted to those involved in the revolt." The secretary of state, moreover, committed the good offices of the United States to guarantee the integrity of honest elections. Lansing added a thinly veiled threat, warning Menocal that any delay "would probably force this Government to take such action as might destroy the moral effect of the Constitutional Government's successes."[42] Two days later, the State Department restated the requisite importance of amnesty and fair elections to the restoration of peace; both considerations, as the cardinal points of the Santiago settlement, constituted the minimum basis for ending the dispute.[43]

The Failure of Compromise

Within twenty-four hours, the settlement arranged in Santiago collapsed in Havana. First and foremost, the specter of partial elections guaranteed by Washington aroused considerable apprehension in Conservative circles. If, in fact, original estimates of Liberal electoral strength had any substance — and most observers believed they did — the partial elections ordered earlier by the Supreme Court virtually guaranteed a Liberal sweep. Menocal, no doubt aware of the central position of amnesty in the proposed settlement, chose to seize the issue of pardons to undermine the Santiago accord. "This is not a revolution of the people," he rebutted angrily, "but is almost wholly a military sedition of officers who have been disloyal to the Government." To grant insurgent leaders an "indiscriminate" pardon on the scale proposed by Washington, Menocal suggested, "would have a disastrous effect upon the morale of the army and upon public opinion." The rebels had violated their oaths, "scandalously broken discipline" by rising in arms against the constitutional government, imprisoned constituted and lawful authorities, destroyed public archives, and appropriated public funds. Such an amnesty, the president exhorted, "would not only crush the authority and moral force of the Government but would provoke deep discontent in the loyal forces." Circumstances warranted not an amnesty but, on the contrary, "just and exemplary punishment of the principal perpetrators and instigators of such crimes." Only through these means could "future government in Cuba be set upon a firm foundation and the integrity of her institutions preserved."[44] Of the corollary issue of honest partial elections Menocal's communication contained little more than perfunctory acknowledgment. Indeed, Gonzales detected that Menocal "seemed indifferent as to the elections."[45]

No one in the State Department seemed to appreciate fully the implications of Menocal's rejection of the Santiago agreement. In a single stroke, the Conservative chieftain irrevocably committed the United States to "constituted" authority, while shattering the most promising — and, perhaps, for Menocal the most threatening — opportunity for peace. Growing daily more absorbed with European developments, Lansing responded with a conciliatory counterproposal. On March 3, Lansing, apparently unaware that in principle the basis of the Santiago accord had already been shattered, again raised the question of elections. The State Department suggested that Menocal offer an amnesty to insurgents other than army officers, thereby facilitating the partial elections: "The immediate question is not amnesty but the right of those in complicity with the present insurrection to cast their votes in the partial elections to be held under decree of the Supreme Court."[46] Lansing had paid little attention to the details of the Santiago agreement and the position of amnesty. After the failure of the February 10 coup, the "immediate question" became amnesty.

Menocal repeated his determination to suppress the uprising without resorting to concessions tending to compromise the integrity of his administration. Bowing in the end to clamor from the State Department, Menocal issued vague pardons to all insurgents except former army officers, civil officials, and "pernicious leaders and flagrant criminals."[47] Havana had skillfully yielded in form to the demands of the United States without accepting the substance of the Santiago settlement.

Menocal's opposition to American policy maneuvers received full support, if not inspiration, from the legation. Partly out of anger at what Gonzales understood to be a usurpation of the legation's authority in Cuba by naval officers in Oriente and partly on grounds of policy, the minister opposed the negotiated peace in Santiago. The settlement, Gonzales protested, ignored the "intricate past political history" of Cuba and disregarded any consideration of future political repercussions. The revolution had failed, Gonzales emphasized; insurgent Liberals, defeated and without a legitimate cause, had become mere bandits. The only effective means of ending the habit of revolution in Cuba, and thereby permitting the island to live in tranquility as a self-governing republic, necessarily involved unconditional submission of the insurgents. "Anything like compromise," Gonzales warned Washington, "would be acclaimed victory by revolutionists and another step away from stable government."[48] Protesting naval intermeddling in Cuba internal affairs, Gonzales further challenged the authority of naval officials to negotiate a settlement with insurgent representatives.[49] The legation urged Washington to scrap the settlement and order American armed forces to move against the insurgent-held city as the only satisfactory remedy of the situation. As an alternate to the agreement of amnesty, Gonzales suggested that rebel officers surrender to American naval authorities and permit enlisted men to accept the government's offer of pardon; the United States, Gonzales added, would offer its good offices to save the most important national figures of the revolt from severe or capital punishment.[50]

Unaware of the turn of events in Havana and Washington, American officials in Santiago continued to perfect the details of the March 1 agreement. All decrees issued by Liberal authorities received the sanction of American representatives. Shortly after the transfer of power to civilian Liberals, Belknap reiterated his guarantee of fair elections and reissued his promise to open the port and clear all government ships menacing maritime traffic outside the bay; Belknap also pledged to keep opposition forces out of the city.[51]

On March 4, authorities in Santiago received the first indication that the settlement had somehow miscarried. Having already privately repudiated the agreement, Menocal now publicly refused to renew the cease-fire and ordered government forces in Oriente Province to advance on Santiago.

Reports of an imminent government attack stunned Liberal and American officials in Santiago. The Liberal governor, José García Muñoz, appealed immediately to Belknap for American intercession to prevent a renewal of fighting.[52] Apparently still uninformed that the settlement had failed to win final approval in Havana and outraged by the threat to the peace fashioned laboriously only days earlier, Belknap denounced the *menocalista* violation of the terms of the Santiago agreement. In a strongly worded proclamation, Belknap outlawed all government operations in Oriente Province and ordered Menocal's troops to stay outside the city:

I hereby declare that any military activity, beyond that necessary to restore and preserve order and tranquility, is prejudicial to the peace and welfare of this province and I do further hereby solemnly warn any and all persons against taking military operations in the Province of Oriente, except under the orders of the Military Commandant [Fernández] of this province; and I do hereby further solemnly warn all persons under arms, not under command of said Commandant, against committing or taking part in any and every hostile act within this Province and against advancing into this Province with intent to disturb peace.[53]

Believing that only ignorance of the settlement on the part of local *menocalista* commanders could account for the announced offensive against Liberals in Santiago, Belknap dispatched naval officers to inform the advancing government forces of the armistice.[54]

By March 5, the peace accord had publicly collapsed.[55] In Havana, Menocal and the American minister repudiated outright the negotiated settlement.[56] In Washington, Lansing, pressed by the international crisis, chose the path of least resistance and yielded to Havana. "You understand," Lansing later said to Gonzales in justification of his original support of the Santiago negotiations, "that the United States is facing a serious international situation outside the Western Hemisphere and that the Department's recommendations are based on this fact as well as its consideration for the welfare of Cuba."[57] In Oriente, *menocalista* field commanders repudiated the settlement and announced their intention to subdue the revolt without further concessions to insurgent Liberals.[58] Colonel Matías Betancourt, the government military chieftain in Oriente, scorned Belknap's proclamation of March 4, asserting that he accepted orders only from Havana.

By March 7, government troops had pressed their advance to the outskirts of Santiago. Fierce resistance in the suburbs intensified as fighting moved closer to the city.[59] The American consulate urged Washington in vain to secure an immediate armistice as the "only means of preventing great disaster and bloodshed."[60] In Santiago, Belknap appealed to Fernández to withdraw his forces in order to avoid an armed confrontation with *menocalista* troops and thereby save the city from major destruction. After lengthy discussions, during which Belknap pledged that Santiago would remain under the control of Liberal civil authorities, Fernández agreed to withdraw Liberal military forces.[61] On March 8, at the request of the Liberal government, Belknap landed some four hundred officers and men to assist local authorities in preserving order.[62]

Throughout the first week of March, Belknap remained committed to the original settlement. As late as March 11, Belknap reiterated his support of the Liberal administration in Santiago. "There shall be," the naval chief vowed, "no fighting in the city as long as I have the power to prevent [it]. No force shall be allowed to fight its way in."[63] Confident that the dispute could be settled politically, Belknap refused to allow government troops to occupy Santiago until both sides had arrived at a negotiated settlement; repeatedly, the naval commander counseled compromise and mediation. Belknap sensed that Liberal leaders in Santiago, including many former regular army officers and provincial officials prominent before the revolution, feared the penalties resulting from an unconditional surrender. Without concessions from Havana, Belknap warned, the conflict would continue interminably.[64]

By mid-March, pressure from Washington had revoked consular and naval commitments to the negotiated settlement. The State Department reprimanded Consul Griffith for an inappropriate display of sympathy for Liberals during their administration of government in Santiago.[65] Admiral Belknap was censured by Mayo for having overreached his authority.[66] Belknap ended his advocacy of a mediated peace. In accordance with his orders, the naval chieftain prepared to relinquish Santiago to *menocalista* forces.[67] "I supposed," Belknap concluded ruefully, "that our Government has made up its mind to let the Cuban Government put the insurrection down irregardless of private losses, as a good precedent. It will discourage other revolutions to have this one fail."[68] From March 15 to 16, sea and land units from Havana proceeded to occupy the eastern capital. To prevent disorders coincident with the occupation, *menocalista* troops remained positioned outside Santiago while American forces continued to patrol the city.[69] On March 25, the navy evacuated all land forces from Santiago, leaving the city in control of government authorities.

The Mediation Impulse Localized

The presence of naval patrols off various points of the coast of insurgent-held zones continued to involve American representatives in direct and frequent communication with local insurgent leaders. Like Belknap in Santiago, naval officials elsewhere in Oriente Province perceived a negotiated end to the dispute as the most effective way to discharge their responsibility for American lives and property. Almost without exception, naval commanders found Liberal representatives in their respective districts predisposed to negotiate an end to the conflict. Throughout March and early April, quite spontaneously and without official sanction, naval authorities in collaboration with local American consular agents organized a number of peace conferences, bringing together representatives of both sides of the dispute to discuss peace. On March 12, one such session in Guantánamo convened aboard the U.S.S. *Montana*.[70] On April 13, the commander of the American patrol in Nipe Bay, Admiral H. K. Hewitt, organized a conference between the district rebel chieftain Blas Masó and government officials, encouraging them to negotiate a settlement of the two-month-old conflict.[71]

A second series of conferences, by far the most promising after Santiago, occurred in Manatí between Hewitt and the staff of insurgent General Felipe Leyva. Liberals pledged to lay down their arms in exchange for amnesty guaranteed by the United States and elections supervised by American representatives.[72] Impressed by the reasonableness of Liberal conditions and detecting in this offer an opportunity to end the revolt, Hewitt urged Washington to endorse the terms proposed by Liberals in Manatí. "I feel certain," Hewitt explained, "that if the United States sees fit to act on their request, quiet and order will quickly be restored. Otherwise I fear much more property will be destroyed and the safety of unprotected Americans greatly endangered."[73]

The tentative Manatí accord collapsed owing to further opposition from Havana. For the second time in almost as many weeks, the promise of a negotiated peace was spurned by the American legation in the capital. A settlement of this type, Gonzales protested, would be tantamount to "the recognition of the justice of the rebellion and admission of the Government's defeat." Any arrangement offering less than a complete and unconditional victory of the government was simply unacceptable. "While apparently urging a course calculated to quell the immediate disorders," Gonzales insisted, "he [Hewitt] does not seem to consider the effect which justification of the rebellion might have on the future peace of Cuba."[74] Without the appropriate minimum guarantees, insurgent Liberals in Manatí withdrew their offer and retired into the interior.[75]

As the rebellion moved into its third and fourth months, and the hopelessness of Liberal leaders increased, naval representatives assumed still another function. Throughout May and April, naval authorities organized temporary cease-fires to encourage contending forces to come together. In this manner, American officials hastened the collapse of organized Liberal resistance by intervening in behalf of insurgent leaders to arrange with local *menocalista* authorities terms for the surrender of Liberal partisans. The presence of naval officials permitted insurgent leaders, desirous of abandoning the field but unwilling to surrender unconditionally, to secure satisfactory conditions, guaranteed by American authorities for renouncing armed struggle. Most commonly, naval commanders arranged with local government representatives the terms for the exile of Liberal leaders. The opportunity for Liberal leaders to leave the field with appropriate guarantees encouraged many prominent insurgent chieftains to abandon the struggle. These desertions directly contributed to a localized collapse of the political protest and generally weakened the Liberal movement. Gradually, as hopes for the Liberal cause grew increasingly bleak, larger numbers of insurgent chieftains appealed to American representatives for assistance in arranging surrender or flight. United States ships anchored off the Oriente coast provided accessible refuge for those insurgent leaders seeking political asylum and wishing to leave the island. The U.S.S. *Machias* provided sanctuary for five Liberal commanders who asked for political refuge. After negotiating with government authorities, naval officials secured permission to arrange for their departure to New Orleans.[76] In early April, U.S. naval and consular officials negotiated with government representatives safe-conduct passes for the leading Liberal insurgents in Oriente, including Rigoberto Fernández and Luis Loret de Mola. In return for arranging the surrender of part of their force, the Liberal leaders secured through American officials a guarantee of safe-conduct and transportation to American-occupied Haiti.[77] By the end of May, virtually all Liberal party chieftains in arms had arrived at some settlement or another with government agents.[78]

The various expedients adopted by American officials in eastern Cuba to protect life and property had the sum effect of bolstering Havana's position in Oriente. Armed intervention, local truces, and the arrangement of exile for insurgent Liberal leaders contributed to a general collapse of organized Liberal resistance. An effective negotiated settlement, however, at one point so close to consummation, continued to elude U.S. efforts. Faced with two governments at different ends of the island, each finding support from different agencies of the United States government, Washington followed the course of least resistance.

The capture of José Miguel Gómez at Caicaje and the expulsion of Liberals from Santiago within weeks of one another virtually assured the collapse of the organized Liberal challenge to Menocal. Flushed with military success, Menocal's confidence soared. By late March, the Conservatives had committed themselves to a complete military suppression of the revolution without further compromise or concession.[79]

5.

Liberals, Bandits, and Social Protest: The Persistence of Insurgency

The Politics of Insurgent Leadership

By mid-March, the Liberal politico-military challenge no longer constituted a direct threat to the Conservative government. On the diplomatic front, insurgent Liberals had failed to achieve even their most modest objectives, namely, a favorable hearing from the United States. In the field, the Liberal protest had gradually lost all qualities of an organized national uprising. Liberal armies operating in Las Villas and western Camagüey, the forces most distant from the main body of insurgent concentrations in Oriente, had been largely routed and dispersed. The battle of Caicaje resulted in the capture of the principal — and most prestigious — political and military directors of the Liberal movement. In the east, the evacuation of Santiago, followed by the *menocalista* occupation of the city, had undermined Liberal governmental authority in Oriente Province.

Diplomatic reversals and successive military setbacks in Caicaje and Santiago convinced many national Liberal leaders in the field of the futility of further armed opposition to the Conservative government. The protest had earlier lost the active support of a considerable number of civilian party leaders who, in response to the American notes of February 13 and 18, refused to mortgage their political careers to a movement opposed in Washington and apparently doomed in Cuba. The long-range repercussions of Caicaje, moreover, transcended the immediate effects of the loss of Gómez and the insurgent General Staff. Civil and military insurgent chieftains, demoralized by the capture of the *jefe máximo* of the insurrection and now convinced that Caicaje signaled the

65

final collapse of the movement, felt relieved of any further obligation to support the Liberal protest. After mid-March, insurgent leaders in increasing numbers reached private peace settlements with government authorities. Some Liberal chieftains surrendered in exchange for personal guarantees; others, with the assistance of American authorities, chose to abandon the field of armed struggle for exile abroad. The nationally prominent leaders of the Santiago takeover, including Rigoberto Fernández and Luis Loret de Mola, privately made peace with the Conservatives and were allowed to leave Cuba for refuge abroad.[1] By early spring, hundreds of key figures of the Liberal uprising had found safety in the United States, Jamaica, Mexico, Haiti, and the Bahamas.[2]

Through capture, death, and exile, the Liberal protest had been deprived of most of its nationally important chieftains. Civilian leaders who had originally organized the movement, together with army officers who had seconded the party leadership in mid-February, gradually disappeared from the field. When, in April, Menocal followed Washington's lead in declaring war on Germany, several more prominent leaders, including Gerardo Machado, abandoned the field as an expression of solidarity with the homeland in the moment of the international crisis. Cuba's declaration of war, Orestes Ferrara wrote in New York, made Liberals "understand that our duty was to maintain internal peace above any other cause."[3]

The continuing insurgency, furthermore, precipitated a crisis in the Liberal party. By early spring, disagreement over strategy and purpose had split the party into town and country polarities. In Havana, prominent Liberals who had earlier either repudiated the movement or, after initially joining, quickly abandoned the protest when the coup stalled in the capital, condemned the insurgent leadership remaining in the field; other Liberal leaders, arrested earlier for their part in the conspiracy and released on parole, likewise urged rebel leaders to support the Conservative government.[4] In early May, congressional Liberal leaders caucused in Havana to order insurgent commanders in the interior to cease all further field operations and surrender to government authorities.[5]

During April and May, virtually all leaders of any political or military stature had abandoned the field.[6] The collapse of the insurgent national leadership deprived the movement of central direction. With the capture or death of ranking political and military leaders, and the flight, defection, and exile of others, direction of insurgent forces continuing to operate in the field passed to subaltern commanders. The majority of chieftains who remained under arms after early May were politically anonymous — figures largely unknown nationally who had achieved at best secondary regional positions in the Liberal party and the armed forces. Many had secured local prominence only as a result of their field successes in the course of the insurgency.

Having occupied only minor posts in the Liberal party or subaltern commands in the revolt, these insurgent chieftains possessed insufficient national stature to permit them to bargain for personal guarantees and amnesty concessions from government authorities. Most surviving chieftains lacked official party position; virtually all of the insurgent rank and file had little more than nominal political affiliation. Surviving insurgent leaders in the field lacked the popularity and national prestige necessary to attract national attention and sympathy to their plight. The lack of financial resources, political connections, and appropriate family ties, moreover, precluded life in exile as a viable alternative to the field. Fernández and Loret de Mola left Cuba with some $194,000.[7] When Carlos Mendieta finally made his way out of Cuba in April 1917, he settled in Jamaica and resumed his medical practice in exile.[8] Without prominent family links, important political associations, and national stature, minor insurgent commanders in the field after mid-March could expect to receive from the Conservatives only the severest penalties. Their fate at government hands was of little consequence to the party: since they were politically anonymous and nationally unknown, their condition would not attract national attention or generate public sympathy. They could not reasonably expect to receive, like Machado, the guarantees traditionally the result of widespread publicity attending surrender and trial. Neither could they reasonably expect, like José Miguel Gómez, Rigoberto Fernández, and Luis Loret de Mola, U.S. diplomatic intervention in their behalf.[9] Without the necessary legitimizing political affiliations, they were viewed as "common criminals."[10] Punishment for the insurrection would fall fully on the anonymous participants of the movement. Accounts of the treatment accorded to Liberals captured by government forces circulated throughout insurgent camps. Few could reasonably expect to escape the fate of Gustavo Caballero — one of the more prominent Liberal leaders to emerge in Camagüey in March — who was captured by government forces in April and killed en route to Havana under mysterious circumstances.[11] If Caballero could be murdered by his captors with such impunity, what possible fate awaited lesser known figures?

Convinced of the virtue of the Liberal cause, many subaltern commanders had followed the party civilian and military leadership into the field unquestioningly. By the end of April, with the disappearance of the nationally prominent leaders of the Liberal protest and the repudiation of the insurrection by party spokesmen in Havana, local insurgent commanders remained in the field to work out the accommodations most appropriate to their particular needs. The majority remained nominally committed to original Liberal objectives and assumed direction of armed bands determined to succeed where the national leadership had failed. Indeed, success offered the only viable alternative to long prison terms and, quite possibly, to death.

The lingering commitment to the revolution among insurgent Liberal leaders remaining in the field after Caicaje and Santiago stemmed also from a continuing, if misplaced, confidence in the ultimate triumph of the Liberal cause. Many retained their arms in the belief that the insurgency would start anew in the late spring when the sugar harvest came to an end. Others continued the armed struggle in the expectation that a much-rumored coup, reportedly scheduled in Havana for May 20, would block Menocal's inauguration for a second term. The swift collapse of the Liberal plot in the capital on February 9 and 10 had permitted many of the original conspirators to rejoin army ranks undetected. The continued existence of Liberal sympathizers within the armed forces encouraged many to remain in the field in the anticipation of a second antigovernment plot in the capital.[12] Lastly, if everything else failed, insurgent Liberals in Camagüey and Oriente believed that, despite growing differences with the urban sector of the party, the Liberal congressional delegation in Havana would boycott Congress and block the quorum necessary to ratify congressional confirmation of the president's disputed election victory.[13]

The Social Content of Insurgency

However effective the combination of American diplomacy and Cuban military measures may have been in suppressing the Liberal political challenge, by early spring Havana had still failed to put an end to the insurgency. On the contrary, the situation that many American authorities had originally feared the most had developed. The collapse of central insurgent authority had decentralized the leadership of the armed struggle and transformed a national movement into a protest largely regional and local in nature. By early April, the insurgency had reorganized around decentralized field units, distributed throughout the eastern provinces; each arrogated to itself more or less autonomy and was only nominally committed to vindicating the moribund Liberal cause. The organized political challenge had come to an end without a cessation of the insurgency.

By mid-March, in the wake of military and diplomatic reversals, the main bodies of Liberal troops in Oriente had dispersed into mobile guerrilla units. Days after the evacuation of Santiago de Cuba, insurgent troops under Fernández and Loret de Mola scattered into small irregular units of twenty to thirty men.[14] The establishment of guerrilla columns, moreover, necessitated the organization of new commands destined to survive in the field long after Fernández and Loret de Mola had left Cuba. The main body of insurgent armies in Songo, Guantánamo, and Manatí similarly retired into the interior, reorganized into guerrilla units.[15] Estimates of the total number of insurgents operating as guerrillas in late March and early April varied. In Camagüey, some three to four thousand armed officers and men remained in the field.[16] In Oriente, various estimates placed guerrilla forces between five thousand and seven thousand men.[17]

As the leadership of the insurrection decentralized, the social base of the insurgency broadened. In addition to — and increasingly, in the course of the spring, independent of — the original political grievances, the armed protest embraced local issues. The populist appeal of the Liberal party and its flamboyant leadership had early attracted to the insurgent banner workers, farmers, and peasants in virtually all the eastern provinces. The ''ignorant and incapable class,'' the American consul in Havana reported, made up the majority of the Liberals' support.[18] In the Guantánamo valley, the revolutionary movement won widespread support among sugar workers in the region. As late as May, observers speculated that there would be a "continued increase in the drift of the laboring classes to the ranks of the bandits and revolutionary force."[19] Throughout the spring, Afro-Cubans in increasing numbers joined the partisan bands operating in the east.[20]

Local social and economic grievances, independent of national political issues, gained increasing prominence as the rebellion entered the third month, now without national direction. In 1917, a way of life was coming to an end in eastern Cuba. Throughout the latter half of the nineteenth century, the eastern provinces had remained largely impervious to the currents then transforming sectors of western Cuba into the bastion of the sugar latifundia. Sugar estates in the east, by comparison, were primitive family enterprises, without the capital and technological resources of the west and incapable of participating in the modernization impulse of the nineteenth century.[21] By the turn of the century, Oriente contained the largest number of independent farms with the smallest average acreage.[22] A variety of different communities and economic enterprises survived intact into the twentieth century. The sugar estates continued to coexist forbearingly with the coffee plantations, the single independent farms, and the innumerable unincorporated rural communities. To be sure, the sugar latifundia occupied an important place in the eastern landscape. Typically, however, the latifundia in Oriente were more traditional than commercial, more family than corporate. In 1899, only one-half of 1 percent of the farms in Oriente were over ten *caballerías* (333 acres), constituting some 26.9 percent of the area under cultivation.[23] For generations, much of the land in these backwater rural areas was held in common, often without formal title; family land claims reaching back to the century of conquest and settlement often rested on local tradition and occupancy. Few of the landowning families had more than a vague notion of the size or value of their properties.[24]

The collapse of European beet sugar production and the rise of sugar prices early in World War I forecast a profound transformation of the economic purpose of land in Oriente and Camagüey. Very soon after

August 1914, a drive was begun to bring eastern Cuba under the regimen of the modern sugar latifundia.[25] Cane fields spilled out of the traditional sugar regions in western and central Cuba and advanced implacably eastward; miles of imposing timber forests succumbed to the expanding fields of frail stalks of cane. Teresa Casuso recalled:

> I remember, in Oriente, the great impenetrable forests that were set aflame, whole jungles that were fired and razed to the ground to make way for the sugar cane. My parents were in despair for that lost wealth of beautiful, fragrant tropical wood — cedar, mahogany, and mastic, and magnificent-grained pomegranate — blazing in sacrifice to the frenzy to cover the countryside with sugar cane.[26]

Newly organized sugar conglomerates, representing enormous sums of American capital, appeared throughout eastern Cuba. Old estates, traditional holdings, and family farms passed under new foreign management; larger sugar producers absorbed smaller companies.

The expansion of the zones of sugar cultivation, moreover, adversely affected other agricultural enterprises in eastern Cuba. In Oriente, coffee and cocoa planters lost their workers and, ultimately, their land to sugar. By 1919, coffee and cocoa production had ceased in nine Oriente municipalities, including Santiago, Mayarí, Holguín, Banes, Gibara, Puerto Padre, Victoria de las Tunas, Campechuela, and Niquero. Several coffee plantations, such as El Olimpo and others in Songo and Palma Soriano, were converted directly into sugar plantations.[27]

Much to the bewilderment and confusion of the people of Camagüey and Oriente, scores of small landowners, farmers, and peasants were transformed into a rural proletariat in less than a decade. Those who resisted the pressures to abandon the soil found themselves driven to search for new land deep in the inhospitable mountain ranges of Baracoa and the Sierra Maestra, far from traditional transportation routes and local agricultural markets.[28] The concentration of land in sugar latifundia, Ramiro Guerra y Sánchez wrote, uprooted the farmer, destroyed the rural landowning and independent farming class, impoverished the rural population, and converted the countryside into a satellite of a foreign power.[29]

Dislodged as an independent property-owning class, moreover, an entire sector of eastern Cuba's population found itself further displaced as a labor force. A necessary coefficient of the success of the new sugar conglomerates arising in Oriente was the availability of a plentiful supply of cheap labor. For this, the sugar companies turned to Haiti and Jamaica. Starting as early as 1913, increasing numbers of Antillean laborers arrived in Cuba to work in the newly organized cane fields of Camagüey and Oriente. In 1917, a record number of Jamaicans and Haitians arrived in Cuba.[30] Between 1913 and 1921, some 180,000 workers were legally contracted in Haiti and Jamaica to cut cane in eastern Cuba.[31] Many thousands more were suspected to have been introduced into the island illegally.[32]

The arrival of West Indians in such numbers in less than a decade further contributed to the general disruption of Oriente society. Between 1907 and 1919, the population of Oriente showed an extraordinary increase of some 60 percent, from 455,086 to 730,909.[33] A community largely beyond the main reaches of the twentieth century and, by virtue of isolation and temperament, for generations impervious to outside influences, was suddenly subjected to a wave of foreign immigration totally without precedent. Foreign languages, strange customs, and new religions swept through the province, undermining the region's long tradition of cultural stability.

The increase of the provincial population in Oriente, however, although consistent with population trends across the island, concealed an entirely different demographic drama occurring at the local level. Sugar not only appropriated land but also displaced people. Considerable numbers of barrios in those municipalities experiencing severe socioeconomic dislocations suffered sharp losses of population. Indeed, between 1907 and 1919, at least five barrios situated in the new sugar districts of eastern Cuba disappeared altogether.[34] Coffee- and cocoa-producing municipalities, most notably Gibara, Mayarí, Holguín, Puerto Padre, and Baracoa, suffered the largest losses. Fully one-third of the twenty-three barrios of Baracoa experienced a decline in population; more than half of the fourteen barrios in Cobre lost population. Similar developments were experienced in Alto Songo, Bayamo, Guantánamo, and Jiguaní.[35]

In early 1917, as the Liberal party plotted against the Menocal government, eastern Cuba found itself in the throes of a socioeconomic upheaval. The traditional world of generations of *orientales* crashed suddenly in their midst — in full view, without warning, without apparent reason. A society made up in the main of self-sufficient farmers was reorganized into a community consisting largely of dependent farm workers, frequently working for foreign corporations, eating foreign-produced foods, often living in company towns, and buying from company stores.[36] Land in eastern Cuba ceased to produce for the local population and became instead the preserve of products destined for foreign markets. The loss of control over the economic purpose of land, furthermore, increased Cuba's dependence on foreign food imports. Between 1914 and 1916, food imports increased dramatically.[37]

	1914	1916
Meat	$11,269,163	$18,427,137
Cereals	15,393,569	26,151,554
Fruits	772,057	1,247,812
Vegetables	5,602,017	10,362,443

"The small Cuban population," one observer commented, "cannot produce $300 or $400 worth of sugar per capita and at the same time produce their own food."[38] The loss of self-sufficiency, moreover, occurred almost simultaneously with the first of a series of relentless price increases, especially in food. Between November 1916 and October 1917, the price of rice increased 75 percent in one typical company store in Oriente; flour increased by 46 percent and beans some 50 percent.[39]

Well before the outbreak of "La Chambelona," the rural population of Camagüey and Oriente was in a rebellious mood. Rage among the peasants, farmers, and small landowners mounted; popular reaction against the disruption of Oriente society increased. As early as October 1914, some four thousand peasants marched angrily against local government authorities in Baracoa to protest the loss of their land. A confrontation of tragic proportions between the demonstrating peasants and the armed forces was avoided only after Emilio Soto, the local Liberal candidate for Congress, pledged himself to seek alternative means to recover the lost land.[40] As late as July 1917, peasants continued to protest maneuvers designed to dispossess them of their land.[41]

By February 1917, the prevailing mood in eastern Cuba favored the plot brewing in Havana. Indeed, the Liberal conspiracy found virtually an entire province poised at the brink of rebellion. Supporters of "La Chambelona" in Camagüey and Oriente brought to the insurgency a complexity of grievances that went well beyond the political dimensions of the Liberal protest. That the insurgency would survive well after the collapse of central political direction was in no small measure due to the socioeconomic nourishment the original Liberal protest received locally in Camagüey and Oriente. The disappearance of Liberal chieftains no doubt facilitated this process and served to diffuse the leadership regionally and invigorate the politically bankrupt insurgency with local socioeconomic issues.

The autonomy devolving on local insurgent columns after the disappearance of national leadership permitted partisan bands to turn their attention increasingly to local grievances, thereby generating support locally. Three months after the abortive coup in Havana, the armed protest had acquired characteristics of large-scale social banditry. The men and women who become social bandits, Eric Hobsbawm posited, are products of the imposition of capitalism by external forces — "insidiously by the operation of economic forces which they do not understand and over which they have no control."[42] Bandits, Hobsbawm wrote elsewhere, tend to reflect "the disruption of an entire society, the rise of new classes and social structures, the resistance of entire communities or peoples against the destruction of its way of life."[43]

Well before the outbreak of the February revolution, acts of individual rebellion were on the increase in both Camagüey and Oriente. Displaced from the land, deprived of a livelihood, many *orientales* channeled protest into banditry. The livestock and wares of the large latifundia and foreign estates, together with company stores, were subject to increasing attacks. Several rural rebels very quickly distinguished themselves and acquired province-wide reputations as popular symbols of *oriental* resistance to foreign technology and capital. Such personalities as José "Cholo" Rivera and Rafael Valera became the scourge of the estates. Indeed, as early as November 1914, banditry had reached sufficient proportions to prompt Secretary of *Gobernación*

Hevia to pledge publicly new energetic measures to combat the prevailing wave of "lawlessness."[44]

In the early spring of 1917, what had begun as an armed protest by the Liberal party had reorganized around local issues under the direction of provincial chieftains. Even as early as February 28, the French consul in Santiago reported the interior "filling with guerrillas difficult for the insurrection leaders to control."[45] Newly reconstituted insurgent bands enjoyed the protection of the provincial population throughout the spring. "In the great part of the country," the American consul in Caimanera reported in mid-April, "the rebels find welcome shelter among the inhabitants."[46] Sheltered, protected, and supported by the local population, armed partisans attacked sugar estates, seized livestock, and made off with food and supplies; goods seized from estates were often redistributed among the communities of the interior.[47] By the spring, the protest in eastern Cuba had to a considerable extent evolved into a peasant cry for vengeance on the propertied, a fury of energy directed toward curbing the estate and righting individual wrongs. "The Liberals," one observer remarked of the revolt, "do not want to fight, they do not want to kill or destroy, but being underofficered the men who have private grievances against some of the plantation owners or managers have avenged them in spite of the influence of their officers. The destruction of property is done a great deal by private individuals not by the revolutionists."[48]

The decentralization of the insurgent command and the subsequent dispersals of Liberal armies into local guerrilla units converted a difficult situation into an impossible one for Conservative authorities in Havana. The widened social base of the protest had pushed the insurgency beyond the limited political objectives inherent in the original plot. "The revolutionary forces operating in this province," the American consul in Caimanera reported in late May, "have now degenerated into groups of bandits headed by notorious characters having no political significance."[49] Supported by the interior population, partisan bands successfully eluded superior government forces; when insurgent bands met government units of comparable size, the guerrilla forces proved to be formidable adversaries.

Nowhere were the underlying reasons for the insurrection in Oriente and Camagüey in early spring seen so clearly as in the relationship between armed bands and American property owners. To be sure, the estates of all foreigners, as well as the property of Cubans, were attacked. The destruction of American-owned estates, however, assumed important symbolic significance in the spring. The decentralization and dispersal of the rebel forces increased the difficulty of the sugar estates in negotiating private settlements with local insurgent units. No single commander exercised complete and effective authority over the farflung bands located throughout the sugar districts of eastern Cuba. "The great difficulty in which I find myself," one estate manager wrote, "is that there is no one single chief, or head with whom I can treat, there being present in our neighborhood seven men acting as Captains, Colonels and Generals, constantly giving unintelligible orders and counterorders and always finding a group ready to obey."[50] In the absence of adequate protection from Havana, planters in the eastern interior had on several earlier occasions successfully negotiated settlements with insurgent chieftains in which the estates offered food, supplies, and shelter in exchange for guarantees of the security of estate property and personnel. By early spring, these informal arrangements were becoming increasingly unworkable. "We did not ask for any [government] protection before," the assistant manager of the Miranda Sugar Company cabled the New York office, "while the Liberals were organized and under recognized leaders, but now the situation is different — for the rebels are scattered throughout the country and we fear the small bands that come across our property may do us some damage."[51]

The inability of government forces to act either adequately in the protection of property or decisively in the suppression of the revolt assumed a new urgency in April as past informal pacts between planters and rebels proved increasingly ineffective. One group of American citrus colonists in Oriente petitioned Washington for assistance in the face of the new developments in the province. "For nearly two months," the planters wrote, "the rebel forces were held in restraint by rebel chiefs that were in our neighborhoods, and we owe it to their efforts that our colonies were left undestroyed at the time. After the government 'successes' in the Southern part of the Province, large hordes of rebels invaded our territory. The leaders lost control and our business places, farms, and homes have been raided or burned, our horses and cattle have been carried away or killed."[52]

Political considerations heightened the danger to U.S. property. Social grievances joined political protest as insurgents sought to settle scores with Americans. Increasingly, surviving Liberal units grew anti-American. In the aftermath of the stillborn Santiago settlement and the subsequent *menocalista* occupation of the city, the insurgent forces felt themselves betrayed. Disappointment in Washington's failure to follow through with ratification of the Santiago agreement turned to resentment as American authorities, in violation of their pledge to Liberal chieftains, relinquished control of Santiago de Cuba to government troops.[53] In Manzanillo, the American consul reported in mid-April the prevalence of bitter anti-American feelings among large sectors of the local population.[54] Consul Griffith noted with some concern the growing resentment against the United States in Santiago. "There is," Griffith reported, "a decided feeling of resentment and hatred against the Americans among the liberals here and insurgents as they openly claim the Americans deceived them."[55]

Scattered into small irregular units, weakened militarily by a reduction in size, and pursued by superior government forces, the insurgents revised their tactics to conform to the new realities. By early spring, local socioeconomic grievances had joined national politico-military frustrations. Having failed to secure American assistance through negotiations, the few Liberals remaining in the field committed their resources to compel U.S. intervention through an organized campaign against property. Indeed, after mid-March, insurgents organized their campaign primarily around the destruction of estates. Political grievances had fused with social protest. The guerrilla units formed out of the main Liberal army in Santiago de Cuba were not so much designed to engage government forces as organized to destroy property. The tactical content of the waning Liberal protest had been established by mid-March. Rigoberto Fernández, soon after evacuating Santiago, spoke of a "program" of destruction of property to force the intervention of the United States.[56] In late March, the State Department learned that Liberal forces dispersing into guerrilla units were "returning into the hilly country and increasing their operations of burning, robbing, and destruction of property with greater activity."[57] In Guantánamo, guerrilla bands retired into the interior with the intention of waging a war of destruction in the surrounding countryside.[58] In southeast Oriente, the guerrilla force under General Blas Masó demanded American assistance to re-solve the conflict under threat of stepping up activities against property. "They seemed to be determined," Griffith reported, "through acts of violence, pillage and burning of property to bring on if possible Ameri-can intervention and they have no hesitancy in openly making declara-tions to this effect."[59] As far west as Cienfuegos, insurgents mounted operations against property.[60] If the campaign against property failed to secure U.S. intervention, insurgent Liberal chieftains intimated the further necessity of sacrificing American lives.[61] If the United States declined to intervene, one rebel leader warned Commander H. K. Hewitt, insurgent Liberals would force the United States to intervene to deliver American property interests from complete destruction. "They are now respecting life and property," Hewitt wrote in late March, "but if the United States does not intervene, they state they intend to start a wholesale campaign of destruction, and if that does not avail, they may even go so far as to threaten the lives of Americans."[62]

By mid-April, the lingering political protest had combined with social banditry and assumed unmanageable proportions. Throughout the spring, guerrilla forces attacked sugar properties virtually at will.[63] The persistent insurgency continued to disrupt normal sugar operations throughout the eastern provinces. Mysterious fires destroyed entire cane fields. The revolt continued to disrupt and disperse labor. Railroads, still not fully recovered from the effects of the early weeks of the revolu-tion, remained favorite targets of insurgent bands. "The destruction of native and foreign close by," the president of the Bayate Sugar Com-pany wrote, "has been tremendous. It runs into the millions. The rebels want intervention in the worst way, and the leaders say that if Wilson will not intervene on account of destruction, they will be compelled to wake him up by killing Americans, the most prominent ones will be taken first. In that way none of us are safe."[64]

The attack on property served to alienate the insurgents further from organized Liberal party support. Key party leaders looked with horror at the force they had unleashed in the eastern third of the island. The revolt had acquired a social dimension never intended by its architects. Too many ranking members of the Liberal party held substantial interests in the very sugar properties under seige in eastern Cuba. And with sugar profits peaking in the early spring, the persistent insurgency threatened both the completion of the 1917 harvest and, more important, the planting for the 1918 crop. In New York, Orestes Ferrara, himself on the board of directors of the Cuba Cane Sugar Corporation, quickly disassociated himself from the insurgency after Caicaje and Santiago. The revolt, Ferrara declared disapprovingly in mid-March, had "gone crazy and was destroying property right and left."[65] As long as the revolution was "purely political," Ferrara's attorney in New York, Martin W. Littleton, informed the State Department, Ferrara did not disguise his sympathy and support for the Liberal cause. "Now that the revolution has come to a point where it will end in anarchy," Littleton explained, "he is very much opposed to it because anarchy means the ruin of individual rights and property, and he is a large holder of property himself."[66]

Prelude to Intervention

Growing attacks on property involved American interests much more directly in the Cuban dispute. Throughout the early spring, the protracted rebellion impinged increasingly on vital American interests in Cuba. Confidence in Havana's ability to restore order in the east gave way gradually to apprehension and official skepticism. The European war added on Washington pressures of a different sort to end the continuing insurgency. From the very outset, Wilson could not entirely dismiss the possibility of German complicity in the Cuban revolution. "I am very free from G[erman] suspicions," Josephus Daniels recorded Wilson as saying, "but so many things are happening we cannot let Cuba be involved by G[erman] plots."[67] The declaration of war on Germany in April heightened American concern over the disorders in Cuba. The persistence of the insurrection, many in Washington feared, offered Germany an opportunity to establish undetected submarine bases at any of the many deserted coves and harbors along the Cuban coast; also, the Liberals' anti-Americanism raised for many the possibility of active collaboration between the insurgent forces and German agents.[68] Menocal skillfully played on these apprehensions in the United

States and refused to allow American fears to rest. After Cuba's declaration of war, Havana attempted to discredit the Liberal cause by continually characterizing the insurgents as pro-German sympathizers serving the Central Powers as a fifth column in Cuba. Occasionally, the government reported "uncovering" a German conspiracy involving members of the Liberal party.[69] With direct American involvement in the European war, moreover, the security of sugar production in Cuba transcended traditional concerns for the safety and protection of the property of U.S. nationals abroad. After April, precisely when insurgents in Cuba began to attack property, sugar passed under the purview of strategic national interests vital for the war effort. In early May, just weeks after the declaration of war, the Council for National Defense informed the State Department of the "utmost importance" of Cuban sugar production to the Allied Powers and the United States. "Every possible step," the council urged Lansing, "should be taken to safeguard the production of this commodity."[70]

Despite the heightened importance of sugar, the armed dispute in Cuba continued without sign of ending. A sense of uneasiness began to settle over Washington as American authorities despaired of Havana's ability to end the insurgency. As early as February 28, the military attaché had predicted that the Cuban armed forces lacked the capacity to sustain a protracted campaign against the insurgent forces without considerable American assistance.[71] Most naval observers in Cuba concurred. "To appreciate the difficulty attendant upon the supression of an insurrection conducted in this island along the lines [of a guerrilla war]," the commander of the U.S.S. *Dixie* mused, "we have only to recall the fact that the Spaniards with 200,000 or more men in this island were unable to accomplish a similar task even though their campaign was conducted along lines of the utmost severity and extending over a long period of time."[72]

By early spring, the performance of the Cuban armed forces had confirmed earlier misgivings. Government encounters with insurgent forces decreased — by design, American observers suspected. The Cuban armed forces, one naval commander reported, displayed little enthusiasm for arduous field operations against the guerrilla forces. The field command limited government operations to offensive actions in which the government possessed a clear superiority; otherwise, the army rarely ventured beyond the security and safety of the cities.[73] "There is a decided lack of energetic activity on the part of government forces," the American consul at Caimanera wrote, "which leaves no doubt in my mind as to the fact that the troops of the Government are, in most cases, actually avoiding contact with the revolutionaries and bandit forces."[74]

In Havana, however, Gonzales's optimism never wavered. The legation throughout the conflict opposed any settlement potentially capable of compromising the authority of the Menocal government. Within a national setting, this necessarily committed Gonzales to mobilizing maximum support internally for Conservative authorities. Within the context of Cuban-American treaty relations, the minister's task involved reassuring Washington that Havana possessed the ability to restore peace to the disaffected provinces unassisted. On March 30, Gonzales confidently predicted that the "prospects for an early pacification in Oriente are excellent."[75] Two weeks later, the legation relayed its expectation of an "early suppression of bandits."[76] As late as May 16, Gonzales continued to report uncritically about Menocal's confidence in a "quick disappearance of the rebellion."[77]

Reports from the eastern provinces failed to justify Gonzales's optimism. While the legation in Havana held out the expectation of imminent peace, observers in Oriente and Camagüey continued to proclaim the hopelessness of the situation. "Menocal can not put down the revolution," the president of the Bayate Sugar company insisted, "without American intervention."[78] In Caimanera, the American consul reported daily occurrences of "destruction and pillage" in his district. "Strongly recommend," H. M. Wolcott wired the State Department, "superior force of American marines be sent here with authority [to] pursue revolutionists until subjugated."[79] Just a day before Gonzales reassured Washington of an "early suppression" of the insurgent forces, one naval observer in Oriente reported:

I am given the impression that, unless the rebellion shortly terminates by some political arrangement, it will be very shortly necessary for the United States to send a considerable force here to protect the important American enterprises and the communications as well as to facilitate our own measures for naval security along these coasts.

Nothing has occurred in the last two and one-half weeks to convince me of the military power of the Cuban Government to quell this rebellion within the very near future, whereas I believe that one month's continuation of the present conditions will seriously damage the military interests of the United States.[80]

Indeed, by the spring, many American authorities expected not an end to the revolt but a revival of the insurgency as the completion of the sugar harvest released thousands of laborers from employment in the cane fields and the mills.[81]

The persistent and almost unanimous accounts from eastern Cuba disputing the claims advanced by the legation strained the credibility of Gonzales's reports. These differences might have been minimized in Washington but for disconcerting reports of unusually close personal ties existing between Gonzales and President Menocal. Minister Gonzales "is completely dominated by the Menocal Government," one American resident complained to Washington, "and it is absolutely useless to appeal to him for protection as he constantly assures us that the Government has the matter well in hand, and that everything will be all right in a very short time. . . . Either he is totally ignorant of the conditions prevailing throughout the Island, or he is deliberately minimizing these conditions and keeping this knowledge from our Government in Washington."[82] Leon J. Canova, chief of the Mexican Affairs Division in the State Department and a former resident of Cuba, reported learning from his sources on the island that "unfortunately Minister Gonzales appears to send only such information as he obtains from the Palace. He has the reputation of not being a good mixer, and therefore has a very limited circle of friends from which to draw information. In the Legation there is no one who is really in close touch with the Cuban situation."[83] Hugh Grosvenor, a British attorney in Havana and a personal friend of Undersecretary of State Frank L. Polk, informed Washington that Gonzales had become "unusually intimate" with the Cuban president's family. "At the time of the last election . . . it appear[ed] evident that his friendship carried with it such bias that he became inaccessible to any Cuban who was not endorsed by the President's clique." Grosvenor passed on to the State Department a charge prevalent in Cuba that Gonzales could not be trusted with confidential information. One high

Cuban official reported seeing Gonzales bring ''confidential dispatches from the Department to the Palace and discuss his answer with the President.''[84]

The continuing crisis reached a climax in mid-May, when political disturbances in American-occupied Haiti and Santo Domingo necessitated the transfer of marines stationed in Cuba as well as the naval patrols off the Oriente coast.[85] On May 10, Lansing learned that the Navy Department could not spare additional marine units for service in Cuba.[86] The prospect of withdrawing the American garrison from Cuba and leaving behind an insurgency still in progress caused considerable alarm in Washington. ''It is obvious,'' J. H. Stabler, chief of the Latin American Division, noted, ''that at this time the marines cannot be withdrawn from Cuba, where they are affording protection to American lives and to sugar properties, without being replaced by other forces.''[87] Unwilling to transfer to the Cuban government increased responsibility for security of sugar estates in eastern Cuba, the State Department tentatively proposed replacing the departing marines with army units. On May 14, the War Department agreed to raise whatever military force necessary for duty in Cuba.[88] A day later, Lansing instructed the legation to secure from Menocal authorization to transfer troops to Cuba:

> The Department regarded the situation in connection with the production of sugar so necessary to the United States and the Allied Powers as extremely serious. You are therefore instructed to present this matter again to General Menocal and to use your influence with him to induce him to agree to the sending of a force of American troops in order to protect sugar production, which must not be interrupted. . . .
>
> In bringing this matter to President Menocal's attention you may say to him that this Government has every confidence in his ability to cope with the situation in Oriente Province, but that in view of the fact that so much depends upon a supply of sugar for the United States and the Allies it desires to aid him in bringing peaceful conditions at the earliest moment to Cuba, and therefore it wants to cooperate with him.[89]

The State Department proposal evoked immediate opposition in

Havana. As early as May 13, in response to earlier hints suggesting the possible necessity of having to deploy additional American armed forces in Oriente, Gonzales admitted the difficulty of determining 600 miles away the validity of appeals for assistance. "But Menocal stated last night," Gonzales hastened to add, that "[he] did not consider additional United States forces needed as precaution."[90] Responding three days later to Lansing's instruction of May 15, Gonzales offered Washington a detailed chronicle documenting government achievements and successes in the field. With some six thousand troops in the eastern districts and another two thousand officers and men available immediately for service if necessary, Gonzales repeated his expectation of a "quick disappearance of the rebellion."[91]

The Morgan Mission

Havana's opposition to further U.S. armed involvement in Cuba, seconded by Minister Gonzales's own reservations, forced the State Department to reconsider the proposed intervention. The persistence of conflicting reports from sources at opposite ends of the island, moreover, further persuaded the State Department to delay action pending a thorough review of conditions in Cuba. The central issue in May 1917 was the need to weigh Havana's immediate political requirements against U.S. long-term needs. Armed intervention, if in fact unwarranted by conditions in Cuba, had the potential to create new problems and compound old ones. The intervention proposal carried the inherent risk of impairing Menocal's ability to govern and reviving in full Liberal hopes for a favorable hearing from the United States. In either case, intervention offered no solution. A decision to abandon intervention, on the other hand, necessarily involved risking the interruption of sugar production and, quite possibly, the loss of the following year's crop.

As a preliminary to any final decision, the State Department sought an independent review of conditions in eastern Cuba. In mid-May, Washington dispatched to Cuba Henry H. Morgan, the former American consul general in Hamburg, to study politico-economic conditions in Camagüey and Oriente. Holding a joint appointment as consul general at large for the State Department and special representative for the Council of National Defense, Morgan arrived in Cuba in late May.

After a short stay in Havana, Morgan reached Santiago on May 29. The consul general gave immediate priority in Oriente to consultation with ranking American diplomatic, military, and business representatives and extensive travel to the interior sugar districts.

All doubts remaining about the wisdom of intervention were immediately laid to rest by Morgan's reports. The revolt no longer posed a serious political threat, Morgan conceded. The unwillingness of planters in eastern Cuba to clear burned areas in preparation for the 1918 crop, however, owing largely to a general lack of confidence in Havana's ability to guarantee the security of future sugar production, posed the greatest single threat to the following year's harvest. Labor had not fully recovered from the effects of the February revolution. More important, conditions in the sugar districts offered little hope of quieting sufficiently in the near future to meet the labor requirements of the 1918 *zafra*. The labor shortage dating from the first weeks of the revolution continued to handicap planters and sugar production. The only certain means of inspiring confidence among the planters and providing minimum assurances of safety to labor, Morgan counseled, lay in sending "American Marines to the province to cooperate with Cubans but with authority to pursue and destroy rebel bands where ever located."[92] Several weeks later, the State Department received a comprehensive report of conditions in eastern Cuba, detailing the urgency of the need for American armed forces. Morgan again reassured Washington that the Liberal protest no longer posed a political threat to Conservatives in Havana. The small quantity of arms and ammunition recovered from the insurgent forces, however, raised speculation among the planters that another revolution was being planned for the 1918 harvest season. A repetition of the 1917 disorders, Morgan warned, threatened to destroy not only the 1918 crop in Santa Clara, Camagüey, and Oriente, but all future sugar production in eastern Cuba. "I am of the opinion," Morgan wrote, "that the only way to forestall such an uprising will be to send an armed force into the country as it is the only force the rebels respect and fear."[93] A week later, Morgan issued a third request for American armed forces. "No confidence whatever," the consul general insisted, "can be placed in the Cuban troops, for they are not competent to control the situation." United States troops would act in conjunction with Cuban forces; the joint operations would receive maximum publicity throughout the island, Morgan suggested, and serve to inspire confidence among the planters.[94] Some weeks later, Morgan again appealed for armed forces. He sensed "an undercurrent of unrest running through Cuba regarding the political situation, which nothing, in my opinion, will quiet except the arrival of our troops on the island."[95]

In the face of conflicting estimates of politico-economic conditions in eastern Cuba, Morgan's reports resolved the debate. In a very real sense, ultimate resolution of the policy debate generally, and armed intervention specifically, rested entirely on Morgan's evaluation of conditions on the island.[96] At no time did Morgan share Gonzales's optimism.

The tenor of Morgan's reports from Cuba revived in full plans to send troops to Cuba. Indeed, Morgan's first report sufficed to persuade Lansing to prepare for armed intervention. "It would appear from [Morgan's] report," Lansing explained to the White House, "that it would be well, if possible, to send troops to that region in order to insure confidence on the part of the planters and induce them to continue the production of cane."[97] A week later, the Council of National Defense, also following Morgan's reports with considerable attention, concurred and pressed for the immediate organization of an American expeditionary force to protect sugar production.[98] Further distribution of Morgan's dispatches from Cuba among other government wartime agencies, including the National Food Administration and committees of Allied governments, served to confirm the decision to intervene militarily. By early June, Washington had concluded that "the presence of a large force of American troops in the eastern end of Cuba is absolutely imperative to aid restoration of order if necessary and particularly to give confidence to the laborers who are afraid to return to work in the cane fields and mills."[99]

Widespread social banditry in eastern Cuba abated somewhat by early summer. In July 1917, Menocal suspended constitutional guarantees. This, the president explained to the American minister, enabled the government to "imprison persons believed to be German intriguers when under ordinary conditions they can be held only three days unless there is proof of the lawlessness."[100] In fact, the suspension of constitutional guarantees marked the inauguration of a systematic government campaign of selective terror and intimidation in Camagüey and Oriente.

As early as April, a reign of terror had descended on rural communities in the eastern interior. Between April 2 and April 5, some fifty persons were summarily executed by an army patrol on the property of the Elia and Jobabo estates.[101] Throughout the summer government agents moved against suspected rebels and rebel-sympathizers; assassinations reached near epidemic proportions. "A large number of murders are being perpetrated in this province and Camagüey by hired assassins," Consul Morgan reported from Santiago de Cuba on August 31, "the victims being members of the Liberal party who took part in the last revolution."[102]

Not all insurgent bands dissolved, however. In early June, the *New York Times* correspondent in Havana reported learning that the rebellion continued in the "mountainous regions of Oriente province."[103] As late as July 31, the American vice-consul in Antilla reported the existence of "mountaineers" near the Oriente towns of La Maya and Songo, well armed, some with new rifles, and all with plenty of ammunition.[104] Many survivors retreated deeper into the mountain ranges of the eastern interior, there to remain as a community of outcasts in much the same fashion as the *palenques* and bandits of the nineteenth century.[105] Periodically, in the years that followed, the capital press published brief back-page accounts of the results of army encounters with the bandit remnants of "La Chambelona." In December 1917, the bandit chieftain "Nando" Guerra eluded a government ambush in San Jerónimo, Camagüey. Later that same month, Silvio Hernández was killed in Ciego de Avila. In January 1918, Justo and Enrique Hernández were captured and killed by a Rural Guard patrol in Céspedes, Camagüey. In January 1920, Augusto Puente Guillot met his end at the hands of the Rural Guard unit in Boniato, Oriente. Ultimately, the capital press lost interest in reporting the fate of the bandit survivors of "La Chambelona."[106]

In early summer 1917, Havana and Washington completed final preparations for the arrival of marines. Not without some irony, the U.S. estates demanded the protection of American armed forces against the very conditions created by American capital.

6.

The "Sugar Intervention": Marines in Cuba

The Diplomacy of Armed Intervention

The arrival of American armed forces in eastern Cuba resulted in large measure from a general lack of confidence in Havana's ability to put an end either to the revolt then on the wane or to uprisings in the future. To be sure, by July 1917, most American officials recognized that the Liberal revolution was virtually at an end. The planters of eastern Cuba, however, as the principal casualties of the fighting in the spring, could find in Havana's military performance little inspiration, and less incentive, to prepare for the 1918 crop. This was the essence of Consul Morgan's reports: American support — visible, publicized armed support — was the necessary minimum guarantee for the future success of the Cuban sugar crop.

All participating official agencies in Havana and Washington, however, for different reasons shared a common interest in couching the armed intervention in forms disguising its mission. Consul Morgan, who on several occasions reported the revolt at an end, proposed justifying the intervention "under the guise of co-operation with the Cuban Government in suppression of the insurrection."[1] Some weeks later, Morgan publicly elaborated on his scheme in Santiago de Cuba: "It is demanded that the next crop be the largest which Cuba has ever had, and that it must not suffer the slightest interruption, and for this reason the United States Government as an ally of Cuba will send down here, if it is necessary, forces, who in cooperation with Cuban troops will guarantee the crop absolutely."[2]

Morgan's allusion to politico-military requirements as justification for the presence of American armed forces, however, caused considerable alarm in Havana. Always sensitive to the impact of U.S. policy on

Cuban politics, the Gonzales legation opposed any official rationale suggesting even remotely that armed intervention responded to either the insurgent protest or Menocal's inability to deal with the rebellion. The State Department shared the legation's apprehension. Washington, too, feared antigovernment forces would misinterpret the intervention. An imperfect interventionist construct, appearing to capitulate to Liberal solicitations, risked reviving a revolt politically at an end. The State Department, further, felt the necessity to minimize offense to Cuban officials who had consistently denied, publicly and privately, the need for American troops and for whom intervention remained a potential source of political embarrassment. Under these circumstances, Washington could not impose on Cuba an intervention sanctioned within the context of Cuban-American treaty relations without risking injury to Menocal's position nationally and, quite possibly, in the process reanimating the moribund insurrection.

The final public policy rationale for the intervention had little connection with the political events of the preceding five months. Instead, Washington invoked the exigencies of the international situation and Cuba's participation in the world war as public justification for the arrival of American armed forces. The status of Cuba as an Allied belligerent, the State Department announced, placed responsibilities on the Cuban people for the duration of the war. Without directly alluding to the insurgency, Washington denounced any interference with Cuba's contribution to the war effort — the production of sugar. Since Cuba and the United States had joined in a conflict waged "for the highest rights of humanity and in defense of principles of international law," the time had arrived "when all internal political questions must be set aside in the face of the grave international danger":

> Therefore, as the Allied Powers and the United States must depend to a large extent upon the sugar production of Cuba, all disturbances which interfere with this production must be considered as hostile acts, and the United States Government is forced to issue this warning that unless all those under arms against the Government of Cuba return immediately to there [sic] allegiance it may become necessary for the United States to regard them as its enemies and to deal with them accordingly.[3]

The appeal to wartime considerations offered policymakers an ideal means of disguising the purpose of intervention. As early as May 15, alluding to the "extremely serious" sugar situation, Lansing instructed Gonzales to use his influence with Menocal to secure Havana's approval for the sending of American troops of Cuba "to protect sugar production, which must not be interrupted." "These troops," Lansing suggested to the legation, "should be ostensibly sent to Guantanamo for purposes of training and could be in readiness to give protection to property and to enforce the proclamation of this Government."[4]

The proposal to disguise the intervention as drill and training maneuvers won immediate support at all levels of the policy officialdom. On July 12, Undersecretary of State Polk instructed Gonzales to exert all his "tact and diplomacy" to secure an invitation from Havana to send troops to train in a warm-weather climate.[5]

Formulated in the guise of Allied collaboration, Havana could acquiesce gracefully, without apparent compromise of national sovereignty, and, indeed, seek to mobilize national support around the arrival of American troops without fear of incurring the political liabilities otherwise attending U.S. intervention. For Menocal, the arrangement, far from weakening his government, served as powerful testimony to Cuba's devotion to, and participation in, the Allied cause.[6] In Washington, the proposed intervention schema promised at once to guarantee an adequate supply of sugar while minimizing the likelihood of adverse political repercussions.[7] Once set in the context of wartime collaboration, American intervention was not an issue of national debate in Cuba but a matter of international urgency beyond the purview of partisan review. The fear of being branded pro-German sympathizers deterred those who might otherwise have been tempted to seize upon the presence of American troops as a demonstration of Menocal's inability to govern or as a sign of Liberal success.

On July 14, Menocal dutifully offered the United States "training camps" in Oriente Province to allow American troops to "train in mild winter climate." This invitation, Gonzales added, offered the "tactful commander" an opportunity to "impress eastern Cuba" with the presence of American armed forces by organizing "extensive marches from Guantanamo."[8] Washington subsequently expanded Havana's offer of camp sites near Santiago de Cuba to include "all of Oriente and possibly other provinces of Cuba.''[9] At a White House conference in mid-August, the State Department learned that an unexpected increase in Marine Corps enlistments eliminated the need to send army units to Cuba.[10]

The Schema of Intervention (I)

After two months of deliberations and preparations — five months after the Liberal challenge had ended — marines arrived in Cuba. In August 1917, the first contingent of American armed forces, the Seventh Regiment of marines, made up of some 938 officers and men, disembarked and established camp in the Guantánamo naval station.[11]

The organization of the American military mission in Cuba conformed to the constraints imposed on the intervention by prevailing politico-diplomatic circumstances. The presence of American marines in Cuba did not technically constitute an intervention. On the contrary, Havana had publicly invited the United States, as an Allied cobelligerent, to train troops in a warm-weather climate. Within the context of the policy agreed on by Washington and Havana, field operations sought to reconcile disparate and often rival claims made on the expeditionary force, including the military objectives of the intervention, the political needs of Havana, and the economic requirements of Washington.

American troops arrived in Cuba to meet not only the objectives stated by politicians and diplomats in Havana and Washington, but also the needs of the sugar producers underlying these objectives. Indeed, American armed forces in Cuba performed a mission common to all the armed interventions in the past. Throughout the first year of the ''sugar intervention,'' the American expeditionary force assumed responsibility for the security of the cane fields, mills, warehouses, wharf facilities, and the supporting transportation and communications infrastructure. More than the protection of property, American armed forces were to guarantee the processes of sugar production, including planting, harvesting, manufacturing, and distribution.

Had the intervention responded directly to the issues of property, little would have distinguished the arrival of marines in Cuba in 1917 from earlier armed interventions. The mission of American armed forces, however, and the methods available to the marine command to accomplish this mission, remained consistently circumscribed by, and subject to, the policy rationale adopted at the outset to justify the American military presence. The fiction used to organize a politically inoffensive intervention, in defining the context of the American mission, determined the structure of intervention. The American command found itself obliged to organize field maneuvers behind the politico-diplomatic protocol between Havana and Washington according to which American armed forces were in Cuba only to drill and train. As guests of the Cuban government, American military authorities were enjoined to observe the limitations inherent in their invitation and operate behind the understood political injunctions. Any disclosure, implied or real, any action inconsistent with the stated public mission of American troops in Cuba, Gonzales cautioned the marine field command, threatened to cause Menocal considerable political embarrassment and, indeed, jeopardize the very arrangement by which the United States had stationed marines on Cuban soil.[12] As early as November 1917, the presence of American armed forces in eastern Cuba had aroused anti-American protests and denunciations against Conservative authorities for their apparent collusion with Washington to violate Cuban sovereignty. Popular indignation subsided only after officials of the U.S. command had reassured local authorities of the purely wartime character of marine operations.[13]

The publicly stated purpose of the intervention also eliminated an otherwise troublesome source of conflict locally. Distributed wholly among communities committed to the February revolution both by virtue of political temperament and by early complicity, and among whom charges of U.S. duplicity during the Santiago negotiations enjoyed widespread credence, American forces operated as unwelcomed intruders in districts often still under arms. The anti-American sentiment among existing insurgent bands continued unabated.[14] Under these circumstances, the arrival of American armed forces under any pretext other than ''training'' risked exacerbating unsettled conditions in Oriente and Camagüey. Indeed, many feared that the slightest disclosure of the unstated purpose of the American mission in Cuba would serve only to encourage further destruction of sugar properties. ''I wish to express the opinion,'' Gonzales warned his superiors in the State Department, ''that if the idea becomes prevalent in Oriente that Americans are attempting to prevent the burning of cane it is an open question whether it would incite burning."[15]

From the moment marines arrived in eastern Cuba the legation demanded strict observance of the protocol of the intervention. Fearful that any departure from the proclaimed purpose of American armed forces in Cuba would undermine Menocal's authority nationally, Gonzales insisted that all field operations conform to the letter and spirit of the stated policy rationale. In December 1917, upon the arrival of an additional 1,000 officers and men of the Ninth Regiment and the subsequent consolidation of all marines in Cuba into the Third Provisional Brigade, Gonzales denied the marine commander's request to expand field operations in eastern Cuba. To avoid any possible misunderstanding with Cuban authorities, moreover, the brigade commander requested Gonzales to withhold from Menocal news of the arrival of the additional marines.[16] Angered by the apparent contravention of the spirit of the original settlement, Gonzales protested the subterfuge employed by the marine command and opposed any further distribution of armed forces in Cuba.[17] The Ninth Regiment subsequently relocated in the naval station and remained encamped at Guantánamo for the duration of its year in Cuba.[18]

Havana's offer of mild weather training camps provided all parties concerned with an expedient arrangement through which to satisfy the diverse requirements of the intervention. In October 1917, the marine command established permanent camps on Cuban territory with headquarters at San Juan Hill near Santiago, two companies in Camagüey, one at Guantánamo, another at San Luis, and a last one at Alto Cedro.[19] Some weeks later, an additional two companies established camps near Bayamo.[20]

The distribution of marines in camp sites throughout the sugar districts of eastern Cuba allowed the American expedition to supervise production centers under the pretext of training exercises. From camps established strategically throughout Camagüey and Oriente, the marine command placed the eastern third of Cuba under surveillance. A system of periodic patrols, organized under the guise of "practice marches," allowed marine companies to visit various sugar-producing districts, important transportation and communication centers, and the larger provincial cities.

The underlying assumption about the intervention from the outset, and the premise around which the enterprise was organized, was that the mere presence of American armed forces, appropriately publicized and visibly placed, would suffice to underwrite order and guarantee successful sugar harvests for the duration of the war. Indeed, the intervention was undertaken to meet the specific demands of the planters of eastern Cuba. Most American authorities in Cuba and the United States believed that the arrival of marines would immediately create the salutary conditions necessary to give the planters the confidence to return to sugar production and would provide labor the necessary security to resume work by discouraging attacks on the sugar estates. This was the compelling message relayed by Morgan to the State Department and the basis upon which Lansing approached the White House. The limited number of interventionist forces, scattered and isolated throughout eastern Cuba, and the distribution of permanent camps, suggested that Washington viewed the intervention as a nonhostile operation. "Your entire command," Gonzales informed the marine commander, "could not protect one medium size plantation from incendiary cane fires if there was any determined purpose to start such fires."[21] American military forces served rather as deterrents than as actual restraints. "The marines are in Cuba," Gonzales insisted, "not as guards for sugar cane nor as police officers, but for the general moral effect of their presence in discouraging any possible contemplated disturbance of the peace of the country."[22]

Under these conditions, practice marches fulfilled a variety of purposes. Most important, periodic patrols into the surrounding countryside served to reassure the far-flung sugar estates that American armed forces remained close at hand. In addition, marines gathered intelligence data, learned of planters' specific problems, and, in general, collected information that was subsequently passed on to the appropriate military and diplomatic authorities in Havana and Washington. Practice marches also facilitated reconnaissance of the surrounding countryside. In anticipation of possible emergencies in the future, marine companies on patrol studied road conditions, bridge and rail facilities, communication systems, and water supplies, and noted and recorded the existence of potential camp sites in the interior.[23]

Responsibility for surveillance of specific regions of eastern Cuba was distributed among the various marine companies. The companies in Camagüey patrolled primarily the eastern half of the province and the north coast. Practice marches from Bayamo maintained points west, particularly Manzanillo, under periodic supervision. The Alto Cedro company regularly dispatched mounted units to the Oriente north coast, while the camps in San Luis and Guantánamo patrolled the provincial interior.[24]

Sites selected as marine camps conformed to strategic imperatives. Primary considerations included proximity to the sugar districts and to railroad transportation, and accessibility to communication systems. The limited number of marine camps distributed in Camagüey and Oriente also served to minimize suspicion of the American mission in Cuba. As the 1918 harvest approached, pressure from planters to increase the number of permanent marine camps mounted. Occasionally, local political agitation heightened demands for the establishment of additional camps. Supported by the legation, the marine command resisted the estates' appeals to distribute the interventionist forces into new encampments. Too many marine positions, officials feared, threatened to belie the public purpose of the American presence. "It appears to me desirable," the marine commander Colonel M. J. Shaw wrote, "to continue the impression to the Cuban people that the mission of the regiment here is for training." Any further distribution of marines, Shaw feared, particularly in response to the requests from sugar estates, would have made it increasingly "difficult to insure credence."[25] Gonzales supported the field command, also fearing that the creation of new marine positions involved a breach of faith:

> The Cuban government consented to the marines coming for training purposes, and also to their distribution to certain points. While this original plan has been extended, the points covered now should not be further increased without definite reason and advance understanding with the proper Cuban authorities. If there should be an outbreak this policy would, of course, be immediately changed, and the marines and the Cuban forces distributed to the best advantage. While the principal officers of the Cuban government understand quite well what we are doing, we owe them as much protection as possible from adverse public which our course might arouse.[26]

Rather than establish new permanent camps, the itinerary and schedule of practice marches were modified from time to time to meet changing needs. Political disorders in Antilla in 1918 led immediately to a request for the establishment of a new marine camp in the area of the municipality. Afraid such a move would have a "bad general effect," Shaw pledged to keep the city under close surveillance. A marine officer was dispatched to Antilla to collect intelligence data from local Cuban and American authorities. By May, the marine command had rerouted the practice marches of the district company to include Antilla.[27]

The anomalous character of the intervention dictated close cooperation and constant communication among legation officials, the marine command, and local and national Cuban authorities. The legation served as the coordinating center of the intervention, constantly defining the American mission in Cuba and determining the appropriate diplomatic and military responses. Gonzales never abandoned his commitment to the original conditions of the intervention. Accordingly, the legation demanded from the marine command complete compliance with the letter and spirit of the agreement. The U.S. military force in Cuba, Gonzales informed the newly arrived marine commander in late 1918, was "nominally and officially in Cuba for training purposes and not as guards or police purposes":

> There exists a tacit understanding between the president and myself that it may be used for the latter purpose, but except in the event of a sudden and vital emergency, it must be employed only on the authority of this legation which should have had opportunity to obtain the consent of the president of Cuba.[28]

In the event a "sudden and vital emergency" precluded consultation and collaboration with officials in Havana, Gonzales added, "effort should be made to obtain a call for action from local Cuban civil or military authorities."[29] Under no circumstances were marines authorized to act without prior legation approval. "No action," Gonzales warned the marine command, "must be taken or representation of any sort made involving our Government on any authority in Cuba unless it comes from the Legation."[30]

To minimize friction between Havana and Washington, marines were instructed as a matter of course to cooperate fully with local civil and military authorities. Dispersed in isolated districts throughout the interior provinces, in companies of approximately one hundred officers and men, distant from supplies and often in the midst of a hostile population, it behooved the marine command to establish cordial relations with local authorities. Marine units organized operations with the prior knowledge of provincial and municipal authorities.[31] Language difficulties often made assistance from Cuban authorities necessary. None of the officers and men stationed in Camagüey knew any Spanish beyond the few words necessary to get around the city.[32]

In collaborating with Cuban officials, moreover, particularly military authorities, American armed forces performed another service vital to the U.S. mission in Cuba. The very organization of the intervention delegated direct responsibility for the security of sugar production to the Cuban army. At the request of the United States, the Cuban government concentrated some seven thousand troops in the sugar districts. Only an American force of equal size, most authorities agreed, offered any comparable guarantee to sugar production.[33] Ill-prepared to assume the task assigned to the larger Cuban army, marines provided moral support and technical assistance to the Cuban forces stationed in the eastern sugar districts. Marines formed the "valuable backbone" of the Cuban military force assigned to the eastern provinces, supervising the activity of the Cuban army, inspecting the measures devised by the Cuban General Staff, and furnishing whatever information and suggestions were deemed necessary to enhance the efficiency of the island's sugar garrisons.[34] Periodic courtesy calls during practice marches to Rural Guard posts and provincial army commands became an essential feature of marine patrols. These visits provided the forum through which Cuban and American authorities exchanged intelligence information and field reports. Suggestions designed to improve conditions in the Cuban armed forces were made either locally or passed on to the Cuban General Staff through the military attaché office in the legation.[35]

The arrival of marines in August 1917, and the subsequent organization of practice marches, contributed to restoring a measure of calm in the sugar zones of eastern Cuba, particularly among the planters.[36] The "moral effect" of the marines' presence did, indeed, inspire confidence on the estates. Planters returned to sugar production with an enthusiasm surpassed only by their elation at the soaring prices of sugar. Thousands of new acres of land in Oriente continued to pass under the regimen of cane.[37] Labor returned to the fields and mills. Planters reported the destruction of cane and equipment at an end; incidents of destruction and theft of livestock and supplies dropped sharply.[38] In 1918, Cuba produced a record harvest.

The Schema of Intervention (II)

The establishment of peace in rural Cuba coincided with increasing unrest in urban centers. By mid-1918, the major threat to sugar production was no longer rebellion in the countryside but labor protests in the cities. The latest threat, in fact, did not directly involve sugar production. Strategically located in the island's economic infrastructure, sugar production necessarily shared the vagaries experienced by the supporting commercial and industrial sectors. In 1918, these affiliate sectors, including communications systems, shipping, and railroads, were the targets of labor organizers. Rising prices, poor working conditions, and the workers' struggle for recognition of newly organized unions contributed to a new mood of labor militancy. Throughout 1918 and 1919, strikes and labor protests swept across the island, directly affecting every major sector of the economy. General strikes on two occasions brought the island to a standstill.[39] By December 1918, American authorities had come to perceive labor as the greatest single source of danger to sugar production.[40] At no time since the February revolution did events in Cuba threaten sugar production as seriously as the labor protests between 1918 and 1919. Strikes affected the very substructure of the sugar system. Labor agitation against the railroads both interrupted the internal movement of sugar and prevented machinery and repair equipment vital to production from arriving at the mills. Stevedore strikes tied up sugar cargoes on Cuban docks, prevented the unloading of necessary supplies, and paralyzed trade in Cuba. Spontaneous sympathy strikes often halted the planting and harvest of cane in the fields and interrupted the manufacturing processes in the mills.

In adversely affecting sugar production, as well as virtually every other sector of commerce and manufacturing, labor-management disputes quickly transcended purely internal concern. Strikes reverberated internationally. In addition to condemning the traditional proletarian challenge to foreign capital, American authorities ascribed to labor protests in Cuba qualities justifying U.S. intervention within the context of the Platt Amendment. The December 1918 railroad strikes in Oriente, the American consul in Santiago charged, were politically inspired and sought to overthrow the Menocal government.[41] The marine command saw Liberals and Germans behind the rash of strikes in January 1919.[42] A railroad strike in March 1919, Gonzales suspected, was a political movement directed against the government supported by "Spanish agitators of dangerous anarchistic" tendencies and radical workers "predicating impossible demands bordering on Bolshevism."[43]

Measured against the requirements imposed on Cuba by the Platt Amendment, labor protests challenged Havana's ability to discharge its treaty commitment to the protection of life, property, and individual liberty. By late 1918 and early 1919, workers' protests had reached sufficient proportions to lead American authorities to review labor struggles within the context of Article III of the Platt Amendment. Labor struck directly at the property interests to which Havana, and ultimately, through treaty responsibility, Washington, was committed to protect. In the past, the intervention clause had been applied only in those instances where political disturbances had threatened economic interests. If, however, American intervention in Cuba was essentially a response to the inability of Havana to provide minimum guarantees to life, property, and individual liberty, it hardly mattered that in this instance, between 1918 and 1919, the source of the menace to foreign capital came from labor. In either case, political disorder or labor unrest, property interests suffered similar hardships. For the purpose of policy considerations, moreover, the distinction between political upheaval and labor protest was further blurred the moment American authorities ascribed to strikes partisan undercurrents.

American officials perceived sufficient peril in labor protests to warrant the invocation of the Platt Amendment. The legation reported in early 1919 that a railroad strike had caused "tremendous losses to American interests"; this "menace to property interests," Gonzales wrote, "is as great as would be active revolution."[44] In Washington, the chief of the Latin American Affairs Division, F. L. Mayer, feared that conditions in Cuba appeared to be drifting toward a revolutionary situation, placing sugar production again in serious jeopardy. Alluding to the intervention clause of the Platt Amendment, Mayer urged an increase of marines. Although the strengthening of American armed forces in Cuba was technically a violation of the original 1917 agreement, Mayer conceded, it was fully warranted by the circumstances that made Article III applicable to conditions prevailing on the island.[45] In Havana, the military attaché shared the State Department view, recommending an additional two thousand marines to safeguard sugar production.[46] Gonzales urged the State Department to inform the Cuban people:

> Apart from treaty obligations of the United States to maintain and uphold in Cuba a government adequate for the protection [of] life and property, it has a most direct and compelling interest in the orderly harvesting and shipment of the present sugar crop, it views with grave concern and displeasure the unpatriotic and base motives of those who, whether for anarchical or political ends or both, have inveighed the workers in essential industries to paralyze the country on the empty pretext of abetting the demands of workers in non-essential industries. The Government of the United States has therefore determined in exercise of its treaty rights to suggest to the Government of Cuba, if work on the railroads, in the harbors and in other essential industries is not resumed within twenty-four hours, the adoption of certain drastic and thorough-going measures to enforce such resumption, and to lend to the Government of Cuba the necessary moral and material aid and support to carry out these measures.[47]

By late 1918, the United States military response to labor activity conformed entirely to the requirements of the Platt Amendment. In December 1918, some 1,120 officers and men of the First Regiment arrived at the naval station in Guantánamo.[48] The Navy Department readied some additional 6,000 marines in Philadelphia and Quantico for possible service in Cuba. The Atlantic Fleet, transporting an additional marine complement of some 1,000 officers and men, organized an itinerary of courtesy calls on select Cuban cities in February 1919.[49]

At the same time, the necessity of immediately responding to mounting labor demonstrations in Cuba obliged American authorities to modify the field operations of the interventionist forces. The marine command promptly rerouted practice marches and reconnaissance patrols to include visits to strike centers. The organization of new camp sites placed American troops in closer proximity to disaffected urban districts. As early as December 1917, labor protests in Manzanillo had prompted the establishment of a permanent camp in Bayamo to place marines closer to centers of labor activism in western Oriente.[50]

In all essential forms, American military operations continued to observe the protocol of the original 1917 agreement. "It appears to me," Shaw wrote, "that it is desirable that the presence of our troops on Cuban territory be known to the fullest extent with a view to exercising a deterrent effect upon those who would foment strikes or disorders."[51] When marine camps failed to deter labor protests, "practice marches" to centers of unrest sought in a more direct manner to encourage workers to return to their jobs by demonstrating U.S. support for management. Cuban authorities frequently sought to intimidate labor leaders by disclosing to union officials that Washington was prepared to use marines to break strikes. In one instance, Menocal informed leaders of striking machinists of American opposition to the strike and Washington's willingness to apply whatever force necessary to compel the workers to end the strike.[52] The appearance of marines at strike centers gave credibility to Havana's threats.

As long as the American mission in Cuba consisted largely of guaranteeing the security of sugar production in the former insurgent provinces, camps distributed between Camagüey and Santiago de Cuba adequately met military needs. By 1919, however, with the threat to sugar production national in proportion, camps and patrols established in 1917 were no longer satisfactory. In January 1919, senior American army, navy, and marine officials in Havana recommended moving the marines in eastern Cuba further west to Santa Clara, the center of Cuba's sugar districts commanding the important railroad junctions linking the western provinces with the east. "Evidence of a thorough [labor] organization," the military attaché warned, "capable of quick united action as demonstrated during the recent general strike in Cuba, rendered the question of our being prepared for another such strike and being in a position to protect lives and property should the occasion arise one which warrants the moving of the regiment of Marines now stationed at

Guantanamo Naval Station into Cuba territory and placing them at Santa Clara."⁵³ In Washington, the State Department instructed the legation to secure from Menocal the necessary authorization to move marines from Guantánamo to Santa Clara. The entire regiment, Undersecretary Polk proposed as a palliative to anticipated resistance from Cubans, would not be moved to Santa Clara at once. Rather a company, dispatched ostensibly for training purposes, would establish camp in Santa Clara and serve as the nucleus around which increases would be made incrementally in response to local conditions.⁵⁴

Havana refused to authorize any further extension of American military operations in Cuba. To "avoid mistaken interpretations that would be prejudicial," Menocal insisted that Washington confine marines to the areas originally agreed upon in eastern Cuba.⁵⁵ The sudden appearance of American armed forces as far west as Santa Clara as part of a wartime training program, at the precise moment Wilson journeyed to Paris to negotiate peace, Menocal pointed out, would strain public credibility in the stated American mission in Cuba and undermine the position of his administration internally.⁵⁶

Unwilling to impose the project on reluctant Cuban authorities, Washington adopted alternative measures to combat strikes. Marine forces in the field received reinforcements from the Guantánamo naval station. On January 20, two companies left Santiago de Cuba for Camagüey, ostensibly for "target practice"; a week later, three companies of marines from the naval station joined the headquarters command in Santiago.⁵⁷ Practice marches increased in numbers and range throughout the two eastern provinces.

Marine maneuvers through strike districts, preceded by appropriate publicity, tended to provide management and Cuban authorities the vital margin of support against labor. The movement of marines from Santiago to Camagüey, in one instance, was organized in such a manner as to give the deliberate impression that American armed forces had arrived to give military support to the Cuban government against the workers.⁵⁸

In those districts beyond authorized marine operations, Washington dispatched naval patrols to pay courtesy calls. Havana, Matanzas, and Ciefuegos received visits varying in length from the Atlantic Fleet. In early March, a general strike ended only after four cruisers and ten submarine chasers called on Havana and Cienfuegos.[59]

By the middle part of 1919, American armed forces had completed their mission in Cuba. Major political and social disputes had been contained without serious damage to the sugar system. In 1918, Cuba had provided a sugar crop that sold for record prices. Most expected an equally successful harvest in 1919. Ominous political murmurs, however, precluded immediate withdrawal of American forces. Already in 1919, preparations for the 1920 national elections had been accompanied by more than the usual partisan denunciations and threats of revolution. Only a successful and peaceful presidential election remained in the way of the withdrawal of marines.

7.

Electoral Intervention in the Plattist System, 1919-1921

Preparations for Elections

With the settlement of World War I at Versailles, domestic politics again reclaimed national attention in Cuba. National politics revived quickly from the moratorium imposed on partisan activities during the war years. Recovery in 1919, however, could not have failed to reflect the shadow cast by the events of 1916-1917. Preparations for the 1920 national elections fully revived the rancor that lodged below the surface of national order. Very early, traditional partisan antagonism, heightened by the disputed electoral struggle of 1916 and the subsequent February revolution, generated more than the usual preelection tensions. Almost a full two years before the scheduled presidential elections, the political scores left unsettled in 1916-1917 surfaced to raise again the specter of civil war.

In Washington, American officials followed electoral developments in Cuba with growing uneasiness. Once again, in early 1919, Cuban political oratory evoked an all too familiar augury. No one in the State Department needed to be reminded that Cuban political leaders had on two separate occasions turned to arms to settle disputed national elections. Confronting the prospect of another quadrennial crisis, Washington prepared to subject the Cuban political system to closer supervision and scrutiny, seeking in political intervention the means with which to regulate the conduct of elections and impose on Cuba the minimum standards deemed necessary for peaceful elections. This perforce involved Washington in guaranteeing, to the satisfaction of all contending factions, the integrity of the electoral system. The State Department had concluded by early 1919 that only elections offering all participants appropriate guarantees, and thereby inspiring national confidence and lending a measure of legitimacy to election results, promised to halt revolutions stemming from disputed elections. Indeed, in supporting Conservative authorities against the charges of electoral abuse in 1916-1917 and assisting Havana suppress the Liberal response to voting frauds in 1917, Washington had implicitly assumed responsibility for the conduct of national elections in 1920.

Prepared by previous experience with Cuban electoral politics to anticipate some of the central issues traditionally associated with presidential contests, in early 1919 the State Department outlined to Menocal the minimum requirements necessary to guarantee peaceful elections. Undersecretary Frank L. Polk stressed that Havana's most immediate responsibility was to organize and preside over elections capable of inspiring national confidence. This involved, first, public assurances from Menocal pledging his administration to fair elections, without which, Polk feared, revolution "was almost certain."[1] The public assurances the State Department asked from Conservative authorities, however, were perceived meaningful by Washington only insofar as Havana further consented to a far-reaching overhaul of the electoral system. Indeed, whatever hopes the State Department had for peaceful elections in 1920 rested largely on reorganizing an electoral system discredited among Liberals in 1916-1917. Only a general reorganization of the electoral order promised to provide the institutional setting capable of lending some degree of credibility to Menocal's commitment to honest elections. Abuse of the electoral code in 1916-1917 had been compounded by the inability of regulatory agencies to respond effectively to charges of fraud. Recurring allegations of irregularities in voter lists, moreover, including in several instances returns far in excess of registered voters, raised the necessity of reviewing the accuracy of the voter registrations around which the 1920 elections would be organized. To avoid a repetition in 1920 of political disorders associated in the past with disputed elections, the State Department emphasized to the American legation the "utmost importance" of persuading Conservatives to reform the electoral code and reorganize voter registration lists. Polk again reminded the legation of the "great importance" Washington attached to immediate public assurances from Menocal guaranteeing the honesty of the 1920 contest. Lastly, Washington sought from Havana an invitation for an American commission to supervise the reform of the electoral system and to help Cuban authorities conduct the elections. All these measures, Polk emphasized, were "absolutely necessary to secure peace in Cuba."[2]

State Department requests evoked mixed reactions from Conservatives in Cuba. The projected electoral code reforms received cautious endorsement. Few disputed the need to revamp voter registration lists. The request for an invitation for an American commission to assist Cuban authorities in conducting the elections, however, met immediate opposition. The presence of U.S. officials supervising the conduct of national elections, Secretary of State Pablo Desvernine protested, promised only to promote political unrest and threatened to saddle the Conservative party with political liabilities of considerable magnitude in an election year. The opposition, Desvernine feared, would seize this arrangement as evidence that Washington had lost confidence in the Menocal government.[3]

The Cuban response to what many in Washington perceived as modest proposals angered officials in the State Department. Vexed by Havana's refusal to comply with recommendations considered by the Washington policy officialdom as the minimum requirements for future peace, the State Department alluded to the possibility of having to reconsider American policy toward the Menocal government. In supporting constitutional governments, Polk warned, the United States "must take into consideration their attitude in regard to the freedom of elections and proper government administration."[4]

Mounting tensions between Menocal and Washington ended when Gonzales, who had been vacationing in the United States, returned to Havana. Gonzales, too, opposed the commission project. Always solicitous of Havana's political sensibilities, the minister shared President Menocal's fears. "Where would he or his party stand before these people," Gonzales queried Polk privately, "if he invited intervention in his own administration and himself openly impugned the sovereignty of the state!"[5] The American legation urged a compromise upon the State Department. Unwanted electoral reforms imposed on recalcitrant Cuban authorities, the American minister counseled, would necessarily meet immediate resistance in government circles and suffer ultimate collapse as a result of administrative sabotage. Gonzales instead urged recourse to personal diplomacy in the form of the "solicitation of friends having vital concern in the peace and welfare of Cuba and as necessary for our personal confidence."[6] Under this arrangement, the legation offered to assume responsibility for securing an informal government pledge to conduct honest national elections.

Within a week, Gonzales had obtained from Menocal both a commitment to electoral reforms and an invitation for General Enoch H. Crowder to visit Cuba to reorganize the electoral code.[7] On February 12, 1919, Menocal formally issued a public request to General Crowder to assist the Cuban government in revising the island's electoral laws in order "to remove the constant source of irritation, criticism, and mortification" attending past elections.[8]

The State Department perceived these developments as the opening through which to secure some measure of control over the conduct of the 1920 contest. Crowder's minimum objective consisted of a general reorganization of the island's electoral system. Specifically, Polk's verbal instructions to Crowder stressed the importance of reforming the Cuban electoral code to avoid a repetition of the legal difficulties of 1916-1917.[9] Quite apart from legal work, however, the State Department hoped privately that Crowder would remain in Cuba throughout the campaign to supervise the administration of the new code. Polk privately cautioned Crowder against making any public statement proposing supervision of elections for fear that premature disclosure would antagonize Menocal. "[I] told him," Polk confided to his diary, "it would be better to recommend certain reforms publicly and make private recommendations to the President of Cuba that it would be useless unless this Government controlled elections."[10]

General Crowder arrived in Cuba in March 1919. For the better part of the next six months, Crowder studied the political context of the electoral code through consultation with the president, government ministries, congressional leaders, and Cuban jurists. By August 1919, after an exhaustive study of all elections since 1908, in which virtually every variety of known fraud was catalogued, Crowder had completed his work on the electoral code.[11] The new law placed greater responsibility on judicial agencies to resolve electoral disputes. The electoral board drew representatives from all parties equally. The code strengthened the authority of the local appellate system over election quarrels. Presidential candidates could not seek office on more than one party ticket. Additional reforms included new voter registration cards, improved channels of communications to relay outlying returns to Havana immediately, and safeguards against padded voter registration lists.[12] Crowder also recommended a new census preliminary to the reorganization of voter registration lists. In July 1919, the Cuban government authorized the establishment of a census bureau under Cuban directors supervised by an American adviser. At Crowder's recommendation, the U.S. War Department appointed Major Harold E. Stephenson to direct the census project in Cuba. With the completion of the census in early fall, the government allotted several months to permit party registrations and complete the distribution of new voter identification cards.[13] By 1920, the revised voter registration lists based on the new census figures had been completed.[14]

Liberal Politics and American Supervision

The reorganization of the electoral system had a generally salutary effect on the leaders of the Liberal party. Many Liberals viewed Crowder's correction of the more conspicuous abuses of past elections as tantamount to a vindication of party charges in 1916-1917.[15] The elimination of the most obvious defects of the electoral system in 1919, however, failed to inspire among Liberal leaders more than a guarded hope for honest elections in 1920. Liberals argued that, in the end, Conservatives retained full custody over the electoral process, however much reformed and reorganized. Having neutralized the deterrent value of revolution as a source of restraint on election fraud and, indeed, having eliminated armed protest from the political equation as a means of redressing grievances, U.S. policy in 1916-1917 had removed all controls over honest elections from the hands of the opposition. Responsibility for elections in 1920, Liberal party spokesmen insisted, now rested with authorities in Washington.[16] As early as December 1918, José Miguel Gómez outlined in tentative form the party position:

If we must tolerate in Cuba intervention in everything, whether in the sanitary department or in the treasury, or in the supply department; if the American army occupies the country, if Minister Gonzales addresses manifestos and dictates to the Cuban people, if the Executive himself has to tolerate intervention by Desvernine and others, and if all this with the consent of the president government; if they rob us of the result of the elections, if they dictate restrictions on the free exercise of electoral rights, if they do not permit us to resort to revolution in order to carry out sane reforms; then in this lamentable case, let us hope they intervene in the only thing in which they have never intervened before and that is real elections which form the only method to save the country. Elections directed by the present government would not make it worthwhile for me to accept a nomination as there would be no justice exercised.[17]

Several months later, the Liberal National Assembly authorized the party's executive committee to seek Washington's assistance if and when, in the judgment of the party leadership, circumstances warranted American supervision of elections.[18]

Throughout the first half of 1919, pressure mounted within the Liberal party to secure U.S. supervision of every stage of the election campaign.[19] In October 1919, the executive committee dispatched Fernando Ortiz to Washington to present the Liberals' case directly to American authorities. In several informal discussions with State Department officials, Ortiz reviewed political developments in Cuba. There was little in the record, either past or present, Ortiz emphasized to the State Department, to provide Liberals with anything more than remote hope for honest elections the following year. The Liberal executive committee, moreover, was prepared to formally request American supervision of elections, without which, Ortiz predicted, Cuba would experience political dislocations dwarfing those of 1917.[20]

The State Department was sufficiently moved by Liberal arguments to raise again with Conservative officials in Havana the issue of American supervision. Within days of Ortiz's return to Cuba, the newly appointed assistant secretary of state, William Phillips, expressed to the legation his fear that to forego supervision left only "the alternative of facing serious political disturbances or a condition equally serious, as a result of failure to supervise." Doubting Menocal's ability, and perhaps willingness, to guarantee the integrity of the 1920 elections, Phillips urged the legation to secure from Havana an invitation for Crowder to supervise the conduct of the campaign. "What would be more natural," Phillips asked rhetorically, "than for Cuba to invite General Crowder (who is now thought to enjoy, as he long has done, the confidence of the majority of Cubans), to interpret and apply the new law."[21]

Renewed American efforts to secure approval for electoral supervision continued to meet opposition in Havana. Gonzales reported that Menocal appeared "astonished" at the American proposal. The appointment of Crowder as election supervisor, Menocal feared, would be interpreted in Cuba as a defeat of his policies and a blow to his administration capable of impairing his ability to govern for the remainder of his term. Indeed, Menocal threatened to resign before submitting his administration to the humiliation of American supervision.[22] Reflecting administration views, Secretary Desvernine detected in the American supervision project a Liberal plot to discredit the Conservative government. Writing directly to Crowder, Desvernine pleaded Havana's case privately, warning that the imposition of supervision would inevitably result in the resignation of President Menocal. Only the *miguelista* faction of the Liberal party, Desvernine insisted, stood to derive any benefit from the chaos certain to result from the collapse of the Conservative government.[23]

Havana's opposition to supervision continued to receive the support of key American officials. Apparently swayed by the power of the Conservative arguments, Crowder expressed serious reservations about imposing supervision on uncooperative Cuban authorities. Crowder's own lack of enthusiasm for supervision, all the more important because of his central importance to the project, slowed Phillips's drive. Without the cooperative participation of all political parties, Crowder cautioned the State Department, supervision was "unthinkable" and foredoomed to failure.[24] The Conservatives' position was also endorsed by the legation in Havana. The issue of supervision, Gonzales wrote, represented nothing more than a mask behind which lurked the malevolent spirit of *miguelismo*. To acquiesce in Liberal demands for supervision was tantamount to vindicating the February revolution, thereby generating in 1920 both "a boom for the presidential aspirations of Jose Miguel Gomez," and encouragement for revolution in the future.[25]

In the face of strong opposition from both Cuban and American authorities, the efforts in 1919 to secure Menocal's endorsement of supervision came to nothing. Whatever sentiment for supervision did exist in Washington diminished in late November when Gonzales secured from Menocal the long-awaited personal pledge guaranteeing the integrity of national elections the following year.[26] More important, efforts to impose supervision failed, largely due to the contradiction of purpose in the policy officialdom in Washington. The proponents of supervision failed to generate much support at the policy levels throughout the State Department. Indeed, the attempt at supervision in 1919 comprised little more than informal recommendations promoting a potentially worthy, if not immediately urgent, enterprise. State Department probes seemed designed to secure from Havana some form of essential guarantees that would make supervision unnecessary. Apart from the election abuses predicted by the Liberals for 1920, nothing had occurred in 1919 to warrant a concerted push for supervision. On the contrary, if Menocal's threat to resign commanded any credibility, as it apparently did with Crowder and Gonzales, electoral intervention threatened to provoke a political crisis of monumental proportions. Deference to Conservative sensibilities and respect for the imperatives of Cuban politics argued powerfully for circumspection in 1919.

In a larger sense, Liberal advocacy of electoral supervision failed to win support in 1919 due to Washington's antipathy to the Liberal party and, in particular, to José Miguel Gómez. Much of the Washington officialdom involved in rescuing Menocal in 1916-1917 had not fully forgiven the Liberal chieftain for his part in the February rebellion. The diplomatic wounds opened by "La Chambelona" had not fully healed. Forced in 1919 to choose between offending Menocal, whose pro-American sentiments had been the Cuban president's outstanding virtue in Washington's estimate, or assuaging the apprehension of Liberal leaders, many of whom had caused policymakers much distress in 1917, the State Department opted for the incumbent Conservative.

Menocal himself had come by 1919 to appreciate the depth of anti-Liberal sentiment in Washington and quickly learned to play upon American fears in order to force concessions to Conservative policies in Havana. Menocal had only to invoke the specter of *miguelismo* to induce in Washington the desired policy response. Important individuals at key levels of policy, sharing with the Cuban president a deep hostility toward Liberal politicians, needed little additional inducement to rebuff the *miguelista* overtures for supervision. Given the numerical superiority of registered Liberals, there was considerable fear among American authorities that elections held under the rigors of impartial supervision would guarantee the Liberals a triumph at the polls.[27] Minimally, as Conservatives reminded Washington, supervision threatened to place severe political liabilities on the incumbent party and, in discrediting the administration, enhance the Liberals' national appeal in 1920.

As early as February 1919, when the *miguelistas* mounted their initial efforts to secure supervision, Gonzales hastened to register in Washington his opposition to the Liberal party. "If I'm going to attempt to save a bank from threatened insolvency," Gonzales wrote Polk privately, "I would not care to have professional safecrackers for my associates in the work. And Gomez, Ferrara, and their immediate following are professional political burglars."[28] Polk shared the minister's sentiments. In mid-1919, Polk instructed Crowder to "intimate unofficially" to the appropriate authorities in Cuba "that we were not very friendly toward Gomez, he was an enemy to the United States and a grafter."[29] Menocal, who otherwise needed little additional encouragement to subvert the electoral process in order to promote the Conservative cause, received from Washington full support, however "unofficially," for policies couched in anti-*miguelismo*. Indeed, American hostility against the Liberals ran so deep that the military attaché in Havana proposed armed intervention as a necessary, if only a last, alternative to a Liberal victory at the polls in 1920. "If it should eventuate," Colonel Paul W. Beck counseled, "that the Liberals are successful at the polls (and it now looks as though such is probable) the only hope for the continuity of the Cuban Republic lies through intervention by the United States."[30]

Changing of the Guard, Cuban Politics, and Policy Démarche

The State Department that had endorsed two administrations of *menocalista* policies experience major personnel turnovers between late 1919 and early 1920. In December 1919, after seven years in Havana, Gonzales was replaced by Boaz W. Long. Leo S. Rowe and Sumner Welles assumed positions of chief and assistant chief of the Division of Latin American Affairs. In February 1920, Bainbridge Colby replaced

Lansing as secretary of state. Two months later, William Phillips was promoted to assistant secretary of state. In June, Norman H. Davis replaced Polk as undersecretary of state.

The rapid turnovers between 1919 and 1920 placed in policymaking positions career diplomats and officials with considerable experience in Latin America generally and Cuba specifically. Long arrived in Havana with a wide background of foreign service experience. Welles and Phillips, New England patricians, had committed themselves to careers in foreign service. Rowe was an academic with a professional interest in events of the Western Hemisphere. All four men had a particular interest in Latin America. Norman Davis carried to Washington familiarity with Cuban politics and personalities as a result of nearly two decades of business and social associations in Havana. Lastly, Secretary Colby, unfamiliar with Cuba, came to rely heavily on the counsel of his subalterns. These changes in the State Department prompted Crowder to predict optimistically that "we shall have for the future what we have not had in the past, a definite Cuban policy."[31]

Concurrent with personnel turnovers in Washington, election-year politics in Cuba moved at an accelerating pace. In early 1920, a power struggle between the *zayista* and *miguelista* factions of the Liberal party ended when José Miguel Gómez emerged as the party's presidential candidate and thereupon promptly expelled his rival Alfredo Zayas. Zayas subsequently organized the *Partido Popular Cubano* (PPC), obtained the PPC presidential nomination, and cast about for allies among the anti-*miguelista* ranks. Sensing the unlikelihood of perpetuating Conservative rule for another four years, and determined to thwart at all costs Gómez's presidential aspirations, Menocal endorsed the PPC and arranged to deliver the support of the Conservative party to Zayas. The PPC and the Conservative party joined together to form the *Liga Nacional*. In return, Zayas pledged to assist Menocal to return to the presidential palace in the 1924 national elections.[32]

Only the newly enacted electoral code, which specifically prohibited a candidate from seeking office on two tickets, stood between Zayas and the Conservative party nomination. In early March 1920, the Conservatives introduced in Congress legislation designed to amend the code to permit dual party nominations. Menocal explained in advance to the State Department that this would guarantee orderly government in

Cuba. More to the point, Menocal appealed to appropriate prejudices in Washington and bluntly disclosed in private that the amendment would prevent Gómez from winning the election.[33]

By early 1920, however, the change of personnel in the State Department deprived Menocal of his long-standing support. The proposed modification of the electoral code evoked immediate opposition in Washington. The administration's partisan assault on the code, Colby protested angrily, threatened to undermine national confidence in the electoral system so laboriously prepared by General Crowder. Colby denounced the contemplated revision of the law as "unwise and unnecessary to the conduct of fair and honest elections in Cuba, giving rise to misunderstanding and capable of jeopardizing the national elections later in the year."[34]

Over Washington's objections, the Conservatives secured rapid congressional passage of the administration's revision of the electoral code. On March 27, Menocal signed the amendment into law. In Havana, Minister Long, disappointed and very much vexed over the rush of events, expressed to Menocal his personal regrets that the Conservatives had chosen to disregard U.S. counsel. Menocal's "very precipitous" act, Long feared, raised an ominous augury very early in the election year.[35] "I am terribly disappointed at Menocal's action," Long admitted. "Apparently the man has played the game very fairly with us for seven years, but in this case, the first I recall of its kind, our word has been disregarded."[36] The State Department, presented with a *fait accompli*, consoled itself by protesting Menocal's action and cautioning against any "further tinkering" with the electoral code.[37]

Washington's second warning, however, went unheeded. Menocal's success in amending a substantive portion of the electoral code without evoking, as a consequence, as much as a single public hint of opposition from Washington, enormously weakened the credibility of the stated American commitment to honest elections. In a political system conditioned to respond to the dictates of public diplomacy, Washington's silence in March 1920, could not have been interpreted as other than an endorsement of *menocalista* actions. Indeed, speculation increased that the administration's amendment of the electoral code, conceived wholly and unabashedly in a partisan spirit, could not have been undertaken without prior consultation and approval of the appropriate authorities in

Washington — a view that Conservatives did little to discourage.[38] The administration's success, moreover, in confining knowledge of American opposition to the proposed revision to the inner councils of the executive office, and the State Department's decision to limit its protest to high-level diplomatic communications, added a further measure of credibility to widespread conjecture.[39] In fact, the reputation of the Crowder code very quickly suffered, in regard to both its capacity to generate confidence in the conduct of elections and its expression of U.S. commitment to the integrity of the electoral system, when the belief spread that Washington lacked interest in defending the code against questionable partisan assaults.

Between March and April 1920, Conservative politicians seized upon these conditions as encouragement to attack the electoral code. New amendments, all designed to make the code even more advantageous to the government ticket, were rushed to the floor of the national Congress. One amendment authorized the administration to hire temporary employees for the duration of the election campaign — a practice outlawed in the Crowder code for having led in the past to government recruitment of political thugs and henchmen to harass the opposition. Another amendment proposed lifting the injuction against absentee registration, a move designed specifically to facilitate enrollment in the new PPC. By late April, Crowder, very much disheartened, concluded ruefully that all the "evils of 1916 are, in all probability, to be practiced in 1920 upon a scale undreamed of in Cuban politics."[40]

The Conservatives' assault on the electoral code revived in full Liberal appeals for supervision. The events of early spring had confirmed the Liberals' worst fears by providing the party leadership with palpable evidence of Menocal's determination to secure for the *Liga* ticket, at all cost, a victory at the polls. In March 1920, the president of the Liberal party, Faustino Guerra, called on the American minister to request an appointment to confer informally and unofficially with Secretary of State Colby in Washington. Without minimal assurances from the State Department, in which the United States would assume some formal responsibility for the conduct of the balloting, Guerra explained, the Liberal party could not participate in the elections later that year.[41] Within a week, Colby had declined Guerra's offer to visit Washington, insisting that any effort to "transfer the forum of political activity from the Island of Cuba to Washington is harmful to the best interests of Cuba and is fruitful of endless misunderstandings.''[42]

The significance of Guerra's message did not go unnoticed in Washington. For the first time, a prominent Liberal had given clear, if only private, expression to a tactic long rumored to be under active consideration in the inner councils of the Liberal party hierarchy — a boycott of elections. In Washington, State Department officials immediately reviewed the implications of the Liberal warning. Although officials in Washington were of the opinion that it was a hollow threat, designed to force the United States to supervise elections, no one was prepared to dismiss such an eventuality entirely.[43] In Havana, meanwhile, Long reported that rumors of a Liberal boycott increased daily. ''Such a withdrawal,'' the minister informed Washington, ''might be a prelude to civil war.''[44] Colby was sufficiently concerned about the rumored boycott to address himself directly to the Liberal threat:

> The withdrawal of any political party from participation in an election . . . is regarded by this Government not only as undemocratic, but as tending to undermine the foundations of popular government. Such withdrawal would in the view of this Government, mean that the leaders of the party thus counseling their followers to abstain from exercising the political duties of citizenship have in reality urged them to withdraw from the political life of the country. Such a proceeding would be regarded in the United States as a grave injustice to the Cuban people, and would place any party adopting such a policy not only beyond the pale of the political life of the country, but as indicative of their incapacity to participate in a fruitful and constructive way in the development of democratic institutions. The withdrawal of any element from the national elections will in no way influence the policy of the United States to regard the result of a fair election as expressive of the national will.[45]

On April 5, Long informed Guerra that the State Department had declined to meet with Liberal representatives in Washington. The Liberal party president received the news with considerable disappointment, repeating to Long that the Conservatives' determination to retain control of the presidential palace precluded any reasonable expectation of fair elections. "If there is no supervision," Guerra vowed, "we cannot go to the polls."[46]

Electoral Politics and American Diplomacy

By April 1920, with balloting little more than six months away, there seemed little prospect of avoiding a repetition of the political convulsions that had attended the last national elections. American authorities were frustrated by their inability to orchestrate events along the lines desired in Washington. The rush of events in 1920 had overtaken the diplomatic *modus operandi* that had been more or less effective in the past in directing the course of events in Cuba. Seeking to mediate political difficulties without direct and public involvement, the State Department failed to contain Conservative excesses and discourage Liberals from plotting an election boycott. A disregard for American counsel induced Washington to review Cuban politics in light of the recent developments and reexamine policy approaches to Cuba.

By the spring of 1920, Washington had arrived at some understanding of the dimensions of the political drama unfolding in Cuba. It required no prophetic gift to foresee the reappearance of all the combustible elements that in 1917 had exploded into revolution. Indeed, no Cuban elections had possessed a greater potential for precipitating a civil war than the contest in 1920. The previous national elections and the abortive revolution had already polarized the political order. Three years was too short a time to dim the memories of 1916-1917 among Conservatives and Liberals. The 1917 revolution continued to rankle with government authorities. For three years Menocal had nursed the wounds inflicted by the *miguelistas*; for Conservatives the 1920 election offered an opportunity to avenge political scores still outstanding. The issue was not so much to keep the Conservatives in power as it was to block Gómez and the Liberals. For this purpose, Menocal could, with little difficulty, embrace ex-Liberal Alfredo Zayas, the president's opponent in 1916, whom he had earlier considered "unworthy" of the presidency.[47] By no other means than backing Zayas, the apostate Liberal, could Menocal have reasonably attempted to deprive Gómez and the Liberals of the presidency. As early as March 1920, Menocal disclosed to the legation his determination to defeat the Liberals at the polls. A *miguelista* victory, the president explained, would serve only to place a premium on treason and revolution; a Gómez defeat, on the other hand, promised to advance the cause of morality in national politics.[48] Menocal invited American participation in his crusade against the Liberals, soliciting from the State Department a public condemnation of the Liberal candidate.[49]

Not until mid-1920 did the implications of Havana's single-minded determination to frustrate a Liberal victory arouse concern in Washington. What alarmed American officials was not so much the enmity among the power contenders, in the past heightened and exaggerated during election campaigns; rather, U.S. concern lay in the growing realization that Menocal was prepared, if necessary, to provoke another civil war to block a *miguelista* triumph. More and more reports reached Washington that the Conservatives would not under any circumstances relinquish power to the Liberals, whatever the outcome of the elections. In the course of his census work, Major Stephenson reported learning that Menocal had pledged to use whatever means necessary, "even at the cost of violence and bloodshed," to prevent a Liberal government.[50] Indeed, Conservatives were predisposed to provoke an American intervention as an alternative preferable to yielding power to the *miguelistas*.[51] In the State Department, Colby informed his staff that Menocal was prepared to "be the first man in Cuba to revolt" if José Miguel Gómez won the election.[52]

Quite apart from obvious partisan undercurrents motivating Conservative-*Liga* officials, the 1920 election involved decisive, if not immediately apparent, issues of vital concern to the Cuban armed forces. The army command in 1920, reorganized in the wake of the February revolution, had substantial reason to fear a *miguelista* election victory. Officers who had staked their careers on the ability of the Menocal administration to survive the *miguelista* armed challenge in 1917, commanders who had benefited directly from the defections produced by the February revolution, and all military personnel who had gained professionally and personally from the army reorganization in the aftermath of the 1916-1917 defections and had fought the Liberals in 1917 shrank in horror at the specter of a Liberal government. Two successive Conservative administrations and a revolution later, a Liberal government threatened to undermine the military order resulting from eight years of *menocalista* rule. The officers who had remained loyal in 1916-1917 faced an uncertain future under a Liberal administration. Liberal schemes for reorganizing the army, in fact, hinted at the return to active command of the *miguelista* officers who had defected in 1917.[53] Far too many officers had committed their careers to the existing Conservative order to entrust their futures passively to the vagaries of election returns. By early spring, military leaders were fully prepared to intervene to impose a political settlement consistent with — or at least not inimical to — the best corporate interests of the armed forces.[54]

Liberal leaders, for their part, refused to accept passively the prospect of an election defeat through corruption and fraud. Many *miguelista* partisans advocated a more agressive policy against the Conservative government than simply the threatened boycott, and urged the party leadership to return to the field of armed struggle to combat electoral violence. In 1920, Liberals directed the threat of revolution wholly at Washington. In Santa Clara and Camagüey, *miguelistas* vowed a systematic campaign to destroy by fire every cane field and sugar mill in the eastern third of the island.[55] The American consul in Antilla reported learning that in the event of widescale electoral fraud, the Liberals planned a revolution transcending mere destruction of property. American nationals, the consul reported, "will be a special object of attack in the coming trouble and will be shot down wherever encountered."[56]

Tensions mounted as the campaign moved into the summer months. Government misconduct during the campaign exceeded the Liberals' worst fears. Reports reaching Washington corroborated Liberal charges of deep government complicity in election abuses. Havana distributed *botelleros*, armed civilian henchmen protected by the army and police, throughout the provinces to intimidate Liberal voters and illegally seize voter registration cards.[57] Municipalities in which registered Liberals outnumbered the combined strength of the PPC and Conservative alignment passed under the control of progovernment military supervisors. More alarming, in many districts the registered voters far outnumbered the count of the recently completed population census, raising suspicions among Liberal leaders about the accuracy of the American-directed census enterprise. In July, a Liberal judge serving on the electoral board was murdered under mysterious circumstances. Liberal representatives warned Washington that government abuses had created an intolerable situation in Cuba certain to erupt into civil war unless attended to immediately by American authorities.[58] Indeed, conditions had reached a point where even the Conservative governor of Oriente appealed for American supervision as a necessary requirement to "insure public peace."[59]

By early spring, developments in the electoral campaign had convinced the legation that American policy was ill-conceived and ill-prepared to meet the brewing political crisis in Cuba. The Menocal administration, Long concluded, had betrayed its pledge to guarantee honest elections. In a meeting with Menocal and Secretary of State Desvernine, Long reminded the Conservatives that Crowder's efforts had sought specifically to prevent a repetition of past electoral abuses. "Since coming here," Long chided the president, "I [have] learned of past happenings which indicate that many Cubans feared, in approaching elections, a repetition of the 1916 experience."[60] Long suggested to the State Department that the passage of amendments to the electoral code, besides increasing reports of government violation of the law, provided sufficient grounds upon which to reexamine the efficacy of supervision. The minister recommended, in the meantime, an immediate increase in the legation staff to permit surveillance of the administration's conduct of the election. "We might consider," Long urged, "how we could keep a check on the Conservative Party's relation to the election process. The organization of this Legation at the present time is not such as to admit of the keeping of any comprehensive check on what transpires throughout this island in the approaching elections."[61]

The legation's loss of faith in Menocal climaxed a growing disenchantment in Washington with Conservative authorities. As a repetition of the events of 1916-1917 appeared increasingly likely, Washington neared the vortex of Cuban politics. Not yet quite prepared to assume direct supervisory responsibility, the United States reasserted to Havana its responsibility under the electoral code. The United States, the State Department indicated, reserved final authority to determine if conditions warranted an investigation of the conduct of elections.[62]

Throughout the early summer, the State Department grew increasingly involved in the Cuban election. In July, an impatient Secretary of State Colby reminded the Cuban president of his "solemn assurance" of the previous November to guarantee honest elections. Colby expressed anger over the apparent lack of investigation into the death of the Liberal judge, asserting that the administration's indifference to the case had created an "unfavorable impression" in Washington. He warned that "nothing short of the most dilligent activity on the part of all the Government authorities in Cuba . . . will remove this impression."[63]

Convinced that Havana lacked the desire, and perhaps, the ability, to guarantee trouble-free elections, in the late summer the State Department tentatively approved preliminary plans to direct the conduct of the campaign. Two plans came under review in Washington. On one project, Undersecretary of State Davis recommended the immediate appointment of General Crowder to administer personally the electoral code in Havana. Diplomatic notes had failed to convince Cuban authorities of the necessity of meeting the minimal election standards vital to the future peace of the island. Crowder's arrival in Cuba, Davis predicted, promised at once to inspire national confidence and to convert what would otherwise be an electoral disaster into a reasonably tranquil affair. "This one step," Davis counseled the White House, "short of actual supervision . . . may prevent this Government from being obliged to intervene once more in Cuba."[64]

The Crowder project failed to generate any more support in August than it had when proposed a year earlier. Menocal again refused to receive Crowder, repeating his determination to resign before sanctioning American intermeddling in Cuban politics.[65] In 1920, moreover, Menocal's resignation would have compounded an already confused and tense political situation, for Vice-President Emilio Núñez had bolted the government party to support the Liberal ticket. Crowder, furthermore, continued to have little confidence in a project undertaken without the cooperation of the Cuban government.[66]

A second plan, requiring virtually no collaboration with Cuban authorities, gained increasing support in Washington. Reviewing the purport of the June 24 communiqué, in which Washington arrogated to itself final authority to determine compliance with the electoral code, the State Department agreed to supervise the conduct of elections. Under the State Department plan, officials were to be appointed to the six provinces to study the election proceedings and report their findings to the legation at periodic intervals.[67] On July 14, Washington informed the legation of the decision to assign to "observers" the responsibility of gathering election data and, it was hoped, of restraining the administration's excesses.[68] By the end of July, Colby had secured final White House authorization to announce at the appropriate moment Washington's decision to observe the election proceedings in Cuba.[69]

The State Department withheld announcement for three weeks, hoping in that interval to persuade Menocal to honor his November 1919 pledge. By mid-August, however, Washington had concluded that the involvement it had so long hoped to avoid was essential if Cuba was to survive the campaign free of postelection political disorders. The State Department concluded that Zayas lacked the support necessary to win the election legally. Events in Cuba, Sumner Welles concluded, justified Liberal fears of fraud and violence in the absence of U.S. supervision. "A revolt by the Liberal Party," Welles predicted, "is a contingency that may be expected if Zayas should appear to be elected." Reports from Cuba suggested that Menocal had not, in fact, fulfilled his November 1919 pledge, the basis upon which the United States had earlier abandoned supervision. Only "radical measures," Welles concluded, could save the rapidly deteriorating political situation in Cuba.[70]

The government's conduct of the election in Cuba confirmed the State Department appraisal of the situation. Military intervenors continued to displace elected Liberal authorities. Government harassment of the opposition included intimidation of voters, theft of *cédulas*, and, with increasing frequency, mysterious assaults on, and even murders of, Liberal officials and candidates. By late summer, a satisfactory settlement of growing political tensions had reached a new urgency as Cuba's wartime boom and prosperity collapsed. Mass unemployment, street demonstrations, and rising prices added new stresses to an already strained political system. Labor conditions heightened American concern that economic grievances would ignite the political situation. "We are advised," Davis wrote the White House, "that widespread alarm exists lest the attempt be made by party leaders to use the dissatisfaction of this element in order to promote serious disturbances in connection with political meetings which are now being held."[71] Suddenly, on August 24, the Liberals dramatically announced their decision, in the absence of adequate guarantees for the safety and lives of Liberal candidates, officials, and voters, to withdraw from the campaign and boycott the balloting. This resolution, Guerra warned the legation, meant inevitably revolution.[72]

The first serious election crisis had erupted. This time no one in Washington doubted the sincerity of the Liberal announcement to withdraw or, for that matter, questioned the authenticity of Liberal charges against the Conservative government. A day after the Liberal announcement, Colby instructed the legation to outline American policy publicly. Alluding to the Platt Amendment, Colby warned Liberals that responsibility for the maintenance of a government adequate for the protection of life, liberty, and property necessarily precluded American sympathy for "any attempt to substitute violence and revolution for the process of government." At the same time, the State Department rebuked the Conservative administration, declaring that Washington was "no less opposed to intimidation and fraud in the conduct of elections as such a procedure might be effective in depriving the people of Cuba of their right to choose their own government." Treaty obligations, Colby concluded, made it "incumbent on the Government of the United States to use all available means to observe the conduct of the electoral procedure in Cuba, as well as the spirit in which the electoral law is being enforced."[73] Minister Long, in Washington for consultation, hastened to add a request that the legation confidentially relate the purpose of the State Department communiqué to Guerra before the Liberal executive committee convened to pass the withdrawal resolution formally.[74]

Colby's message arrived in time to avert an open rupture of the political system. On the strength of the American pledge to observe the elections and the State Department's denunciation of fraud and intimidation, the Liberal leadership agreed to remain in the campaign and go to the polls.[75]

In simply "observing" the campaign, and ultimately the balloting, without actual supervision of the conduct of the election and without authority to correct reported abuses, Washington assumed considerable responsibility for guaranteeing the integrity of the election without, however, a corresponding ability to enforce its recommendations. In the end, it was clear that the State Department, though increasingly involved in Cuba politics, had never intended to go further than observing the campaign. Without establishing the means to exercise on the policy level the restraints some felt warranted by Cuban abuse of electoral procedures, Washington returned to more traditional forms of diplomatic pressure. Throughout the fall, the legation forwarded to Washington periodic summaries of abuses reported from the field. Relying on the information received from Havana, the State Department lodged diplomatic protests with Cuban authorities, demanding immediate investigation and correction of specific abuses.[76] In this manner, the State Department took an increasingly active, if often ineffective, part in the elections. On October 20, recalling the events of 1916, Davis emphasized to Havana the "highest importance" of publicly releasing election returns as quickly as possible.[77] Two days later, the State Department protested thefts of voter registration cards and the unusually large number of appointments of military supervisors. Menocal was urged to remind the military intervenors to observe the strictest neutrality in the election. "It is feared," Colby warned, "that these occurrences, which appear to be well substantiated will give rise to general popular discontent with the manner in which the elections are being conducted."[78] On October 25, Davis again urged Menocal to order the army to abstain from political activities in behalf of any candidate.[79] Three days later, Colby vigorously protested an illegal appointment of a Conservative as mayor of Havana in defiance of a decision by the electoral board and the Supreme Court.[80] Several days before the election, Davis protested the administration's plan to employ military personnel to watch the polls, a clear violation of the Crowder code.[81]

The State Department's attempt to orchestrate honest elections from afar through diplomacy failed to modify appreciably the quality of the administration's campaign. Indeed, diplomatic pressure had been successfully applied in the past only when Havana expected to derive advantage through cooperation. In 1920, Cuban authorities, sensing that Washington's policy options had been greatly reduced, had little reason to heed American advice, particularly when it was inimical to Conservative interests. The Menocal administration continued to display scorn for the electoral laws and disregard for the constitutional rights of the opposition. Liberal officeholders, including judges, mayors, and governors, were summarily removed from elected positions by Conservative authorities. Army units terrorized the Liberal electorate in remote districts. The Ministry of *Gobernación*, the politicized nerve center of the government, issued an inordinate number of permits for firearms to government partisans. Murders of Liberals increased. Between March and October, Menocal issued 335 pardons, 44 to convicted murderers, many of whom subsequently appeared on government payrolls.[82]

The presence of American observers did little to restrain Conservative excesses. On the contrary, American officials charged only with responsibility for recording election practices may very well have contributed to the quality of the government campaign. Government leaders and Conservative-PPC partisans were not slow to discern that the observers' reports had little visible impact on American policy toward Menocal. Because the State Department's efforts to direct elections were conducted at such high official levels as to be unknown to all but a small group of ranking officials in Havana and Washington, all efforts to encourage honest elections were ineffectual. Indeed, the belief that the administration acted with the full approval of the State Department gained widespread currency among government supporters, serving to further embolden Conservative partisans and demoralize the Liberal opposition.[83]

By the fall of 1920, hopes of a reasonably honest election had all but disappeared among American officials. Having accepted the apparent inevitability of a fraudulent election, the State Department shifted its attention to prevent what had been the consequences of disputed balloting in the past — revolution. In mid-September, hinting at possible postelection violence, Long asked that marine patrols increase their practice marches.[84] A week later, the legation asked for an increase in the size of the American expeditionary force to serve as a deterrent to postelection disorders. "The widespread application of fraud," Long wrote, rendered the possibility of a Liberal insurrection quite possible, "more probable in case American force is not increased."[85] The military attaché, Major N. W. Campanole, shared the minister's pessimism, writing that Havana was "disposed to ignore and disregard the expressed interest of the United States for a fair and impartial election"; Havana, Campanole wrote, had created the conditions capable of producing another revolution.[86] The legation's request for an increase in the number of American troops won Colby's support, only to be rejected by the White House. "I feel," Wilson wrote, "that we are authorized to intervene only in case of revolution and not when we may fancy that revolution is impending."[87] President Wilson did, however, authorize

Secretary of War Newton Baker to prepare a full army division for possible service in Cuba.[88]

The approach of national elections on November 1 found Cuba poised
on the brink of civil war. Time and events had overtaken Washington's
policy initiatives. Having failed to persuade Conservative authorities to
comply with the letter and spirit of the electoral code, the United States
prepared to dissuade Liberals from resorting to revolution.

The Election Crisis, 1920-1921

Balloting ended on November 1 without delivering to either party a
clear mandate. Both candidates claimed victory. Communication difficulties and procedural tangles delayed announcement of election results for two weeks. The preliminary results released in mid-November,
however, indicated a Conservative-PPC sweep in five provinces, with
only Havana in the Liberal column. In the midst of charges and countercharges of fraud and corruption, the authenticity of municipal returns,
including several key districts, were in dispute. Liberal allegations of
government fraud, with supporting data, poured into the American
Legation. Ten days after the inconclusive election, Liberals appealed to
Washington to mediate the impasse, asking authorization to dispatch to
the State Department a committee to confer with the appropriate authorities in Washington. Long issued an urgent appeal for instructions.
"I find myself," the minister admitted bluntly, "at somewhat of a loss
to know what to do."[89]

In Washington, the Cuban electoral crisis received immediate attention. Colby declined to receive the Liberal delegation in Washington,
instead urging Liberal leaders to resolve their grievances through the
provisions of the electoral code.[90] This display of proper detachment,
however, concealed a growing alarm among State Department officials.
The deadlock in Havana now allowed Washington to step directly and
actively into the electoral breach. Unresolved elections in 1920 revived
memories of 1916-1917. In 1920, moreover, the election controversy
loomed as a dispute capable of joining pressing economic discontent
with political grievances. As political leaders in Havana maneuvered for
position, the Cuban economy fell prostrate. Unemployment, strikes,
and spiraling prices placed new burdens on a weak political structure.

By late 1920, the State Department no longer believed Cuban leaders capable of resolving the election dispute without a resort to arms. Disillusioned by the inability to manage the course of events on the island by diplomatic means, the State Department lost any further interest in upholding diplomatic protocol in a country over which the United States, by virtue of the Platt Amendment, exercised absolute authority. Washington believed that Havana's indifference to American counsel was largely responsible for creating conditions threatening life, liberty, and property, and justified a forfeiture of Cuba's claim to the trappings of sovereignty. In late December, with the electoral crisis still brewing, the State Department modified Davis's earlier plan and appointed General Crowder as President Wilson's "Special Representative" in Cuba. Crowder received from the State Department sweeping authority over Cuban administration, including supervision of pending partial elections, reorganization of government, and power to institute a variety of measures designed to revive the economy.[91] On December 31, Davis instructed the legation to inform Menocal, "without comment," of Crowder's arrival and to make all necessary preparations for the general to meet with national leaders.[92]

The State Department communiqué jolted Conservative authorities. Menocal protested the lack of prior consultation and American disregard for diplomatic courtesies in preparing for the visit. As a face-saving gesture, Havana asked only for a delay in Crowder's arrival to allow for a formal exchange of notes explaining the purpose of the mission. Otherwise, Menocal, intimated, he would not receive the presidential envoy.[93] The prevailing mood in Washington in early 1921 precluded any further concession to Havana's sensibilities.[94] Undersecretary Davis responded to Havana's protestations bluntly. "You may state to President Menocal and the Minister of Foreign Affairs," Davis instructed the legation, "that on account of the special relations existing in Cuba and the United States it has not been customary, nor is it considered necessary, for the President of the United States to obtain prior consent of the President of Cuba to send a special representative to confer with him regarding conditions seriously affecting the interests of both Cuba and the United States."[95]

Crowder's arrival in Cuba had an immediate salutary effect. Partial elections in the following spring confirmed Zayas's victory. For American officials, Crowder's appropriation of national administration in Cuba provided the vital margin of difference. Cuba, Long wrote several weeks later, was politically "on the rocks" and only Crowder's arrival "here in the nick of time . . . [saved] Cuba from intervention."[96]

8.

Capital, Bureaucrats, and Policy: The Economic Contours of U.S.-Cuban Relations, 1913-1921

United States policy in Cuba between 1913 and 1921 conformed closely to the requirements of an expanding capital stake on the island. Non-military intervention increased in all forms in direct proportion to the expansion of American economic interests in Cuba. To be sure, the complexity of the policy officialdom and the diversity of economic interests precluded perfect symmetry of purpose between policy and capital. On fundamental issues, however, specifically, political stability and opportunity for U.S. capital to expand, policy and capital acted in concert. The Wilson administration, Secretary of State William Jennings Bryan proclaimed to the National Council of Foreign Trade in 1914, had committed itself to "open[ing] the doors of all the weaker countries to an invasion of American capital and enterprise." More than this, the secretary of state reassured the assembled corporate leaders, "my Department is your department."[1] Some years later, Norman H. Davis recalled that Wilson's foreign policy had recognized "an identity of interests between the Latin American republics and the United States — interests both political and commercial." Since "no one questions that peaceful and stable development of the Latin American republics is in the best interest of the United States," Davis concluded, "the policy of this Government evidently should be shaped with that end in view."[2]

In Cuba, the increase of American capital, particularly in sugar, demanded conditions of "peaceful and stable development." The war years had witnessed sweeping changes in the organization and ownership of Cuban sugar production. Newly organized sugar companies appeared throughout eastern Cuba; consolidation of sugar enterprises

129

placed more and more land under fewer and fewer foreign owners.

The Atlantic Fruit Company, incorporated in 1912, expanded operations throughout Camagüey and Oriente. The Cárdenas-American Sugar Company assumed control of some 13,000 acres of cane fields in Matanzas. In the same province, the Matanzas-American Sugar Corporation, incorporated in 1915, secured an additional 10,000 acres. The Manatí Sugar Company, incorporated in 1912 and completed in 1914, acquired in Oriente some 76,500 acres of sugar land and the supporting rail infrastructure. The Cuban Sugar Mills Corporation, organized in early 1917, established new estates around 36,000 acres of virgin land recently acquired in Pinar del Río. The Central Sugar Corporation, founded in 1916, inaugurated operations immediately upon the acquisition of 33,000 acres of land in Las Villas Province.

The Cuba Cane Sugar Corporation launched by far the most ambitious enterprise of the period. Organized in 1916, Cuba Cane did not establish new mills; rather, it assumed direction of existing sugar plantations. Within a year, Cuba Cane had acquired seventeen fully equipped mills, owning outright 353,000 acres and leasing on a long-term basis an additional 194,000 acres. Some 500 miles of railroad, as well as 400 locomotives and 2,500 cane cars, passed under its control.[3]

Older American operations in Cuba modernized and expanded the acreage under sugar cultivation. In 1916, the Cuban-American Sugar Company acquired 325,000 acres, eight sugar mills, two refineries, 500 miles of telephone, and 225 miles of railroad. The United Fruit Company cultivated sugar on some 127,000 acres of land on the Oriente north coast. In Niquero, Oriente, the New Niquero Sugar Company rounded out its expansion at 28,000 acres while leasing an additional 9,000. The Atkins family, resident sugar proprietors in Cuba since the latter half of the nineteenth century, modernized their operations in Camagüey and in 1915 organized the Punta Alegre Sugar Company.[4]

The soaring prices of sugar during World War I provided a powerful stimulus for capital investment and cane expansion in Cuba. In 1913, sugar sold for 2.15 cents a pound; within two years, prices had almost doubled. By 1917, sugar sold for about 5.21 cents a pound.[5] Visiting Cuba in early 1917, Assistant Secretary of the Navy Franklin D. Roosevelt confided in his diary that "development of the Eastern end of Cuba was marked and of course sugar for two years has been a gold mine."⁶ By 1920 American investment in Cuban sugar had reached $400 million and had come to dominate almost half of sugar production on the island.⁷

Sugar investments in Cuba united strategic sectors of American capitalism around a common enterprise. Law firms actively participated in the organization, direction, and management of the newly established sugar combines. More than any other single enterprise, the Cuba Cane Sugar Corporation organized around sugar a network of interlocking interests representing the most powerful financial sectors of the United States. The law firm of Sullivan and Cromwell directed the transactions leading to the organization of the Cuba Cane Corporation in 1915. Sullivan and Cromwell partners occupied central positions in several sugar enterprises. Four attorneys of the firm, including William Cromwell, sat on the board of directors of the Manatí Sugar Corporation; three served as officers.⁸ Sullivan and Cromwell also placed several representatives on the Cuba Cane board; a brother of attorney Frederick Strauss served as chairman of the board.⁹ The Strauss brother represented J. and W. Seligman interests. The J. P. Morgan associates serving on the Cuba Cane board included Cornelius N. Bliss, Jr., W. Ellis Corey, Charles H. Sabin, and Grayson M. P. Murphy. Murphy also sat on the board of directors of Bethlehem Steel (Andrew W. Mellon interests), the owner of considerable mining interests in Cuba, and served as vice-president of the Guaranty Trust Company (Morgan). Cuba Cane board member John D. Ryan sat on the board of the National City Bank at the same time he served as chairman of the board of the Anaconda Corporation (Rockefeller).

Sugar interests linked Cuban sugar enterprises to American refineries. On the Cuba Cane board, sugar refineries were represented by James N. Jarvie, C. A. Spreckels, and Horace Havemeyer. Edward Atkins, president of the Punta Alegre Sugar Company, served as chairman of the board of the American Sugar Refining Company. George R. Bunker sat on the boards of the Guantánamo Sugar and the Cuban-American companies while acting as the secretary of the National Sugar Refining Company of New Jersey. The vice-president of National Sugar Refinery, Thomas A. Howell, served on several sugar boards, including the New Niquero Sugar Company, Cárdenas-American, and the Cuban-American.

The sugar system spawned in the United States a far-flung network of interlocking interests. Reginald Foster and Francis R. Hart, on the boards of United Fruit and Nipe Bay Sugar, also served as director of Old Colony Trust in Boston. Hart, in addition, was associated with the First National Bank of Boston and the Old Colony Investment; Foster served as vice president of New England Mutual. Norman H. Davis, president of the Trust Company of Cuba, held a directorship on the board of the Cuban Telephone Company, a subsidiary of International Telephone and Telegraph, and served on the Cárdenas-American Sugar Company board. W. E. Ogilvie, a director of Cuba Cane, was also president of the Havana Central Railroad and served on the boards of United Railways of Havana and Havana Terminal Railroad Company. Philip Stockton, son of the president of the American Telephone Company, occupied positions on the boards of the First National Bank of Boston, Old Colony Trust, and the American Sugar Refining Company. Various aspects of Cuban sugar, moreover, tended to provide mutually reinforcing links. Old Colony Trust in Boston and Banker's Trust in New York, for example, served as the transfer agents for the United Fruit Company. The First National Bank of Boston, associated with United Fruit, operated three branches and sub-branches in Cuba.

Between 1913 and 1921, the centers of sugar capital and Cuba policy moved toward a confluent relationship. Capital locked directly into policy levels primarily through links among attorneys. Past law school friendships, professional associations, and social ties between the attorneys of government and the attorneys of capital provided the latter direct access to policy circles of state. These relationships, moreover, received an uncommon cohesion through the continuous circulation of lawyers between the capital sector and the policy sector. The practice of recruiting State Department personnel from the offices of New York and Washington law firms, together with the subsequent return of many policy officials to private legal practice, tended to strengthen the bonds between bureaucrats and capitalists. Inevitably, the potential to influence policy decisions increased. The degree to which law firms succeeded in winning favorable policy action for a client often depended on personal ties within the State Department. Indeed, ultimate sucess for a law firm rested on its ability to secure access to the inner recesses of policy formulation. Nor was recourse to this leverage confined solely to

American capital. Sullivan and Cromwell, perhaps among the most successful corporate pleaders, represented some $170 million in Cuba, $70 million of which consisted of Cuban, Canadian, and Spanish capital.[10]

To be sure, specific ties often tended to weaken as the State Department moved during the late 1910s and early 1920s toward professionalization of the foreign service. With the rise of the career officers, the movement of attorneys between private and public service tended to decrease. During the preceding decade, however, many of those directly charged with the formulation of a Cuba policy maintained close relationships with, or were themselves linked personally to, the attorneys representing American capital on the island. Minimally, the policy officialdom shared with corporate lawyers common ideological assumptions according to which the course of U.S.-Cuban relations was determined. More commonly, friendships established in law schools and personal ties formed during private practice provided law firms fairly free access to policy circles. Frederick Coudert of the Coudert Brothers was a close personal friend of Undersecretary of State Frank L. Polk.[11] Before joining the State Department, moreover, Polk had served as legal counsel for Morgan banking interest in New York. Similar ties linked Isidore Lehman, of Lentritt, Cook, Nathan and Lehman, and Secretary of State Robert Lansing. Walter Penfield, a senior partner in Penfield and Penfield, after several years of service in the State Department, had retained close ties with his former colleagues in foreign service.

These associations were reinforced as State Department counselors retired to private practice. In their new capacities, these former policy officials frequently returned among their colleagues in government to plead the case of capital. When Secretary of State Lansing and State Department Solicitor General Lester Woolsey retired from the Department of State, they formed a law firm to represent United Fruit Company subsidiaries.[12] Frank L. Polk left Washington in 1920 to join Stetson, Jennings and Russell, whose clients included several sugar corporations in Cuba and the All America Cable Company, then organizing cable operations in eastern South America. A year earlier, Jordan Herbert Stabler had resigned as chief of the Latin American Affairs Division in the State Department to assume the position of vice-president in the All America Cable Company.

These relationships provided the basis for many of the specific decisions concerning U.S. intervention in Cuba that were made in the course of the February revolution in 1917. American armed forces did not take up garrison positions in Cuba haphazardly. On the contrary, the distribution of marines corresponded specifically to the leverage capacity of law firms in New York, Boston, and Washington. Serving both as solicitors and locators, attorneys pointed out to the appropriate authorities in Washington which properties in Cuba needed priority attention. The Coudert Brothers had sufficient influence in Washington to secure marines for their clients' estates at Cupey and Alto Cedro.[13] Through the efforts of Penfield and Penfield, the United Fruit Company estates at Preston, Felton, Banes, and Nipe Bay received protection from American armed forces.[14] Leventritt, Cook, Nathan and Lehman convinced the State Department to provide naval landing parties to guard the Ermita Plantation, the Confluente Sugar Estate, Santa Cecilia, and the properties of the Guantánamo and Western Railroad Company.[15]

Family ties further contributed to strengthening the links between capital and policy. Sullivan and Cromwell's success in securing marine guards in 1917 for the Manatí Sugar Corporation, the Río Cauto Estate, and the Francisco Sugar Company may have been related in no small measure to the appeal of attorney John Foster Dulles to his uncle, Secretary of State "Bert" Lansing.[16] Paul Fuller, the director of the Bureau of War Trade, was a cousin of Frederick Coudert. William Phillips's marriage to Caroline Astor Drayton in 1910 had linked the assistant secretary of state to the Astor, Roosevelt, and Schermerhorn families. The latter included Sheppard G. Schermerhorn, vice-president of the United Fruit Company.[17] In addition, Phillips's brother-in-law, Andrew J. Peters, former assistant secretary of the treasury and a one-time mayor of Boston, served as director of the Old Colony Trust and the First National Bank of Boston.

The U.S. entry into World War I provided capital with new access to policy. In the catacombs of sprawling wartime bureaucracies, government and capital joined to determine policy. All remaining traces identifying the origins of policy vanished for the duration of the war. With a permanent representative in Cuba, the National Food Administration determined sugar priorities and, in so doing, played a key part in the policy decisions of mid-1917. The decision to send marines to eastern Cuba in June 1917, was made in response to the needs outlined by the

Council of National Defense.[18] Many of the agencies charged with direct responsibility for policy were staffed by individuals linked directly to sugar capital in Cuba. The president of the American Sugar Refining Company, Earl D. Babst, represented the United States on the International Sugar Committee. Cornelius N. Bliss, Jr., on the board of Cuba Cane, served on the War Council. James H. Post, president of the New Niquero Sugar Company and National Refining and vice-president of Guantánamo Sugar and Cuban-American, served on the National Food Administration.

Capital and policy on occasion were fused in a single individual. Such was the case with Norman H. Davis. Before arriving in Washington in 1917, Davis had amassed a considerable fortune in Cuba. Only the short-lived Ports Company enterprise had marred Davis's success on the island. Davis's fortune rested securely on a variety of concerns in Cuba. President of the Trust Company of Cuba, which he organized in 1908, Davis expanded into key sectors of the Cuban economy, including sugar, finance, utilities, and railroads. Davis's portfolio included:[19]

Securities	Amount	Depository
Trust Company of Cuba Building	$ 12,500.00	Trust Company
Buena Vista Company	1,145.00	Trust Company
Cauto Valley Land Company	110,999.00	Trust Company
Cía. de Finanzas "La Continental"	12,212.30	Trust Company
Cía. de los Puertos de Cuba	78,980.02	Trust Company
Cía. de Muelles de Regla	51,400.00	Trust Company
Cía. Fiduciaria	6,500.00	Trust Company
Concha Land Company	9,850.00	Trust Company
Corona Sugar Company	2,945.00	Chase
The Cuba Company	137,125.00	Chase
Cuba Railroad Company	30,750.00	Trust Company
Cuban Telephone Company	300.00	Trust Company
Havana Marina Railroad	—	—
Trust Company of Cuba	240,619.30	Trust Company
American Foreign Banking Corporation	50,012.00	Chase

Bank of New York	94,436.91	Chase
Bankers Trust Company	55,999.00	Chase
Cárdenas-American Sugar Company	—	—
Hires Sugar Company	5,506.00	Chase
Central Sugar Company	—	—
Cuba Cane Sugar Corporation	34,111.80	Chase
Chase National Bank	31,250.00	Chase
Sugar Planters Corporation	10,000.00	Chase
Cuban Colonos Company	14,075.00	Chase
Ambrose B. Gonzales *(The State)*	28,124.77	Mercantile
Republic of Cuba	32,000.00	Morgan
National Bank of Commerce	18,168.75	Morgan
Cuban Sugar Mills Company (Bonds)	11,750.00	Chase
Cuban Sugar Mills Company (Notes)	90,500.00	Chase
Tamarindo Reparto	15,000.00	Trust Company
Trust Company of Cuba (New Balance)	34,857.39	Trust Company

The portfolio of Mrs. Davis included:[20]

Securities	Amount	Depository
Central Teresa Sugar Company	$ 70,000.00	Morgan
Ciego de Avila Company	8,000.00	Trust Company
Cía. Cubana de García	2,000.00	Trust Company
Cuban Telephone	4,866.66	Trust Company
Cuban Railroad Equipment	24,361.40	Morgan
Republic of Cuba	110,000.00	Morgan
Trust Company of Cuba Building	75,000.00	Trust Company
Trust Company of Cuba	10,000.00	Trust Company

Davis's Trust Company of Cuba, moreover, functioned as a strategic nexus of American capital on the island. Holding shares in a variety of enterprises in Cuba, the Trust Company also served as the insuring agency of railroads, utilities, and sugar mills, including the seventeen mills, machinery, and buildings of the Cuba Cane Corporation. The Trust Company of Cuba, in turn, was represented in counsel by Sullivan and Cromwell.[21]

Davis moved with ease among the most important political, economic, and diplomatic representatives in Havana. Active, if not publicly prominent, in Cuba politics, Davis counted among his friends ranking members of virtually all past Cuban governments. He was both active and prominent in Democratic politics in the United States, and his influence in Washington increased during the Wilson years. Davis was also a close personal friend of Minister William E. Gonzales. Indeed, the Gonzales family owed Davis a considerable amount of money. Financial assistance from Davis had allowed Gonzales to meet the financial obligations incurred in his diplomatic post. Without aid from Davis, moreover, the Gonzales family newspaper in Columbia, South Carolina, *The State,* would have ceased publication.[22]

During the second Wilson administration, Davis occupied a number of key positions in Washington. Between 1916 and 1921, Davis moved into those positions of policy that often directly involved the United States with Cuba. During World War I, Davis served as assistant secretary of the treasury, charged with reviewing Allied requests for loans. In mid-1917, he had occasion to review Cuba's application for a $15 million war loan. After consultation with the State Department, the Treasury offered to approve the loan only after Havana had agreed to settle outstanding claims relating to the Ports Company. The Treasury Department further asked Cuban authorities to compensate the railroad companies that suffered property damages in the 1917 revolution, most of which were insured by the Trust Company of Cuba and represented in Washington by Sullivan and Cromwell.[23] Under the conditions imposed by Washington, the American war loan served little more than to allow Havana to meet the claims of foreign capital.

During the critical moments of U.S.-Cuban relations between 1919 and 1921, as national presidential elections edged Cuba to the brink of civil war, Davis served in the State Department as undersecretary of state. With the Bainbridge-Colby State Department still unsettled as a result of the postwar personnel turnovers, and the White House occupied by a paralytic president, considerable policymaking initiative rested with Davis.

American policy between 1919 and 1921 reflected in large measure the related objectives that Davis brought to his new position in the State Department. He shrank in horror at the prospect of elections once again culminating in national political disorders. To be sure, many in the State Department shared these fears. Davis's banking and sugar fortune, however, already battered by the collapse of the Cuban economy in 1920, stood little chance of surviving intact the political tumult attending another revolution.[24] Nor did the political alignments in the 1920 elections show the undersecretary to be entirely neutral. Davis's personal friendship with Liberal presidential candidate José Miguel Gómez went back to the days when the Liberals had authorized the Ports Company project. The Conservatives, on the other hand, led by President Menocal, had caused Davis and his costockholders considerable inconvenience. General Enoch H. Crowder did not conceal his displeasure over the appointment of Davis to the State Department. "Norman Davis," Crowder wrote, "a trusted official of our Government [is] in the State Department alleged to be cooperating with his old friend Jose Miguel Gomez to control the Presidential election in Cuba this year."[25] American impatience with Menocal in the last months of the 1920 campaign may very well have reflected the presence of Norman Davis at policy levels in the State Department. Greater American involvement in the elections at once improved the Liberals' election prospects — if the Liberals' higher voter-registration count was to be believed — and minimized the likelihood of a revolution stemming from disputed returns. Both required U.S. political intervention on a scale hitherto unprecedented. Davis orchestrated the State Department drive. The proposal to send observers to scrutinize the balloting originated in the undersecretary's office; the appointment of Enoch Crowder as special representative of the president reflected Davis' perception of the requirements of American interests in Cuba.[26]

At the field level, policy rationales may often have concealed conflicts of interest. General Crowder's hostility toward the Liberal party may have been related to personal interests vested in the continuity of Conservative administration in Cuba. Originally planning to retire from the army in 1920, Crowder had agreed to accept from the Conservatives a lucrative retainer for services as legal counsel in Washington to the Cuban legation, a position Crowder recognized to be contingent on a *menocalista* electoral victory in 1920.[27]

A conflict of interest may very well have contributed to subverting the 1919 census in Cuba. Under the direction of Major Harold Stephenson, the census, almost from the moment of completion, evoked a storm of Liberal charges of fraud and partiality. Liberal complaints were routinely dismissed in Washington as partisan histrionics. Stephenson, however, did in fact cooperate with Conservative officials, who, in turn, adjusted census data to meet political needs. Under Stephenson's direction, moreover, Conservatives secured all key census positions, including director, subdirectors, and supervisors in all six provincial offices.[28] A year later, under conditions never fully explained, Major Stephenson, now retired from the U.S. Army, completed preliminary plans for organizing a $25 million sugar corporation in Cuba consisting of three mills, 125 miles of railroad, and a subsidiary steamship line.[29] Crowder reacted to the news of Stephenson's private activities with shock and indignation:

> You had an important task in Cuba in taking the population census. Upon the results of your census were built the Electoral Registers for the municipalities. The Presidential campaign has now opened and the accuracy of your work and the impartiality with which you discharged your duties are under review and analysis. It seems that, contemporaneously, you were prosecuting the organization of a sugar company, with capital stock of $25,000,000. Of course, you could make no progress in organizing such a company without availing yourself to the cooperative aid of authorities in Cuba. This would necessarily establish for you a business contact with the Administration that is now contending at the polls for control of the Cuban Government. . . . I think in the light of these facts, you yourself will see how far afield you have gone in interesting yourself in the organizing of a large company.[30]

Cuban politicians, for their part, detected in the sources of American policy a fulcrum upon which to balance national power relationships. In forging a viable political system within the context of the Platt Amendment, Cuban leaders located the appropriate pressure points of American policy, enabling Havana to enmesh U.S. hegemonic power in the very contradictions of the American politico-economic system and thus often neutralize that power. Havana discerned in the American capital stake in Cuba direct approaches to influencing U.S. policy. If, in fact, the purposes of capital and policy were connected, an appeal to the economic interests of capital could often be expected to succeed when an appeal to the diplomatic objectives of policy had failed. In learning to appeal to American capital interests on the island, Cuban leaders showed a keen understanding of the economic dimensions of American foreign policy. In precisely this fashion, Cuban leaders carved out of the Platt Amendment an enclave of considerable political autonomy. Menocal's favorable disposition toward American interests in Cuba won the Conservative president vital State Department policy support leading ultimately to a second term.[31] When it appeared during the Santiago naval negotiations that the tide of U.S. official opinion had changed, Menocal issued a timely statement pledging his administration to a prompt reimbursement of the canceled Ports Company concession.[32]

Cuban national politics reproduced in Havana the capital-policy nexus. The Cuban-American Sugar Company, organized by former Texas congressman R. B. Hawley, had earlier retained the services of Mario G. Menocal to organize and manage the highly successful Chaparra Sugar Estate. In 1917, President Menocal continued to serve on the Cuban-American board of directors. Menocal's secretary of state, Pablo Desvernine, a graduate of Columbia Law School, had represented the Coudert Brothers in Havana a decade earlier. Orestes Ferrara, the Liberal Speaker of the House, and Antonio Sánchez de Bustamante, a prominent Liberal senator, sat on the board of directors of Cuba Cane. The Liberal vice-presidential nominee in 1920, Miguel Arango, who had invested heavily in the Manatí Sugar Corporation, served as the manager for several Cuba Cane Corporation estates in Oriente. The national Liberal ticket in 1920, in fact, linked the Liberal party directly to Cuba Cane, Manatí Sugar, Sullivan and Cromwell, Norman H. Davis, and the Trust Company of Cuba. The unspoken issues of the 1920 presidential election may very well have involved a major struggle for hegemony over the Cuban sugar system between the Cuban-

American Sugar Company, championed by Menocal and the Conservatives, and the Cuba Cane Corporation, represented by the Gómez-Arango ticket. Funds from both corporations found their way into the respective party treasuries.[33] In addition, a Liberal revolution owing to a disputed election in 1920 would have both remedied political grievances and offered partial relief from overproduction and collapsing sugar prices to some sectors of sugar capital. H. C. Lakin, president of the Cuba Company, outlined an intriguing scenario to Norman Davis:

> There seems to be no doubt that the prevailing sentiment in Camaguey and Oriente Provinces is Liberal. It would not surprise me to have sporadic outbreaks in those two provinces at the time of the election. The danger in the western portion of Camaguey is much less than in the eastern portion of that Province or in Oriente Province because apparently Jose Miguel Gomez and Ferrara and other people have become heavily interested financially in several sugar mills between Santa Clara and Ciego de Avila. I do not think they are interested in any sugar properties of Ciego de Avila. As a matter of fact, Americans own most of the sugar properties between Ciego de Avila on the west and San Luis, Alto Cedro, and Antilla on the east.
> . . . The damage to sugar properties east of Ciego de Avila would therefore do little harm to Cuba capitalists, although, of course, the Cuban colono would be badly hurt. A shortage of the sugar crop would help all the rest of Cuba. An attack on American interests, and especially the Cuban-American [Company] would be considered in Cuba, I should suppose, as in effect on the Conservative Party.[34]

The involvement of capital and related interests at various levels of policymaking, both in Washington and Havana, added a dimension to Cuban-American relations central to the direction of American diplomacy. Bh the early 1920s, the requirements of capital and policy in Cuba had converged and produced new approaches to Cuban-American relations.

9.

The Politico-Diplomatic Contours
of U.S.-Cuban Relations, 1913-1921

American policy between 1913 and 1921 represented at once continuity and departure. Before 1916-1917, Washington had accepted, if only reluctantly, treaty responsibilities that necessitated armed intervention in Cuba. After the February revolution, the search for alternatives to armed intervention acquired a new urgency. Military intervention as an involuntary, treaty-dictated response to political disorders in Cuba had become an increasingly unsatisfactory — and indeed a wholly inadequate — interpretation of the Platt Amendment. Between 1916 and 1921, the State Department came to understand, however vaguely, the extent to which American policy could be overtaken by events and manipulated by Cuban politicians. Charged at home with reckless interventionism in the Caribbean, the Wilson policy officialdom increasingly resisted the treaty pressures of further military involvement in Cuba.

The emergent policy of military restraints developed in response to new conditions in Cuba and a greater understanding in Washington of the subtleties of Cuban political processes. With the increase of American capital in the sectors most exposed to the vagaries of Cuban national politics, armed intervention in response to insurrectionary violence offered too little too late. By 1919, the State Department had reached the conclusion that military intervention treated only the symptoms manifested by a functionally imperfect client state.

Between 1913 and 1921, the accent of American policy moved toward the prevention of conditions that in the past had required armed intervention. To be sure, this policy, still incomplete and imperfect in 1916, had failed to prevent the uprising in February 1917. The events of 1916-1917, in the context of international pressures, did, however, increase Washington's eagerness to find alternative systems of intervention that would be superior to the traditional military one. Insofar as

142

these new approaches made a full occupation finally unnecessary in 1917, they were successful. By the end of the decade, Washington had concluded that directly controlling various aspects of Cuban national political processes guaranteed American interests better than merely supporting an incumbent sympathetic to the United States. American interests in Cuba depended on the survival and well-being of a system, not on the interests of a single party or personality — however well disposed to the United States.

In the course of three armed interventions during fifteen years, successive administrations in Washington had adhered strictly to the narrow Root interpretation of Article III of the Platt Amendment. In 1901, seeking to allay the fears of the Cuban Constituent Assembly, Secretary of State Elihu Root pledged that Article III did not "signify intermeddling or intervention in the Government of Cuba." The United States, Root vowed, would intervene only "in order to prevent foreign attacks against the independence of the Cuban Republic or when there may exist a true state of anarchy within the Republic."[1]

The Wilson officialdom expanded the policy context of U.S. diplomatic relations with Cuba. This necessarily involved greater control over a wider range of aspects of Cuban national life. Nothing potentially capable of producing instability could be left unattended. Political and economic developments had rendered the Root approach untenable for the policymakers under Wilson. In seeking to prevent conditions that had in the past obligated the United States by treaty to intervene militarily, the State Department took an enormous step toward assuming greater authority over the Cuban national system.[2]

Politico-diplomatic intervention replaced military intervention. Emphasis no longer fell on restoring order but, rather, preventing disorder. Accordingly, all potential threats to stability passed under the purview of the Platt Amendment in its broadest possible interpretation. In 1920, Undersecretary Norman Davis, consciously paraphrasing Root, insisted the American treaty obligations included responsibility to "prevent action on the part of Cuban authorities which if permitted or continued would jeopardize the independence of Cuba, or the maintenance of a government adequate for the protection of life, property and individual liberty."[3] "It has been," Davis later wrote, "due to the failure to take preventive and corrective means that the United States has repeatedly intervened by force in the Caribbean and in Central America and that military occupations have succeeded military intervention, with all of the attendant evils.'' Davis continued:

> We must note, too, that quite aside from the fears and suspicions this engenders none of the military interventions undertaken by the United States in the Republics to the south has resulted in any permanent benefit either to the people of the state in question or to the people of the United States themselves. We should have learnt by now that the enforcement of peace from the outside does not remove the basic causes which make men resort to revolution. . . . It is futile for the United States to delude itself into believing — as it has done upon so many occasions — that it can impose a lasting peace artificially, by force of arms.[4]

Hence military intervention, besides offering inadequate and incomplete solutions to the problem of instability, also represented an impolitic expression of hegemony.

Since disputed national elections in Cuba had on two previous occasions given rise to insurrectionary protests, Washington appropriated under the widened interpretation of the Platt Amendment greater responsibility for supervising the conduct of elections as a means of preventing political disorders. ''Experience in the past has shown very plainly,'' Secretary of State Colby wrote, ''that free and honest elections are essential 'to the maintenance of a government adequate for the protection of life, property and individual liberty.' ''[5] It therefore behooved the United States, in seeking to prevent disorders, to increase political and diplomatic intervention. ''Upon no other grounds,'' Crowder rephrased Root, ''is 'intermeddling or interference with the affairs of the Cuban Government' justified.''[6]

Increased politico-diplomatic intervention, further, conferred on the American Legation in Havana commensurately greater responsibility for the monitoring and direction of Cuban internal affairs. Indeed, the legation emerged as the coordinating center of the Cuban national system. The arrival of General Enoch H. Crowder in Havana in 1921 as ''Special Representative of the President'' inaugurated in Cuba an era of proconsular diplomacy in which the legation appropriated authority ove virtually every aspect of national administration. The role subsequently played by American diplomatic representatives in Cuba resulted largely from Crowder's perception of the legation's part in this policy system. Crowder contended that only direct and constant supervision of Cuban national administration by American diplomatic authorities in Havana, fully familiar with Cuban law and empowered to intervene directly and freely in politics and finance, offered the United States any reasonable guarantee of stability. The American minister in Havana, Crowder specified, "should and can be the most important man in maintaining a stable government in the country." Crowder concluded:

> Intervention from time to time is to be avoided, if possible. The means by which this Government can fulfill its obligations are those made available by diplomacy. The accomplishment of the desired results is of course greatly facilitated by a most complete knowledge of Latin-American customs, habits and thought, but primarily by great familiarity with the organic law of the country, especially the electoral code.[7]

In 1917, Washington, by condemning the February revolution, sought to put an end to the policy precedents in accordance with which Cubans had in the past formulated strategies of armed struggle. In adopting a "no revolution" policy, however, the State Department increased, rather than lessened, its responsibility for Cuban politics. However adverse Colby may have been to transferring the forum of Cuban politics to the United States, American policy, by increasingly depriving Cubans of control over their own political system, made such a move virtually inevitable. Increasingly, the Cuban political drama was played for the benefit of an American audience.

The reexamination of the Platt Amendment further suggested a search for wider policy flexibility. More than once, the treaty arrangements had limited American policy response to a single military course of action. Before 1920, the Platt Amendment, specifically the intervention clause as interpreted by Root, had become something of a policy liability. Bound by Root's pledge to intervene only after a "true state of anarchy," the United States had failed to develop the politico-diplomatic approaches to prevent anything less. The difficulty confronting policymakers was compounded when Wilson took the view that the Platt Amendment authorized intervention only after the outbreak of revolution. The "contractual right of intervention," Sumner Welles later wrote, "has been exercised on various occasions, but never except in the face of open rebellion which threatened the independence of the Republic and which actually threatened the maintenance of a stable constitutional government." Welles concluded:

> Such actual intervention in or occupation of Cuba as the United States has been obliged to undertake is, of course, at best an artificial method of restoring outward tranquility so that constitutional government may once more be established. Of far greater value is the friendly advice which may be offered to the Cuban Government and to the Cuban people through our representatives.[8]

After the experiences of 1917 and 1920, in short, most American officials had come to recognize the severe limitations inherent in the traditional Cuban policy of the United States.

At the same time, appreciation in Havana of American perceptions of treaty responsibilities allowed Cubans to exploit U.S. policy commitments to the island. Cuban politicians possessed a keen understanding of power relationships and soon developed into agile manipulators of American policy and policymakers. Deprived of full freedom to direct the affairs of state, Cubans quickly located the contradictions and limitations of American power. Insofar as American policy served as the focal point around which Cubans organized a political universe, American policy became something of a pawn moved by all contenders for power on the island. United States armed intervention came to be more frequently — and often more skillfully — wielded as a threat by Cuban politicians against one another than employed as a diplomatic device by Americans in pursuit of policy objectives. Not that the Americans did not use the threat of intervention to evoke a desired response in Havana — they did. Rather, intervention as an active ingredient of Cuban politics was more often introduced on the island by contenders seeking advantage in the competition for national power in a politically and economically truncated system. Indeed, it became clear that the Platt Amendment was one of the most powerful underlying forces in Cuban national politics. So powerful a force was it, that even when the presence of marines in mid-1917 may have been justified under treaty relations, political considerations in Cuba made it inexpedient to invoke the Platt Amendment. American officials went to considerable, indeed, extraordinary, lengths to deny any connection between U.S.-Cuban treaty relations and the "sugar intervention."

The Platt Amendment thus evolved in two fashions. First, the amendment served as the basis for the expansion of U.S. nonmilitary intervention. Second, it increasingly occupied a central position in the Cuban political system. Political parties in Cuba sought sanction for their actions in U.S.-Cuban treaty relations. Cuban actions often conformed wholly to these perceptions. Menocal demonstrated in 1916, and again in 1920, both his capacity to exploit American policy to the Conservatives' advantage and his ability to transfer the responsibility of his actions to the opposition. In 1920, he invoked the requirements of American policy, and his desire to comply with these demands, to justify his efforts to defeat the Liberals. Before the opporutnity to embrace Zayas as the government candidate presented itself to Menocal, the Conservative chieftain, seeking stronger saction to block Gómez, tried to coopt Washington by soliciting a "confidential hint" from the State Department as to the U.S. preference for the Conservative candidate.[9]

Liberals too, for their part, detected the signposts of American policy in the past application of the Platt Amendment and proceeded to formulate strategies accordingly. The Liberal leadership went so far as to justify revolution in the name of the Platt Amendment. Liberals argued that on the evening in November 1916 on which Menocal intercepted election returns and nullified popular sovereignty, there ceased to exist in Cuba a government that guaranteed "life, property and individual liberty." Revolution in February 1917, Liberals maintained, sought only to fulfill the requirements of Article III of the Platt Amendment.[10]

After 1917, the Liberals functioned as a national opposition party without the counterweight leverage traditional and, indeed, essential to the balance of the fragile Cuban political system. Only a closer collaboration with the United States could offset the greater authority that American policy had conferred on the incumbent party, the Liberals concluded, and could make them viable contenders for power. "It is my desire," a defeated Orestes Ferrara conceded to Lansing in 1918, "to do nothing without the approval of your Government.''[11] In the course of this collaboration, Liberals ultimately came to demand of the Americans greater participation in the political system as one means of compensating for their own weakness vis-à-vis the incumbent Conservatives. In the process, the one political party in Cuba that had some claim to populist and nationalist leanings, however sporadic, passed under American influence. The appeal to arms in 1917 had proved incapable of restoring the balance to the regimen of distributive politics; three years later, the Liberals appealed to the United States. In 1920, the Liberals invoked the Platt Amendment, this time not to justify revolution but to sanction U.S. electoral supervision. "It is a case,'' Guerra pleaded in 1920, "of electoral intervention for the maintenance of an adequate government for the protection of life, property and individual liberty, seriously threatened at the coming electoral period.''[12]

After 1916, moreover, the Liberal party proved incapable of containing internal power struggles among party chieftains. In 1918, dissident Havana Liberals deserted the party to organize the *Unión Liberal*. In Oriente Province, Liberals established the *Partido Liberal Provincial*. Disgruntled Liberals in Las Villas organized the *Partido Liberal Unionista*. The desertion of Zayas in 1920 and the subsequent organization of the *Partido Popular Cubano* dealt another blow to the Liberal party.

The Conservative party, too, for its part, did not escape the turmoil of the decade unscathed. In securing by force and fraud the Conservative nomination for reelection in 1916, Menocal stunted the development of intraparty competition and clogged the party mechanism capable of producing viable presidential contenders. Between 1916 and 1919, Conservative politicians nurturing presidential aspirations saw little future in the Menocal-dominated organization. Menocal's opponents within the Conservative party found themselves either seduced by the promises of *menocalismo* or put out of politics altogether. Indeed, in the course of Menocal's second term, many leading Conservatives deserted the party or enrolled in the ranks of the Liberal party. Vice President Emilio Núñez, Menocal's chief conservative rival in 1916, left the party in 1920. Miguel Arango, a longtime Conservative, left the party to serve as the Liberal vice-presidential candidate in 1920. Events between 1919 and 1920 settled the fate of the Conservative party. Determined to thwart the candidacy of José Miguel Gómez, and unable to find among *menocalista* Conservatives even a remotely viable presidential candidate, Menocal went outside the party structure in search of a candidate capable of stopping Gómez. Between 1919 and 1920, a number of disaffected Conservatives deserted the party and organized the *Partido Democrático Nacional.* Another faction abandoned the Conservative party to form the *Partido Republicano.* A third group, headed by former Vice-President Enrique José Varona, claiming to uphold the principles of Conservatism, found the *Partido Nacionalista.*[13] Eight years of Menocal's leadership had reduced the Conservative party to a vehicle of *personalismo.* Renomination in 1916 and opportunism in 1920 all but reduced the Conservative party to insolvency. A Conservative would never again sit in the presidential palace.

The Cuban political system emerged from the *menocalato* institutionally disjointed and functionally impaired. In 1920, a Liberal became the Conservative party presidential candidate and a Conservative became the Liberal party vice-presidential candidate. Political competition had lost even a semblance of meaning and purpose. The politics of personalities had run its course. *Personalismo* had proved incapable of accommodating the growing political and regional heterogeneity of political parties. More important, between 1916 and 1920, *personalismo* was shown to offer only the most ephemeral — and increasingly unsatisfactory — method of distributing the resources and benefits of state. *Miguelismo* had failed the Liberals in 1916-1917; *menocalismo* had betrayed Conservatives in 1919-1920. Reelection had thrown the political system out of alignment, and revolution had failed to restore the balance. By 1920, moreover, new demands had been placed on the Cuban national system by the United States. A new constituency in Washington now demanded greater access to the levers of resource and benefit allocation in Cuba.

By 1920, the Cuban party structure had collapsed. Few had reason to mourn its passing. The United States, for its part, had learned from the *menocalato* to eschew partisan entanglements in Cuba. No longer would a political party or a single individual function as an element indispensable for the well-being of American interest, no longer would a political party or a single individual hold a lien on American support; this too often involved troublesome reciprocal commitments. Political neutrality in Washington would henceforth indicate a well-ordered client state.

Cuban political leaders were powerless, if not unwilling, to arrest the expansion of American control over the national system. Indeed, the fierce partisan struggles of the decade encouraged increased American influence. Political parties, splintered and fractured, incapable of mobilizing sufficient national support, sought the vital margin of support necessary for national ascendancy in informal accommodations to American hegemony. Both Liberals and Conservatives, seeking to use American hegemony to political advantage, perforce consented to a collaboration that itself provided further opportunity for the United States to extend its control over various aspects of the Cuban national system. Cuban complicity served as the necessary coefficient of American hegemony.

In the process of response and counterresponse, the Wilson State Department laid the recognizable cornerstone of a definite policy for Latin America generally and Cuba specifically. The "good neighbor" policy has its sources in the last two years of the Wilson administration. In the old State, War, and Navy Building, the young assistant secretaries and undersecretaries of state developed close relationships with the assistant secretary of the navy. Thirteen years later, Roosevelt would reconstitute the group and return Phillips, Welles, and Davis to policy circles to give direction and orientation to the Latin American policy of the United States.[14] The preference for politico-diplomatic controls over military intervention, the emphasis on proconsular diplomacy, and the ultimate abrogation of the Platt Amendment, already in 1920 something of a liability, would all find formal expression in the "good neighbor" policy.

Notes • Bibliography • Index

Notes

Chapter 1: Politics, Diplomacy, and Reelection: The Cuban Electoral Crisis of 1916

1. Jackson Tinker to William C. Beer, Feb. 7, 1913, Box 6, William C. Beer Papers, Sterling Memorial Library, Yale University, New Haven, Connecticut. Cf. Emeterio S. Santovenia, *José Miguel Gómez* (Havana, 1958), p. 23.

2. "Statement Made by Dudley F. Malone, Third Assistant Secretary of State, to President Menocal in Behalf of President Wilson," May 20, 1913, Department of State, *Foreign Relations of the United States: 1913* (Washington, D.C., 1920), p. 337 (hereafter cited as *FRUS*).

3. George Marvin, "Keeping Cuba Libre," *The World's Work*, XXXIV (Sept. 1917), p. 564.

4. Arthur M. Beaupré to secretary of state, May 5, 1913, 711.37/47, General Records of the Department of State, Record Group 59, National Archives, Washington, D.C. (Hereafter cited as DS/NA, RG 59).

5. Oscar Pino-Santos, *El asalto a Cuba por la oligarquía financiera yanqui* (Havana, 1973), p. 80.

6. Robert F. Smith, *The United States and Cuba: Business and Diplomacy, 1917-1960* (New Haven, 1960), p. 29.

7. See Ralph P. Rokeby to Mario G. Menocal, Jan. 9, 1914, William E. Gonzales Papers, South Caroliniana Library, University of South Carolina, Columbia, South Carolina. Cf. Dana G. Munro, *Intervention and Dollar Diplomacy in the Caribbean, 1900-1921* (Princeton, 1964), pp. 487-88.

8. Joseph Dubé, "The Cuban Ports Company," (Manuscript in author's possession, 1974). Cf. Pedro Luis Padrón, "El escandaloso robo del dragado organizado por José Miguel Gómez y su asociado yanqui Norman Davis," *Granma* (December 26, 1968), p. 2. For some British aspects of the Ports Company affair see J. Fred Rippy, "British Investments in Central America, the Dominican Republic and Cuba: A Study of Meager Returns," *Inter-American Economic Affairs*, VI (Autumn 1952), pp. 96-97.

9. Frederick R. Coudert to Frank L. Polk, June 22, 1916, Drawer 73, File 214, Frank L. Polk Papers, Sterling Memorial Library, Yale University, New Haven, Connecticut. For a full discussion of the Ports Company controversy within the context of the Platt Amendment see Philip C. Jessup, "Memorandum on the Platt Amendment: The Democratic Administration and the War, 1913-1920," part III, Philip C. Jessup Papers, Manuscript Division, Library of Congress, Washington, D.C.

10. In early 1916, Menocal recommended passage of a bill to indemnify the Ports Company stockholders. See Russell H. Fitzgibbon, *Cuba and the United States, 1900-1935* (New York, 1964), pp. 154-56. William E. Gonzales, "Memorandum for Mr. Wright and the Secretary," June 7, 1916, Gonzales Papers.

11. "Record of Sessions of the Constitutional Convention of the Island of Cuba," 7 vols. (Bureau of Insular Affairs Library, National Archives, Washington, D.C., 1901), v. III; Julio Villoldo, "Las reelecciones," *Cuba Contemporánea*, X (Mar. 1916), 237-52.

12. José Manuel Cortina, *La reelección presidencial* (Havana, 1916), pp. 36, 41.

13. Mario Guiral Moreno, "El problema de la burocracia en Cuba," *Cuba Contemporánea*, II (Aug. 1913), 257-67; and Miguel de Carrión, "El desenvolvimiento social de Cuba en los últimos veinte años," *Cuba Contemporánea*, XXVII (Sept. 1921), 19-21.

14. *The State* (Columbia, S.C.), Feb. 5, 1899, p. 1. For an early discussion of this phenomenon see José María Céspedes, "Empleo-manía," *Cuba y América*, III (Apr. 20, 1899), pp. 6-8. See also Enrique Barbarrosa, *El proceso de la República* (Havana, 1911), pp. 20, 32-38, 101-02.

15. Ricardo Navarro, "Report of the Provincial Inspector of Oriente," Apr. 22, 1920, in Cuba, *Census of the Republic of Cuba, 1919* (Havana, 1920), p. 933.

16. Irene A. Wright, *Cuba* (New York, 1910), p. 166.

17. For a general treatment of distributive politics in Latin America see Merle Kling, "Toward a Theory of Power and Political Instability in Latin America," *Western Political Quarterly*, IX (Mar. 1956), 32-33.

18. William E. Gonzales to secretary of state, Jan. 21, 1916, 837.00/1021, DS/NA, RG 59.

19. Enrique Collazo, *La revolución de agosto de 1906* (Havana, 1907), pp. 12-13. For a Liberal view of these events see Rafael Martínez Ortiz, "Juicio acerca de los sucesos políticos de Cuba en 1906," *Cuba Contemporánea*, XV (Oct. 1917), 118-30.

20. See William Howard Taft and Robert Bacon, "Cuba Pacification: Report of William H. Taft, Secretary of War, and Robert Bacon, Assistant Secretary of State, of What Was Done Under the Instructions of the President in Restoring Peace in Cuba," Appendix E, *Report of the Secretary of War, 1906*, 59th Congress, 2nd sess., House Document No. 2, Series 5105 (Washington, D.C., 1906).

21. Mario G. Menocal to Enrique Loynaz del Castillo, Aug. 10, 1912, in Raimundo Cabrera, *Mis malos tiempos* (Havana, 1920), p. 37.

22. José Miguel Gómez to James H. Wilson, Nov. 20, 1912, General Correspondence, James H. Wilson Papers, Manuscript Division, Library of Congress, Washington, D.C.

23. For the *menocalista* position on reelection see Ricardo Dolz y Arango, *El proceso electoral de 1916* (Havana, 1917), pp. 5-7.

24. León Primelles, *Crónica cubana, 1915-1918* (Havana, 1955), p. 27.

25. Ibid.

26. Fernando Freyre de Andrade to Mario G. Menocal, Jan. 14, 1916, in Rafael Rodríguez Altunaga, *El General Emilio Núñez* (Havana, 1958), p. 51.

27. *Diario de la Marina*, Jan. 15, 1916, pp. 1, 5.

28. Enrique José Varona to Wilfredo Fernández, Dec. 6, 1915, in Rodríguez Altunaga, *El General Emilio Núñez*, p. 498.

29. Menocal refused to accept Núñez's resignation and subsequently mollified his dis-

appointed labor secretary by choosing him as the vice-presidential nominee, promising to support him for the presidency in 1920. See Mario Riera Hernández, *Cuba política, 1899-1955* (Havana, 1955), p. 217; and Guillermo Rubiera, "Mario García Menocal y Deop," in Vicente Báez, ed., *La enciclopedia de Cuba,* 9 vols. (Madrid, 1975), IX, 197.

30. Charles E. Chapman, *A History of the Cuban Republic* (New York, 1969), pp. 348-49. See also Carleton Beals, *The Crime of Cuba* (Philadelphia, 1933), pp. 219.

31. *New York Evening Post,* Nov. 12, 1915, p. 6.

32. United States Congress, *Statutes at Large (1903-1905)* (Washington, D.C., 1905), p. 2249.

33. John B. Jackson to secretary of state, Aug. 30, 1910, 837.00/425, DS/NA, RG 59.

34. Enoch H. Crowder, "Memorandum for the Secretary of War," Aug. 6, 1912, 837.6112/2, DS/NA, RG 59.

35. "Message to Congress," Dec. 14, 1913, *Congressional Record,* 63rd Congress, p. 43.

36. See Enrique José Varona, *De la colonia a la República* (Havana, 1919), pp. 214-15.

37. "Statement Made by Dudley F. Malone, Third Assistant Secretary of State, to President Menocal in Behalf of President Wilson," May 20, 1913, *FRUS, 1913,* p. 337.

38. In acknowledging U.S. support after the outbreak of the Liberal revolt in February 1917, Menocal revealed his understanding of American policy: "President Wilson's attitude has been no less gratifying, because his well-known policy during the last four years with respect to Governments which are the product of revolutions had led us to expect what it would be in this particular case." *New York Times,* Feb. 22, 1917, p. 9.

39. See Orestes Ferrara, "Las elecciones de Cuba y el gobierno de Wáshington," *La Reforma Social,* XVIII (Oct. 1920), 125-31.

40. George Bayliss, American consular agent, Antilla, to Frederick Herron, Oct. 9, 1916, File (1916) 710, Miscellaneous Correspondence, American Consulate, Santiago de Cuba, Records of the Foreign Service Posts of the Department of State, Record Group 84, National Archives, Washington, D.C. (hereafter cited as FSP/NA, RG 84).

41. Raimundo Cabrera, "How a Corrupt and Misguided Government Retards Cuba," *New York World,* Dec. 5, 1915, p. E-1.

42. Associated Press to E. M. Hood, Apr. 8, 1916, 837.00/1024, DS/NA, RG 59.

43. *Heraldo de Cuba,* Dec. 11, 1915, p. 2.

44. William E. Gonzales to secretary of state, Jan. 21, 1916, 837.00/1021, DS/NA, RG 59. Leopoldo Horrego Estuch, *Juan Gualberto Gómez, un gran inconforme,* 2nd ed. (Havana, 1918), p. 46.

45. Bernardo Merino y F. de Ibarzabal, *La revolución de febrero. Datos para la historia,* 2nd ed. (Havana, 1918), p. 46.

46. H. M. Wolcott, vice consul, Havana, to secretary of state, Oct. 5, 1915, 837.00/1019, DS/NA, RG 59.

47. P. Merrill Griffith to secretary of state, Mar. 18, 1916, 837.00/1022, DS/NA, RG 59.

48. George Bayliss, American consular agent, Antilla, to Frederick Herron, Oct. 6, 1916, File (1916) 710, Miscellaneous Correspondence, American Consulate, Santiago de Cuba, FSP/NA, RG 84.

49. I am grateful to José Keselman for this information.

50. Franklin D. Roosevelt, Long Hand Diary, Trip to Cuba, Jan. 21-25, 1917, Papers as Assistant Secretary of the Navy, Franklin D. Roosevelt Papers, Hyde Park, New York. As early as 1914, the State Department proposed that the United States seek to frustrate the candidacy of Liberal leader José Miguel Gómez. See Gustave Scholle to William E. Gonzales, Dec. 16, 1914, Gonzales Papers.

51. Chapman, *A History of the Cuban Republic,* p. 338.

52. Jordan Herbert Stabler, "Memorandum: Cuban Elections," Aug. 31, 1916, 837.00/1029, DS/NA, RG 59.

53. See George Bayliss, American consular agent, Antilla, to Frederick L. Herron, Oct. 9, 1916, File (1916) 710, Miscellaneous Correspondence, American Consulate, Santiago de Cuba, FSP/NA, RG 84.

54. J. B. Wright, Division of Latin American Affairs, to secretary of state, Apr. 25, 1916, 837.00/1024, DS/NA, RG 59.

55. Robert Lansing to Joseph P. Tumulty, May 4, 1916, Series 4, File 97, Box 127, Woodrow Wilson Papers, Manuscript Division, Library of Congress, Washington, D.C. American support was conceived as the leverage with which to advance the settlement of the paving issue and the Ports Company controversy. "I recommend," J. B. Wright wrote, "that . . . an expression of support of this Government be deferred for opportune use, should all other efforts to secure a settlement of these matters fail." J. B. Wright to secretary of state, Apr. 25, 1916, 837.00/1024, DS/NA, RG 59. Those most familiar with the Ports Company controversy believed that only the Conservative president could undertake an equitable settlement without widespread criticism nationally. The Liberals, associated with the scandal in the first place, would lack the power to compensate the bondholders. See Norman H. Davis to William E. Gonzales, Mar. 18, 1917, Gonzales Papers.

56. For the most complete biography of Gonzales see Lewis Pinckney Jones, "Carolinians and Cubans: The Elliotts and Gonzales, Their Work and Their Writings," (Ph.D. diss. University of North Carolina, 1952), pp. 587-92.

57. William E. Gonzales to secretary of state, Oct. 28, 1914, 837.00/1011 and William E. Gonzales to secretary of state, Nov. 3, 1914, 837.00/1012, DS/NA, RG 59.

58. Ibid.

59. William E. Gonzales to secretary of state, Jan. 21, 1916, 837.00/1021, DS/NA, RG 59. See also William E. Gonzales, *Concerning Dollar Diplomacy, Crooks and Grafters. Incidents. Paper Read by William E. Gonzales Before the Kosmos Club of Columbia, Relating Experiences While Minister to Cuba and Ambassador to Peru* (Columbia, S.C., 1930), pp. 26-31.

60. Woodrow Wilson to Rafael Conte, May 8, 1916, Series 4, File 97, Box 127, Wilson Papers. *La Lucha,* May 20, 1917, p. 55. Lansing and Wright wrote the substantive portions of the president's message. See Robert Lansing to Joseph P. Tumulty, May 4, 1916, Series 4, File 97, Box 127, Wilson Papers.

61. "La guerrita de febrero de 1917," *Boletín del Archivo Nacional* (Havana), LXI (Jan.-Dec. 1962), 208-12.

62. *New York Times,* Nov. 3, 1916, p. 12

63. Gustave Scholle to secretary of state, Nov. 12, 1916, 837.00/1034, DS/NA, RG 59.

64. One Cuban historian suggests that the Conservatives' decision to intervene in the balloting process occured only after Menocal was reasonably certain that Wilson would win reelection in the United States. See Rodríguez Altunaga, *El General Emilio Núñez,* pp. 214-15.

65. Rubiera, "Mario García Menocal y Deop," p. 199. Secretary of *Gobernación* Aurelio Hevia was alleged to have apologized to Menocal: "I did what I could but in the end the Liberals beat us with their votes." See Riera Hernández, *Cuba política, 1899-1955,* p. 218.

66. J. Buttari Gaunaurd, *Boceto crítico histórico* (Havana, 1954), p. 342. For a detailed chronicle of election irregularities see "Brief Synopsis of Cuba's Present Internal Politics," Oct. 1919, File 1249, Material on Cuba, Enoch H. Crowder Papers, Western Historical Manuscript Collection, University of Missouri, Columbia, Missouri.

67. Alfredo Zayas, "A Statement on the Elections in Cuba, Held November 1, 1916," 837.00/1253, DS/NA, RG 59. Cf. Pedro Luis Padrón, "El 'cambio de paquetes' de Menocal, en 1916," *Granma,* Oct. 24, 1969, p. 2. Returns tabulated up to and including November 2 gave the Conservatives 184,680 to the Liberals' 188,994. See "La guerrita de febrero de 1917," p. 207, and William E. Gonzales to secretary of state, Nov. 21, 1916, 837.00/1047, DS/NA, RG 59.

68. P. Merrill Griffith, "Political Conditions — Santiago de Cuba," Nov. 22, 1916, File (1916) 800, Miscellaneous Correspondence, American Consulate, Santiago de Cuba, FSP/NA, RG 84.

69. William E. Gonzales to secretary of state, Jan. 22, 1917, 837.00/1056, DS/NA, RG 59.

70. Emilio Roig de Leuchsenring, "La ingerencia norteamericana en los asuntos interiores de Cuba," *Cuba Contemporánea,* XXX (Sept. 1922), 38-39.

71. William E. Gonzales to secretary of state, Jan. 24, 1917, 837.00/1057, DS/NA, RG 59.

72. William E. Gonzales to secretary of state, Jan. 22, 1917, 837.00/1056, DS/NA, RG 59.

73. P. Merrill Griffith to secretary of state, Jan. 29, 1917, 837.00/1061, DS/NA, RG 59.

74. H. K. Hewitt, Commanding Officer, U.S.S. *Eagle,* to secretary of the navy, 837.00/1270, DS/NA, RG 59.

75. Primelles, *Crónica cubana, 1915-1918,* p. 239. P. Merrill Griffith to secretary of state, Jan. 29, 1917, 837.00/1061, DS/NA, RG 59.

76. Hugh Grosvenor, "Memorandum," n.d., Drawer 77, File 244, Polk Papers.

77. José Miguel Gómez to Mario G. Menocal, Feb. 3, 1917, in "La guerrita de febrero de 1917," pp. 218-19; and Mario G. Menocal to José Miguel Gómez, Feb. 5, 1917, in ibid. pp. 219-22.

Chapter 2: "La Chambelona": Insurrection in the Plattist System

1. William E. Gonzales to secretary of state, Jan. 22, 1917, 837.00/1056, DS/NA, RG 59.

2. Robert Lansing to William E. Gonzales, Jan. 26, 1917, *FRUS, 1917,* p. 351.

"Memorandum of Statement Made to President Menocal by Minister Gonzales," Jan. 31, 1917, Gonzales Papers.

3. Primelles, *Crónica cubana, 1915-1918*, p. 243.

4. William E. Gonzales to Frank L. Polk, Feb. 4, 1919, Drawer 77, File 243, Polk Papers. William E. Gonzales, "Revolution and History — As Mr. Ford Knows It," (n.d., Gonzales Papers).

5. José Miguel Gómez to Raimundo Cabrera, Feb. 5, 1917, Cabrera, *Mis malos tiempos*, pp. 23-26.

6. Carlos Guas, "¿Quién ordenó el levantamiento de febrero?" *El Mundo*, Jun. 17, 1919, p. 16.

7. Horacio Ferrer, *Con el rifle al hombro* (Havana, 1950), p. 221.

8. Ibid., pp. 218-19.

9. These considerations were expressed by a number of officers in the course of the subsequent courts-martial. See *La Lucha*, Jul. 3, 1917, pp. 2, 8; and ibid., Jul. 4, 1917, p. 8.

10. Herminio Portell Vilá, "La Chambelona en Las Villas," *Bohemia*, LII (May 15, 1960), 36.

11. Luis Solano Alvarez, *Mi actuación militar. Apuntes para la historia de la revolución de febrero de 1917* (Havana, 1920), pp. 19-41.

12. Primelles, *Crónica cubana, 1915-1918*, pp. 245-46. Riera Hernández, *Cuba política, 1899-1955*, pp. 224-26.

13. William E. Gonzales to secretary of state, Feb. 15, 1917, 837.00/1090 and William E. Gonzales to secretary of state, July 16, 1918, 837.00/1489, DS/NA, RG 59.

14. Merino and Ibarzabal, *La revolución de febrero*, pp. 101-03

15. Herminio Portell Vilá, "La Chambelona en occidente," *Bohemia*, LIII (May 22, 1960), 36-37.

16. Orestes Ferrara y Merino, *Memorias: una mirada sobre tres siglos* (Madrid, 1975), p. 204. Cf. Chapman, *A History of the Cuban Republic*, p. 363.

17. Raimundo Cabrera and Orestes Ferrara to secretary of state, Feb. 10, 1917, 837.00/1069, DS/NA, RG 59.

18. Robert Lansing to William E. Gonzales, Feb. 10, 1917, *FRUS, 1917*, pp. 351-52. Dana Munro suggests that the first draft of this telegram contained a threat to withdraw U.S. recognition if Menocal ignored Washington's counsel. The passage was deleted before Lansing signed the wire. See Munro, *Intervention and Dollar Diplomacy in the Caribbean, 1900-1921*, p. 492.

19. Merino and Ibarzabal, *La revolución de febrero*, pp. 89-92. Cf. "La guerrita de febrero de 1917," pp. 223-26.

20. Robert Lansing to William E. Gonzales, Feb. 10, 1917, *FRUS, 1917*, p. 354.

21. P. Merrill Griffith, "City Taken by Military Forces," Feb. 12, 1917, Miscellaneous Correspondence, American Consulate, Santiago de Cuba, FSP/NA, RG 84.

22. José Navas, *La convulsión de febrero* (Matanzas, 1917), p. 10. Juan Jerez Villarreal, *Oriente (Biografía de una provincia)* (Havana, 1960), p. 311.

23. Herminio Portell Vilá, "La Chambelona en Camagüey," *Bohemia*, LIII (May 8, 1960, 13.

24. Lieutenant Colonel Edmund Wittenmyer, military attaché, to secretary, War Col-

lege Division, General Staff, Feb. 20, 1917, File 7298-20, Records of the War Department, General and Special Staff, Record Group 165, National Archives, Washington, D.C. (hereafter cited as WD/NA, RG 165).

25. Wilfredo Ibrahim Consuegra, *Hechos y comentarios. La revolución de febrero en Las Villas* (Havana, 1920), pp. 19-30. As the traditional base of *miguelismo*, Las Villas Province had been an object of particular concern to Conservative authorities in Havana. Just prior to the 1916 elections, Menocal had purged the Santa Clara regimental command of suspected Liberal sympathizers to prevent *miguelistas* from enlisting the regiment in behalf of Liberal candidates in the province. Months before the outbreak of the revolt, hence, the all-important Santa Clara regiment had passed under *menocalista* officers.

26. Ferrer, *Con el rifle al hombro*, pp. 223-24; Solano Alvarez, *Mi actuación militar*, pp. 66-68; Consuegra, *Hechos y comentarios*, pp. 30-35.

27. William E. Gonzales to secretary of state, Feb. 12, 1917, *FRUS, 1917*, p. 355.

28. Consuegra, *Hechos y comentarios*, pp. 19-30.

29. Ferrer, *Con el rifle al hombro*, p. 246.

Chapter 3: Counterrevolutionary Diplomacy: Policy, Politics and the "February Revolution"

1. Cuba, Secretaria de Estado, *Colección legislatura. Leyes, decretos y resoluciones (1 de enero de 1917 a 31 de marzo de 1917)* (Havana, 1927), pp. 209-10, 215-16.

2. José Miguel Gómez to William E. Gonzales, Feb. 19, 1917, in Matías Duque, *Ocios del presidio, 1917* (Havana, 1919), pp. 68-69; Horrego Estuch, *Juan Gualberto Gómez, un gran inconforme*, p. 226.

3. Orestes Ferrara to secretary of state, Feb. 16, 1917, 837.00/1239, DS/NA, RG 59.

4. Raimundo Cabrera and Orestes Ferrara to secretary of state, Feb. 12, 1917, 837.00/1066, DS/NA, RG 59.

5. Robert Lansing to William E. Gonzales, Feb. 13, 1917, *FRUS, 1917*, p. 356.

6. "La guerrita de febrero de 1917," pp. 230-31.

7. In the State Department, the chief of Mexican Affairs, Leon J. Canova, a former resident of Cuba, suspected similar maneuvers. "Menocal's chief advisors," Canova suggested to Lansing, "in his campaign . . . are, with few exceptions, the same men who carried Palma to ruin, and who made necessary the second intervention. They would stop at nothing to continue themselves in power. For a year past, they have openly made their threats and have brazenly stated their intention of winning the elections by hook or crook. They fully realized that there would be a revolt against them, precisely as there had been in 1906, a few months after Palma had assumed the Presidency which he had fraudulently obtained. Therefore they proceeded to force the issue, by persecution and other ways in which they were adept. Had they not done this, there would have been no revolution until Menocal's second inauguration. . . . They succeeded only too well, because, when the wholesale arrests took place early in February, their opponents had but one recourse, which was to revolt." Leon J. Canova to secretary of state, Apr. 30, 1917, 837.00/1426, DS/NA, RG 59.

8. William E. Gonzales to secretary of state, Feb. 11, 1917, *FRUS, 1917*, p. 353.

9. See "Statement of 5 Cuban Revolutionists," in brigade commander, Port-au-Prince,

to major general commandant, June 8, 1917, 837.00/1391, DS/NA, RG 59.

10. James Brown Scott, "The Attitude of the United States Toward Political Disturbances in Cuba," *The American Journal of International Law,* XI (Apr. 1917), 422-23.

11. See Mario G. Menocal to Woodrow Wilson, Mar. 5, 1917, Series 2, Box 158, Wilson Papers; and William E. Gonzales to secretary of state, *FRUS, 1917,* p. 355.

12. William E. Gonzales, "Memorandum," Nov. 9, 1916, 837.00/1044, DS/NA, RG 59.

13. General Hugh L. Scott, chief of staff, to M. E. Hanna, May 3, 1917, Box 28, General Correspondence, General Hugh Scott Papers, Library of Congress, Manuscript Division, Washington, D.C.

14. *New York Times,* Feb. 14, 1917, p. 3.

15. Ibid., p. 10.

16. "Civil War in Cuba," *The Independent,* XIC (Feb. 26, 1917), 344. See also "A Hornet's Nest in Cuba," *Literary Digest,* LIV (Feb. 24, 1917), 455-56.

17. William E. Gonzales to secretary of state, Feb. 14, 1917, *FRUS, 1917,* p. 358.

18. Louis A. Pérez, Jr., *Army Politics in Cuba, 1898-1958* (Pittsburgh, 1975), pp. 28-31.

19. William E. Gonzales to Robert Lansing, Feb. 13, 1917, 837.00/1070, DS/NA, RG 59. A full three days after the abortive coup, Consul General James L. Rodgers continued to fear a revolt of the Havana garrison. See James L. Rodgers to secretary of state, Feb. 13, 1917, 837.00/1073, DS/NA, RG 59.

20. William E. Gonzales to Robert Lansing, Feb. 15, 1917, 837.00/1090, DS/NA, RG 59. "General and widespread doubt exists," Gonzales wrote, "of army's loyalty and the demonstrated disaffection in Santiago and Camaguey is not reassuring. . . . The President's nearest friends even some cabinet members are not confident and I know many of them would be glad of almost any compromise. All of them doubt the army and are apprehensive of result of uprising here."

21. James L. Rodgers to Robert Lansing, Feb. 18, 1917, File (1917) 800, Correspondence, American Consulate General, Havana, Cuba, FSP/NA, RG 84.

22. William E. Gonzales to secretary of state, *FRUS, 1917,* Feb. 12, 1917, p. 355.

23. For Liberal reactions to American public diplomacy, see Orestes Ferrara, "El gobierno de Wáshington y las elecciones en Cuba y Nicaragua," *La Reforma Social,* XIX (Jan. 1921), 29.

24. Robert Lansing to William G. McAdoo, Feb. 17, 1917, vol. 24, Robert Lansing Papers, Library of Congress, Manuscript Division, Washington, D.C.

25. Robert Lansing to William E. Gonzales, Feb. 13, 1917, *FRUS, 1917,* p. 356.

26. Robert Lansing to William E. Gonzales, Feb. 18, 1917, *FRUS, 1917,* p. 363.

27. Pablo Desvernine to Carlos Manuel de Céspedes, Feb. 23, 1917, 837.00/1211, DS/NA, RG 59.

28. See *Diario de la Marina,* Feb. 20, 1917, p. 1. Cf. Leo J. Meyer, "The United States and the Cuban Revolution of 1917," *The Hispanic American Historical Review,* X (May 1930), 163.

29. "La guerrita de febrero de 1917," p. 232.

30. William E. Gonzales, "Revolution and History — As Mr. Ford Knows It," Gon-

zales Papers.

31. William E. Gonzales to Robert Lansing, Feb. 15, 1917, 837.00/1085, DS/NA, RG 59.

32. Gerardo Rodríguez Morejón, *Menocal* (Havana, 1941), p. 117; Ferrer, *Con el rifle al hombro,* p. 232. Cf. Raúl de Cárdenas, *Como funcionó la cláusula intervencionista de la Enmienda Platt* (Havana, 1948), p. 13.

33. William E. Gonzales to Robert Lansing, Feb. 14, 1917, 837.00/1083, DS/NA, RG 59.

34. James L. Rodgers to secretary of state, Feb. 19, 1917, 837.00/1107, DS/NA, RG 59.

35. Pablo Desvernine to Carlos Manuel de Céspedes, Feb. 14, 1917, 837.00/1093, DS/NA, RG 59. *New York Times,* Feb. 16, 1917, p. 8.

36. *New York Sun,* Mar. 18, 1917, p. 7.

37. Colonel E. B. Babbitt, Ordinance Department, "Memorandum for the Chief of Staff," Feb. 28, 1917, File 25458417, Records of the Adjutant General's Office, Record Group 94, National Archives, Washington, D.C. (hereafter cited as AGO/NA, RG 94). William E. Gonzales to secretary of state, Feb. 12, 1917, 837.24/26, DS/NA, RG 59.

38. *New York Times,* Feb. 21, 1917, p. 6.

39. Lieutenant Colonel Edmund Wittenmyer to secretary, War College Division, Feb. 20, 1917, File 7298-20, WD/NA, RG 165.

40. Pablo Desvernine to Carlos Manuel de Céspedes, Feb. 23, 1917, 837.00/1211, DS/NA, RG 59.

41. William E. Gonzales to secretary of state, Feb. 14, 1917, 837.24/27, DS/NA, RG 59.

42. Commander H. B. Price, U.S.S. *Melville,* to commander, Destroyer Force, Atlantic Fleet, "Conditions in Manzanillo and Verbal Request Made for Arms and Ammunition," Feb. 22, 1917, WA 7, Subject File, 1911-1927, Naval Records Collection of the Office of Naval Records and Library, Record Group 45, National Archives, Washington, D.C. (hereafter cited as NRC/NA, RG 45).

43. Log of U.S.S. *New York,* Feb. 24, 1917, Records of the Bureau of Naval Personnel, Record Group 24, National Archives, Washington, D.C. (hereafter cited as BNP/NA, RG 24).

44. Commander A. F. Fecheteler, Battleship Division Six, to commander, Battleship Forces, "Conditions At and Near Manzanillo, Cuba," Mar. 4, 1917, File 27868-56, General Records of the Department of the Navy, Record Group 80, National Archives, Washington, D.C. (hereafter cited as GRDN/NA, RG 80).

45. General Hugh L. Scott, chief of staff, to M. E. Hanna, Mar. 3, 1917, Box 28, General Correspondence, Scott Papers.

46. *New York Times,* Feb. 20, 1917, p. 3.

47. Commander A. F. Fecheteler, Battleship Division Six, to commander, Battleship Forces, "Conditions At and Near Manzanillo, Cuba," Mar. 4, 1917, File 27868-56, GRDN/NA, RG 80.

48. Commanding officer, U.S.S. *Paducah,* to senior officer present, Apr. 15, 1917, WA-7, Subject File, 1911-1927, NRC/NA, RG 45; Robert Debs Heinl, *Soldiers of the*

Sea: The United States Marine Corps, 1775-1962 (Annapolis, 1962), p. 232.

49. "Intervention in Cuba Under the Platt Amendment" (Historical Branch, G-3 Division, Headquarters, United States Marine Corps, Washington, D.C.), p. 18.

50. Confidential War Diary, U.S.S. *Machias,* May 4, 1917, to May 15, 1917, NRC/NA, RG 45; P. Merrill Griffith to secretary of state, Mar. 21, 1917, 837.00/1292, DS/NA, RG 59.

51. See commanding officer, U.S.S. *Dixie,* to secretary of the navy, Mar. 4, 1917, 837.00/1200, DS/NA, RG 59.

52. William E. Gonzales to secretary of state, Feb. 25, 1917, 837.00/1138, DS/NA, RG 59.

53. William E. Gonzales to secretary of state, Mar. 12, 1917, 837.00/1210, DS/NA, RG 59.

54. Confidential War Diary, naval station, Guantánamo, from April 7, 1917, to April 30, 1917, NRC/NA, RG 45.

55. Commander H. K. Hewitt, U.S.S. *Eagle,* to chief of naval operations, "Report of Operations, Nipe Bay Vicinity," Apr. 13, 1917, 837.00/1325, DS/NA, RG 59.

56. Commander H. K. Hewitt, U.S.S. *Eagle,* to chief of naval operations, "Report of Operations, Nipe Bay Vicinity," Apr. 13, 1917, 837.00/1325, DS/NA, RG 59.

57. Commanding officer, U.S.S. *Paducah,* to senior officer present, Apr. 15, 1917, WA-7, Subject File, 1911-1927, NRC/NA, RG 45; Henry H. Morgan to secretary of state, June 7, 1917, 837.00/6351, DS/NA, RG 59.

58. *Times of Cuba,* Apr. 1917, p. 35; Clyde H. Metcalf, *A History of the United States Marine Corps* (New York, 1939), p. 333.

59. E. N. Wise, general manager, Guantánamo and Western Railroad Company, to M. L. Lewis, May 14, 1917, 837.00/1384, DS/NA, RG 59.

60. Diary of John R. Bullard, Mar. 3, 1917, 837.00/1472, DS/NA, RG 59.

61. Raimundo Cabrera and Orestes Ferrera to secretary of state, Feb. 12, 1917, 837.00/1066, DS/NA, RG 59; Raimundo Cabrera and Orestes Ferrara to secretary of state, Feb. 16, 1917, in Cabrera, *Mis malos tiempos,* pp. 126-27; *New York Times,* Feb. 15, 1917, p. 5.

62. Manuel Rodríguez et al. to William E. Gonzales, n.d. (received Feb. 26, 1917), 837.00/1144, DS/NA, RG 59.

63. Willard King to Colonel Edward M. House, Feb. 27, 1917, Box 158, Series 2, Wilson Papers.

64. Santiago Chamber of Commerce, "Petition," in P. Merrill Griffith to Robert Lansing, Feb. 22, 1917, *FRUS, 1917,* p. 365.

65. In Robert Lansing to P. Merrill Griffith, Feb. 23, 1917, *FRUS, 1917,* p. 366.

66. Robert Lansing to William E. Gonzales, Mar. 7, 1917, 837.00/1179, DS/NA, RG 59.

67. Ibid.

68. Waldemar León, "Caicaje: batalla final de una revuelta," *Bohemia,* LIX (June 30, 1967), 100-02; "La guerrita de febrero de 1917," pp. 239-41.

69. Frank Polk, Confidential Diary, Mar. 12, 1917, vol. 1, Drawer 88, Polk Papers.

70. General Hugh L. Scott, chief of staff, to I. A. Barnes, Mar. 13, 1917, Box 28, General Correspondence, Scott Papers.

Chapter 4: Gunboat Diplomacy: Naval Mediations and Liberal Politics in Oriente Province

1. Luis Loret de Mola, "Sobre la guerra civil de 1917," *Boletín del Archivo Nacional,* LX (Jan.-Dec. 1961), 243. Insurgent authorities appropriated some $300,000 from local government and private deposits in the first two weeks of Liberal government. See Bernardo Figueredo to W. A. Merchant, Apr. 7, 1917, Gonzales Papers.

2. P. Merrill Griffith, "City Taken by Military Forces," Feb. 12, 1917, File (1917) 800, Miscellaneous Correspondence, American Consulate, Santiago de Cuba, FSP/NA, RG 84.

3. Luis Loret de Mola to Commander Dudley Wright Knox, United States Naval Station, Guantánamo, Feb. 20, 1917, File (1917) 800, Miscellaneous Correspondence, American Consulate, Santiago de Cuba, FSP/NA, RG 84.

4. Commander Reginald R. Belknap to commander in chief, Atlantic Force, Feb. 27, 1917, WA-7, Subject File, 1911-1927, NRC/NA, RG 45.

5. Rigoberto Fernández to William E. Gonzales, Feb. 14, 1917, File (1917) 800, Miscellaneous Correspondence, American Consulate, Santiago de Cuba, FSP/NA, RG 84.

6. Rigoberto Fernández to American Consul, Feb. 14, 1917, File (1917) 800, American Consulate, Santiago de Cuba, FSP/NA, RG 84; Herminio Portell Vilá "La Chambelona en Oriente," *Bohemia,* LII (Apr. 24, 1960), 124.

7. Dudley Wright Knox to commander in chief, Feb. 18, 1917, WA-7, Subject File, 1911-1927, NRC/NA, RG 45. Cf. Merino and Ibarzabal, *La revolución de febrero,* p. 192.

8. Dudley Wright Knox to commander in chief, Feb. 18, 1917, WA-7, Subject File, 1911-1927, NRC/NA, RG 45.

9. Loret de Mola, "Sobre la guerra civil de 1917," p. 179; P. Merrill Griffith, "Memorandum," Feb. 16, 1917, File (1917) 800, Miscellaneous Correspondence, American Consulate, Santiago de Cuba, FSP/NA, RG 84.

10. Dudley Wright Knox to Luis Loret de Mola, Feb. 16, 1917, File (1917) 800, Miscellaneous Correspondence, American Consulate, Santiago de Cuba, FSP/NA, RG 84.

11. Robert Lansing to American Legation, Havana, Cuba, Feb. 17, 1917, 837.00/1101, DS/NA, RG 59.

12. William E. Gonzales to Robert Lansing, Feb. 18, 1917, 837.00/1105, DS/NA, RG 59.

13. H. D. Butler, "Instructions to Armed Boat Stationed at Entrance to Santiago de Cuba Harbor," Feb. 19, 1917, Area Files, Caribbean, 1911-1927, NRC/NA, RG 45; Reginald R. Belknap to Julia Belknap, Feb. 22, 1917, Box 13, General Correspondence, Reginald R. Belknap Papers, Library of Congress, Manuscript Division, Washington, D.C.

14. Rigoberto Fernández to P. Merrill Griffith, Feb. 24, 1917, File (1917) 800, Miscellaneous Correspondence, American Consulate, Santiago de Cuba, FSP/NA, RG 84.

15. P. Merrill Griffith to secretary of state, Feb. 27, 1917, 837.00/1180, DS/NA, RG 59.

16. Edward M. Wise to P. Merrill Griffith and commander, United States Naval Sta-

tion, Guantánamo, Feb. 25, 1917, File (1917) 800, Correspondence, Guantánamo Agency, FSP/NA, RG 84.

17. Ibid.

18. The Palma Sugar Company et al. to P. Merrill Griffith, "Petition," Feb. 27, 1917, File (1917) 800, Miscellaneous Correspondence, American Consulate, Santiago de Cuba, FSP/NA, RG 84.

19. P. Merrill Griffith to secretary of state, Feb. 27, 1917, File (1917) 800, Miscellaneous Correspondence, American Consulate, Santiago de Cuba, FSP/NA, RG 84.

20. Otto E. Reimer to Charles E. Knoblauch, Feb. 20, 1917, 837.00/1205, DS/NA, RG 59.

21. Commander R. R. Belknap to commander in chief, Atlantic Force, Feb. 27, 1917, WA-7, Subject File, 1911-1927, NRC/NA, RG 45.

22. P. Merrill Griffith to secretary of state, Feb. 27, 1917, 837.00/1180, DS/NA, RG 59.

23. Commander Reginald R. Belknap to commander in chief, Atlantic Force, Feb. 27, 1917, WA-7, Subject File, 1911-1927, NRC/NA, RG 45.

24. Reginald R. Belknap to Julia Belknap, Feb. 28, 1917, Box 3, General Correspondence, Belknap Papers.

25. Ibid.

26. Loret de Mola, "Sobre la guerra civil de 1917," pp. 179-80.

27. Commander Reginald R. Belknap, "Memorandum of Conference on Board, this Date, on the General Insurgent Situation," Mar. 1, 1917, Subject File, 1911-1927, NRC/NA, RG 45; Chapman, *A History of the Cuban Republic*, p. 377.

28. P. Merrill Griffith to secretary of state, n.d. (received Mar. 1, 1917), 837.00/1162, DS/NA, RG 59; Loret de Mola, "Sobre la guerra civil de 1917," p. 182.

29. William E. Gonzales to secretary of state, Feb. 25, 1917, 837.00/1138.

30. Sydney Brooks to Colonel Edward M. House, Mar. 3, 1917, Group Number 466, Series I, 32/8, Correspondence, Edward M. House Papers, Sterling Memorial Library, Yale University, New Haven, Connecticut. Brooks, an English correspondent, was a close friend of House. For some of his published views on Cuba, see "An English View of Cuba," *Forum*, XXXVI (Oct. 1911), 461-70, and "Some Impressions of Cuba," *North American Review*, CIC (May 1914), 734-45.

31. Lieutenant Colonel Edmund Wittenmyer to secretary, War College Division, General Staff, "Political Situation Arising From Cuban Insurrection," Feb. 28, 1917, File 7299-21, WD/NA, RG 165.

32. Commander Reginald R. Belknap to commander in chief, Atlantic Fleet, Mar. 2, 1917, WA-7, Subject File, 1911-1927, NRC/NA, RG 45.

33. Robert Lansing to Josephus Daniels, in Robert Lansing to William E. Gonzales, Mar. 7, 1917, 837.00/1179, DS/NA, RG 59.

34. P. Merrill Griffith to secretary of state, n.d. (received March 5, 1917), 837.00/1172, DS/NA, RG 59.

35. Rigoberto Fernández to secretary of state, July 9, 1917, 837.00/1393, DS/NA, RG 59.

36. Diary of U.S. Atlantic Fleet, "Cuban Situation," Feb. 27, 1917, to Mar. 5, 1917, 837.00/1232, DS/NA, RG 59.

37. Colonel José Jané to William E. Gonzales, n.d., 837.00/1391, DS/NA, RG 59. Belknap also requested Washington to secure an extension of the truce. See Reginald R. Belknap to secretary of state, n.d., 837.00/1391, DS/NA, RG 59.

38. Reginald R. Belknap to secretary of state, n.d., 837.00/1391, DS/NA, RG 59.

39. Rigoberto Fernández to secretary of state, July 9, 1917, 837.00/1393, DS/NA, RG 59; "La guerrita de febrero de 1917," pp. 243-45.

40. P. Merrill Griffith to secretary of state, n.d. (received Mar. 5, 1917), 837.00/1172, DS/NA, RG 59.

41. Ibid.

42. Robert Lansing to William E. Gonzales, Mar. 1, 1917, *FRUS, 1917,* pp. 371-72.

43. Robert Lansing to William E. Gonzales, Mar. 3, 1917, *FRUS, 1917,* pp. 375-76.

44. Menocal's message in William E. Gonzales to Robert Lansing, Mar. 3, 1917, *FRUS, 1917,* pp. 374-75.

45. William E. Gonzales to secretary of state, Mar. 2, 1917, *FRUS, 1917,* p. 373.

46. Robert Lansing to William E. Gonzales, Mar. 3, 1917, *FRUS, 1917,* p. 373.

47. William E. Gonzales to Robert Lansing, Mar. 4, 1917, 837.00/1166, DS/NA, RG 59.

48. William E. Gonzales to secretary of state, Mar. 2, 1917, *FRUS, 1917,* pp. 373-74.

49. "American Consul and Commander of 'USS San Francisco' at Santiago," Gonzales protested, "by arrangement with rebels have not only complicated a serious situation and slapped Cuban Government in the face but have abrogated formal declaration by the Department of State to Cuban people and violated policy of President Wilson as announced to the Chamber of Commerce of Santiago. That announcement of policy had the weight of an order to the representatives of the United States Government. The solemn declarations by the United States Government have been treated as if they were mere 'scraps of paper.' For the honor of my country's word I record this protest." William E. Gonzales to secretary of state, Mar. 6, 1917, 837.00/1179.

50. William E. Gonzales to secretary of state, Mar. 4, 1917, 837.00/1170, DS/NA, RG 59.

51. P. Merrill Griffith, "City Taken by Military Authority," Feb. (sic) 6, 1917, File (1917) 800, Miscellaneous Correspondence, American Consulate, Santiago de Cuba, FSP/NA, RG 84.

52. José García Muñoz to American consul, Santiago de Cuba, Mar. 4, 1917, WA-7, Subject File, 1911-1927, NRC/NA, RG 45.

53. Reginald R. Belknap, "Proclama," Mar. 4, 1917, WA-7, Subject File, 1911-1927, NRC/NA, RG 45.

54. Commander, Battleship Division, to commander in chief, "Conditions At and Near Manzanillo, Cuba," Mar. 4, 1917, WA-7, Subject File, 1911-1927, NRC/NA, RG 45; *New York Times,* Mar. 8, 1917, p. 3. Cf. Loret de Mola, "Sobre la guerra civil de 1917," pp. 179-80.

55. "The first information I had on the subject," Gonzales later recalled, "was the receipt in Havana of a printed proclamation bearing the signature of a United States naval officer at Santiago, recognizing Rigoberto Fernandez as in command of the province of Oriente and 'warning' any opposing forces from entering the province. I was outraged by the act and the usurpation of authority and immediately cabled to Washington protesting

against my proclamation to the Cuban people made on the authority of my government being thus treated as 'scraps of paper.' '' Gonzales, "Revolution and History — As Mr. Ford Knows It," Gonzales Papers.

56. On the same day, Mar. 5, Menocal wrote to President Wilson: "Allow me to . . . express to you once more my most sincere thankfulness for your several messages setting forth without leaving any room for doubt your high policy of upholding and supporting the Constitutional government here in the present unfortunate circumstances." Mario G. Menocal to Woodrow Wilson, Mar. 5, 1917, Series 2, Box 152, Wilson Papers.

57. Robert Lansing to William E. Gonzales, Mar. 7, 1917, 837.00/1179, DS/NA, RG 59.

58. Commander, Battleship Division, to commander in chief, "Conditions At and Near Manzanillo, Cuba," Mar. 4, 1917, WA-7, Subject File, 1911-1927, NRC/NA, RG 45.

59. Loret de Mola, "Sobre la guerra civil de 1917," p. 181.

60. P. Merrill Griffith to secretary of state, n.d. (received Mar. 9, 1917), 837.00/1193, DS/NA, RG 59.

61. Rigoberto Fernández to secretary of state, 837.00/1393, DS/NA, RG 59; Loret de Mola, "Sobre la guerra civil de 1917," p. 181.

62. Log of U.S.S. *San Francisco,* Mar. 8, 1917, BNP/NA, RG 24; José García Muñoz to Reginald R. Belknap, Mar. 8, 1917, in Merino and Ibarzabal, *La revolución de febrero,* pp. 194-96.

63. Commander Reginald R. Belknap to José García Muñoz, Mar. 11, 1917, 837.00/1478, DS/NA, RG 59.

64. Commander Reginald R. Belknap to commander in chief, Atlantic Fleet, Mar. 13, 1917, 837.00/1478, DS/NA, RG 59.

65. Robert Lansing to William E. Gonzales, Mar. 17, 1917, 837.00/1269a, DS/NA, RG 59.

66. Reginald R. Belknap to Julia Belknap, Mar. 16, 1917, Box 3, General Correspondence, Belknap Papers.

67. Colonel José Jané to Mario G. Menocal, Mar. 13, 1917, 837.00/1478, DS/NA, RG 59.

68. Reginald R. Belknap to Julia Belknap, Mar. 16, 1917, Box 13, General Correspondence, Belknap Papers.

69. Commander Reginald R. Belknap to commander in chief, Atlantic Fleet, Mar. 16, 1917, "Situation in Santiago de Cuba," WA-7, Subject File, 1911-1927, NRC/NA, RG 45; William E. Gonzales to secretary of state, Mar. 16, 1917, 837.00/1224, DS/NA, RG 59.

70. Edward M. Wise, consul, Guantánamo, to Rigoberto Fernández, Mar. 12, 1917, 837.00/1391, DS/NA, RG 59.

71. Commander H. K. Hewitt, U.S.S. *Eagle,* to chief, naval operations, "Report of Operations, Nipe Bay Vicinity," Apr. 13, 1917, 837.00/1325, DS/NA, RG 59.

72. General Felipe Leyva et al. to Commander H. K. Hewitt, Mar. 19, 1917, 837.00/1270, DS/NA, RG 59.

73. Commander H. K. Hewitt, U.S.S. *Eagle*, to secretary of the navy, Mar. 20, 1917, 837.00/1270, DS/NA, RG 59.

74. William E. Gonzales to Robert Lansing, Mar. 23, 1917, 837.00/1270, DS/NA, RG 59.

75. Commander H. K. Hewitt to naval operations, "Situation at Manati," Apr. 7, 1917, 837.00/1317, DS/NA, RG 59.

76. U.S.S. *Machias* to naval operations, Mar. 20, 1917, WA-7, Subject File, 1911-1927, NRC/NA, RG 45; Primelles, *Crónica cubana, 1915-1918*, pp. 306-08.

77. Edward M. Wise to secretary of state, n.d. (received Apr. 7, 1917), 837.00/1300, DS/NA, RG 59; Merino and Ibarzabal, *La revolución de febrero*, p. 214; Loret de Mola, "Sobre la guerra civil de 1917," pp. 184-85.

78. Primelles, *Crónica cubana, 1915-1918*, p. 321.

79. Commander Reginald R. Belknap to commander in chief, Atlantic Fleet, "Situation in Santiago," Mar. 20, 1917, WA-7, Subject File, 1911-1927, NRC/NA, RG 45.

Chapter 5: Liberals, Bandits, and Social Protest: The Persistence of Insurgency

1. For the details of the Liberal surrenders see "La guerrita de febrero de 1917," pp. 252-56.

2. Portell Vilá, "La Chambelona en Occidente," p. 82.

3. Orestes Ferrara to Woodrow Wilson, May 13, 1917, 837.00/1480, DS/NA, RG 59.

4. William E. Gonzales to Robert Lansing, June 16, 1917, 837.00/1386, DS/NA, RG 59; Eduardo Guzmán to Comandante Víctor Mesa, Apr. 16, 1917, and Eduardo Guzmán to Colonel M. Varela, Apr. 16, 1917, in Merino and Ibarzabal, *La revolución de febrero*, pp. 222-23.

5. William E. Gonzales to Robert Lansing, May 8, 1917, 837.00/1338, DS/NA, RG 59; *Diario de la Marina*, May 7, 1917, p. 12.

6. For a complete listing of the key surrenders see Rubiera, "Mario García Menocal y Deop," pp. 155-59.

7. Rigoberto Fernández," Exposición al presidente de los Estados Unidos," in Cabrera, *Mis malos tiempos*, pp. 420-30.

8. Miguel de Marcos Suárez, *Carlos Mendieta* (Havana, 1923), p. 117.

9. American authorities consistently advocated leniency and amnesty for, and interceded in behalf of, Liberal leaders as one way of hastening the end of the rebellion. See Robert Lansing to American Legation, Havana, Cuba, Oct. 4, 1917, 837.00/1422, DS/NA, RG 59; "Memorandum on the Platt Amendment," Box 35, Francis White Papers, National Archives, Washington, D.C. Cf. Enrique Roig, *Los acontecimientos políticos de 1917 y el problema de la amnistía*. (Havana, 1918), pp. 63-114.

10. On April 1, 1917, Havana proclaimed that "only outlaws and bandits remain in the field in Oriente." See *Times of Cuba*, May 1917, p. 23.

11. "Gustavo Caballero: 'cadaver' por anticipado," *Granma*, Oct. 25, 1969), p. 2. Cf. Portell Vilá, "La Chambelona en Occidente," p. 82.

12. Menocal also feared some type of Liberal plot. On inauguration day, the govern-

ment garrisoned Havana with troops carefully screened for loyalty. Two American warships called in Havana ostensibly to allow naval officials to join the United States inaugural delegation but, in fact, in the hope that the navy's presence would have a calming effect in the capital. See Confidential War Diary, U.S.S. *Chatanooga,* May 1, 1917, to May 31, 1917, NRC/NA, RG 45.

13. "Relato o apuntes de campaña del coronel Roberto Méndez Peñate," in Cabrera, *Mis malos tiempos,* pp. 404-05.

14. Commander, U.S.S. *San Francisco,* to commander in chief, Atlantic Fleet, Mar. 13, 1917, 837.00/1478, DS/NA, RG 59.

15. P. Merrill Griffith to secretary of state, Mar. 18, 1917, 837.00/1267, DS/NA, RG 59.

16. Ferrer, *Con el rifle al hombro,* p..239.

17. P. Merrill Griffith to secretary of state, May 15, 1917, 837.00/1361; and Robert Lansing to William E. Gonzales, Apr. 25, 1917, 837.00/1325a, DS/NA, RG 59.

18. Gaston Schmutz to secretary of state, Feb. 26, 1917, 837.00/1165, DS/NA, RG 59.

19. H. M. Wolcott, Caimanera, to secretary of state, May 1, 1917, 837.00/1375, DS/NA, RG 59.

20. John J. Jova, American consul, Sagua la Grande, to Charles M. Winans, May 16, 1917, File (1917) 800, Correspondence, American Consulate, Cienfuegos, Cuba, FSP/NA, RG 84.

21. Franklin W. Knight, *Slave Society in Cuba During the Nineteenth Century* (Madison, 1970), pp. 41-43, 156-57.

22. United States Department of War, *Informe sobre el censo de Cuba, 1899* (Washington, D.C., 1900), p. 554.

23. Robert B. Hoernel, "Sugar and Social Change in Oriente, Cuba, 1898-1946," *Journal of Latin American Studies,* VIII (Nov. 1976), 233.

24. Enrique Lavedán, "Los ladrones de tierras en Oriente," *Gráfico,* III (Feb. 7, 1914), p. 10. Cf. Robert B. Batchelder, "The Evolution of Cuban Land Tenure and Its Relations to Certain Agro-Economic Problems," *The Southwestern Social Science Quarterly,* XXXIII (Dec. 1952), 241. For a discussion of the varieties of property ownership see Francisco Pérez de la Riva, *Origen y régimen de la propiedad territorial en Cuba* (Havana, 1946), pp. 24-148.

25. Between 1914 and 1917, some twenty new sugar mills began operations in Cuba — mostly in Camagüey and Oriente. See Oscar Pino-Santos, *El asalto a Cuba por la oligarquia financiera yanqui* (Havana, 1973), pp. 73-81.

26. Teresa Casuso, *Cuba and Castro* (New York, 1961), p. 9. "If things go on like this," *El Mundo* commented editorially, "we will be planting cane in the patios of our homes." Primelles, *Crónica cubana, 1915-1918,* p. 182.

27. Cuba, *Census of the Republic of Cuba, 1919* (Havana, 1920), p. 950.

28. Antonio Núñez Jiménez, *Geografía de Cuba,* 2nd ed. (Havana, 1959), pp. 253-55; Jerez Villarreal, *Oriente (biografía de una provincia),* p. 307. Significantly, the insurgents were often described as "mountaineers." See American vice consul, Antilla, "Post-revolution Conditions in Oriente Province, Cuba," July 31, 1917, 837.00/1408, DS/NA, RG 59.

29. Ramiro Guerra y Sánchez, *Sugar and Society on the Caribbean: An Economic*

History of Cuban Agriculture (New Haven, 1964), pp. 85-93. Cf. Alberto Arredondo, *Cuba: tierra indefensa* (Havana, 1945), pp. 246-48.

30. Some 18,000 Jamaicans and Haitians arrived in eastern Cuba to harvest sugar. See Cuba, Secretaria de Hacienda, Sección de Estadística, *Inmigración y movimiento de pasajeros en el año de 1917* (Havana, 1918), p̃. 5.

31. Cuba, Secretaria de Hacienda, Seccion de Estadística, *Inmigración y movimiento de pasajeros en el año . . .,* 1913-1921 (Havana, 1914-1922).

32. Evelio Tellería Toca, "Mas de un cuarto de millón de braceros importados," *Granma,* Apr. 14, 1970, p. 2; "El jamaiquino y el haitiano," *La Lucha,* Oct. 19, 1919, p. 12; J. Pérez de la Riva, "La inmigración antillana en Cuba durante el primer tercio del siglo xx," *Revista de la Biblioteca Nacional 'José Martí',* XVIII (May-Aug. 1975), 74-88.

33. Cuba, *Census of the Republic of Cuba, 1919,* p. 392.

34. These included Neuvas de Jobosí and Santa Gertrudis in Camagüey and Aguarás, Cuaba, and La Plata (Puerto Padre) in Oriente.

35. This information is drawn from data available in the Cuban censuses of 1907 and 1919.

36. Hoernel, "Sugar and Social Change in Oriente, Cuba, 1898-1946," p. 235.

37. In H. H. Morgan to Herbert C. Hoover, Aug. 4, 1917, 837.50/13, DS/NA, RG 59.

38. *New York Times,* Dec. 23, 1917, p. 7.

39. Hoernel, "Sugar and Social Change in Oriente, Cuba, 1898-1946, p. 238.

40. *Diario de la Marina,* Oct. 11, 1914, pp. 1, 5.

41. A peasant demonstration in Santiago involved several large landowners in the Menocal government. See *La Lucha,* July 2, 1917, p. 2.

42. Eric Hobsbawm, *Primitive Rebels* (New York, 1959), p. 5.

43. Eric Hobsbawm, *Bandits* (New York, 1969), p. 18.

44. Rubiera, "Mario García Menocal y Deop," p. 137.

45. In William E. Gonzales to Robert Lansing, Feb. 28, 1917, 837.00/1155, DS/NA, RG 59.

46. H. M. Wolcott to secretary of state, Apr. 20, 1917, 837.00/1374, DS/NA, RG 59.

47. Statement of N. Arthur Helmar, Division of Latin American Affairs, "Memorandum," Mar. 28, 1917, 837.00/1315, DS/NA, RG 59. Cf. H. M. Wolcott to secretary of state, Apr. 20, 1917, 837.00/1374, DS/NA, RG 59. Loló de la Torriente, *Mi casa en la tierra* (Havana, 1956), pp. 89-93.

48. Statement of N. Arthur Helmar, Division of Latin American Affairs, "Memorandum," Mar. 28, 1917, 837.00/1315, DS/NA, RG 59.

49. H. M. Wolcott, "Political Conditions in Oriente Province," May 22, 1917, File (1917) 800, Miscellaneous Correspondence, American Consulate, Santiago de Cuba, FSP/NA, RG 84.

50. Diary of John R. Bullard, Jobabo, Cuba, Mar. 8, 1917, 837.00/1472, DS/NA, RG 59.

51. L. M. A. Evan to C. Warner, Apr. 8, 1917, 837.00/1788, DS/NA, RG 59. A. H. Lindelie, president of the Bayate Sugar Company, described the insurgent chieftains in mid-March as "neighbors and friends of ours." A. H. Lindelie to Senator A. J. Gronna, Mar. 16, 1917, 837.00/1308, DS/NA, RG 59.

52. Andrew Kobler et al. to American consul, Santiago de Cuba, "Petition," Apr. 20, 1917, File (1917) 800, Miscellaneous Correspondence, American Consulate, Santiago de Cuba, FSP/NA, RG 84.

53. Statement of N. Arthur Helmar, Division of Latin American Affairs, "Memorandum," Mar. 28, 1917, 837.00/1315, DS/NA, RG 59.

54. H. M. Wolcott to secretary of state, Apr. 20, 1917, 837.00/1315, DS/NA, RG 59.

55. P. Merrill Griffith to secretary of state, Mar. 18, 1917, 837.00/1269, DS/NA, RG 59.

56. Commander, U.S.S. *San Francisco,* to commander in chief, Atlantic Fleet, Mar. 13, 1917, 837.00/1478; and P. Merrill Griffith to secretary of state, Mar. 14, 1917, 837.00/1251, DS/NA, RG 59.

57. Duncan U. Fletcher, chairman, Senate Committee on Commerce, to secretary of state, Mar. 19, 1917, 837.00/1248, DS/NA, RG 59.

58. P. Merrill Griffith to secretary of state, Mar. 18, 1917, 837.00/1269, DS/NA, RG 59.

59. P. Merrill Griffith to secretary of state, Apr. 21, 1917, 837.00/1269, DS/NA, RG 59.

60. Charles M. Winans, consul, Cienfuegos, to secretary of state, May 1, 1917, 837.00/1328, DS/NA, RG 59.

61. P. Merrill Griffith to secretary of state, Mar. 14, 1917, 837.00/1251, DS/NA, RG 59. For a detailed account of insurgent operations in Camagüey between March and April, see Merino and Ibarzabal, *La revolución de febrero,* pp. 168-79.

62. Commander H. K. Hewitt, commanding officer, U.S.S. *Eagle,* to secretary of the navy, Mar. 20, 1917, 837.00/1270, DS/NA, RG 59.

63. Statement of N. Arthur Helmar, Division of Latin American Affairs, "Memorandum," Mar. 28, 1917, 837.00/1315, DS/NA, RG 59.

64. A. H. Lindelie to Senator A. J. Gronna, Mar. 16, 1917, 837.00/1308, DS/NA, RG 59.

65. Martin W. Littleton to Frank L. Polk, Mar. 17, 1917, File 228, Drawer 77, Polk Papers; *New York Times,* Mar. 15, 1917, p. 4.

66. Martin W. Littleton to Frank L. Polk, May 7, 1917, 837.00/1358, DS/NA, RG 59.

67. Josephus Daniels, diary, 1917-1921, Box 3, Josephus Daniels Papers, Library of Congress, Manuscript Division, Washington, D.C.; Josephus Daniels, *The Cabinet Diaries of Josephus Daniels, 1913-1921,* ed. E. David Cronon. (Lincoln: University of Nebraska Press, 1963), p. 106. See also Edwin C. Hill, "Love and a Little Luck Thwarted the Cuban Rebels," *New York Sun,* V, Mar. 18, 1917, p. 3. The British, on the other hand, suspected German involvement from the outset and repeatedly expressed these fears to Washington. See *London Times,* Mar. 3, 1917, p. 7. Cf. Robert Lansing, *The War Memoirs of Robert Lansing, Secretary of State* (New York, 1935), pp. 311-12.

68. Commander E. A. Anderson, Squadron Three, Patrol Force, to secretary of the navy, "Plan for Cooperation of Cuban Forces with United States Navy," June 6, 1917, Office of the Secretary, Secret and Confidential Correspondence, 1917-1926, File PD 150-1, GRDN/NA, RG 80. At different points during the insurrection, rumors suggested that Germany had pledged assistance to help the Liberals expel the Americans. At another time, Berlin had allegedly transferred large sums of money to Liberal coffers; a popular

rumor spoke of the presence of German submarines in Cuban waters assisting insurgent bands. For a general review of the scare of German involvement see Victor Hugo Gibean, Jr., "Relations of Cuba With the United States, 1916-1921," (Ph.D. diss., University of North Carolina, 1953), pp. 128-63.

69. *New York Sun,* Mar. 7, 1919, p. 1; and *New York Times,* Mar. 13, 1917, p. 1. Cf. Pedro Luis Padrón, "La sublevación liberal de 1917," *Granma,* Oct. 25, 1965, p. 2.

70. Robert Lansing to Newton Baker, May 10, 1917, 837.00/1347a, DS/NA, RG 59.

71. Lieutenant Colonel Edmund Wittenmyer to secretary, War College Division, General Staff, "Political Situation Arising from Cuban Insurrection," Feb. 28, 1917, File 7299-21, WD/NA, RG 165.

72. Commanding officer, U.S.S. *Dixie,* to secretary of the navy (operations), Feb. 25, 1917, WA-7, Subject File, 1911-1927, NRC/NA, RG 45.

73. Lieutenant Commander Austin Kautz, U.S.S. *Machias,* to commander in chief, Atlantic Fleet, May 3, 1917, File 27557-87, NRC/NA, RG 45.

74. H. M. Wolcott to secretary of state, May 3, 1917, 837.00/1375, DS/NA, RG 59.

75. William E. Gonzales to secretary of state, Mar. 30, 1917, 837.00/1278, DS/NA, RG 59.

76. William E. Gonzales to secretary of state, Apr. 16, 1917, 837.00/1311, DS/NA, RG 59. Cf. Munro, *Intervention and Dollar Diplomacy in the Caribbean, 1900-1921,* pp. 498-99.

77. William E. Gonzales to secretary of state, May 16, 1917, 837.00/1357, DS/NA, RG 59.

78. A. H. Lindelie to Senator A. J. Gronna, Apr. 14, 1917, 837.00/1357, DS/NA, RG 59.

79. II. M. Wolcott to secretary of state, May 1, 1917, 837.00/1327, DS/NA, RG 59.

80. Commanding officer, U.S.S. *Paducah,* to senior officer present, Apr. 15, 1917, WA-7, Subject File, 1911-1927, NRC/NA, RG 45.

81. Confidential War Diary, United States Naval Station, Guantánamo, Cuba, from Apr. 7, 1917, to Apr. 30, 1917, NRC/NA, RG 45.

82. In J. G. White to Henry Morgenthau, Mar. 12, 1917, 837.00/1231, DS/NA, RG 59.

83. Leon J. Canova, Mexican Affairs Division, to secretary of state, Apr. 30, 1917, DS/NA, RG 59. Canova's information may have come from Liberal sources. For a good many of his fifteen years in Cuba, Canova was associated with the Liberal party. During the government of José Miguel Gómez, Canova served as chief of the Government Bureau of Information connected with the Cuban Department of Agriculture, Commerce, and Labor. See Leon J. Canova to William E. Gonzales, June 4, 1913, Gonzales Papers.

84. Hugh Grosvenor, "Memorandum," n.d., File 244, Drawer 77, Polk Papers.

85. Robert Lansing to Newton Baker, May 18, 1917, 837.00/1350, DS/NA, RG 59.

86. Robert Lansing to American Legation, Havana, Cuba, May 11, 1917, 837.00/1326, DS/NA, RG 59.

87. Jordan Herbert Stabler to secretary of state, May 18, 1917, 837.00/1379, DS/NA, RG 59.

88. Newton Baker to Woodrow Wilson, May 14, 1917, Box 4, Newton Baker Papers, Library of Congress, Manuscript Division, Washington, D.C.

89. Robert Lansing to American Legation, Havana, Cuba, May 15, 1917, 837.00/1438, DS/NA, RG 59.

90. William E. Gonzales to secretary of state, May 13, 1917, 837.00/1348, DS/NA, RG 59.

91. William E. Gonzales to secretary of state, May 16, 1917, 837.00/1357, DS/NA, RG 59.

92. Henry H. Morgan to secretary of state, May 30, 1917, 837.61351/12, DS/NA, RG 59.

93. Henry H. Morgan to secretary of state, May 30, 1917, 837.61351/17, DS/NA, RG 59.

94. Henry H. Morgan, "Re Situation in Oriente Province, Cuba, and the Necessity for Sending One Regiment of U.S. Troops to That Part of the Island," June 28, 1917, 837.00/1394, DS/NA, RG 59.

95. Henry H. Morgan to Jordan Herbert Stabler, Aug. 3, 1917, 837.00/1477, DS/NA, RG 59.

96. Morgan left Washington apparently charged with the singular responsibility of providing information around which to determine the necessity of intervention. The commander of the U.S.S. *Chatanooga,* transporting Morgan from Havana to Santiago, learned that the measures to be adopted by Washington would be determined wholly by Morgan's recommendations. See U.S.S. *Chatanooga,* Confidential War Diary, May 1, 1917, to May 31, 1917, NRC/NA, RG 45.

97. Robert Lansing to Woodrow Wilson, May 31, 1917, 837.504/199a, DS/NA, RG 59.

98. Minutes of Meeting of the Council of National Defense, June 8, 1917, Box 451, Daniels Papers.

99. Frank L. Polk to American Legation, Havana, Cuba, July 12, 1917, 837.00/1394, DS/NA, RG 59.

100. William E. Gonzales to secretary of state, July 14, 1917, 837.00/1396, DS/NA, RG 59.

101. Rubiera, "Mario García Menocal y Deop," p. 157. The Elia estate was one of the newly organized sugar properties in eastern Cuba, established in 1915 in the *municipio* of Guáimaro, Camagüey.

102. Henry H. Morgan to secretary of state, Aug. 31, 1917, 837.00/1415, DS/NA, RG 59; Buttari Gaunaurd, *Boceto crítico histórico,* p. 377. Cf. Vicente Menéndez Roque, *Ortros días* (Havana, 1962), pp. 117-18.

103. *New York Times,* II, June 3, 1917, p. 4.

104. American vice-consul, Antilla, "Post-revolution Conditions in Oriente Province, Cuba," July 31, 1917, 837.00/1408, DS/NA, RG 59.

105. See Francisco López Leiva, *El bandolerismo en Cuba (Contribución al estudio de esta plaga social* (Havana, 1930), pp. 20-36. Banditry was endemic to Oriente Province. As late as 1957, Raúl Castro's guerrilla column encountered — and incorporated into the insurgent forces — some 200 bandits *(escopeteros)* operating in the Sierrra Cristal range of northeastern Oriente. See Euclides Vázquez Cándela, "El Segundo Frente Oriente 'Frank País': pequeña república insurgente," *Revolución,* Mar. 11, 1963, p. 8.

106. These accounts are found in *La Lucha,* Dec. 28, 1917, Jan. 11, 1920, and Dec.

25, 1918; and *Diario de la Marina,* Jan. 11, 1920.

Chapter 6: The "Sugar Intervention": Marines in Cuba

1. U.S.S. *Chattanooga,* Confidential War Diary, May 1, 1917, to May 31, 1917, NRC/NA, RG 45.

2. *El Cubano Libre* (Santiago de Cuba), May 25, 1917, in Henry H. Morgan to secretary of state, June 21, 1917, 837.61351/17.

3. Robert Lansing to William E. Gonzales, May 15, 1917, *FRUS, 1917,* p. 407.

4. Ibid., pp. 406-07.

5. Frank L. Polk to American Legation, Havana, Cuba, July 12, 1917, 837.00/1394, DS/NA, RG 59.

6. Mario G. Menocal, "Cuba's Part in the World War," *Current History,* IX (Nov. 1918), 315-18; José A. Martínez, "La entrada de Cuba en la Guerra Universal," *Cuba Contemporánea,* XIV (May 1917), 5-11.

7. In soliciting Havana's prior approval to station troops on the island, the State Department hastened to disclaim any implicit modification of basic treaty relations between the United States and Cuba. The American request, Washington insisted, was made in response to the international crisis and occurred outside the context of treaty relations. Washington meant to establish no precedent by bringing American wishes to place troops in Cuba to the attention of Cuban authorities. "This is a war measure," Polk cautioned,"and has no bearing upon the treaty rights of the United States to send troops to Cuba and to the Naval Station at any time it considers necessary." Frank L. Polk to American Legation, Havana, Cuba, July 12, 1917, 837.00/1394, DS/NA, RG 59.

8. William E. Gonzales to secretary of state, July 14, 1917, 837.00/1395, DS/NA, RG 59.

9. Frank L. Polk to Newton Baker, July 18, 1917, 837.00/1395, DS/NA, RG 59.

10. Robert Lansing to American Legation, Havana, Cuba, Aug. 17, 1917, 837.00/1407, DS/NA, RG 59.

11. Confidential War Diary, United States Naval Station, Guantánamo, Cuba, Aug. 1, 1917, to Aug. 30, 1917, NRC/NA, RG 45.

12. William E. Gonzales to Colonel J. E. Mahoney, United State Marine Corps, Jan. 3, 1918, 837.00/1455, DS/NA, RG 59.

13. Colonel M. J. Shaw, commanding officer, Seventh Regiment, to major general commandant, "Report of Operations," Nov. 3, 1917, 837.00/1398, DS/NA, RG 59.

14. "I get the impression," Colonel Shaw wrote in November 1917, "that in their hearts the Cubans do not welcome our advent into Cuban territory." Ibid.

15. William E. Gonzales to secretary of state, Oct. 13, 1917, 837.00/1428, DS/NA, RG 59.

16. William E. Gonzales to Colonel J. E. Mahoney, United States Marine Corps, Jan. 3, 1918, 837.00/1455, DS/NA, RG 59.

17. Colonel J. E. Mahoney to William E. Gonzales, Dec. 29, 1917, 837.00/1455; and William E. Gonzales to Colonel J. E. Mahoney, Jan. 3, 1918, 837.00/1455, DS/NA, RG 59.

18. Truman S. Strobridge, *A Brief History of the 9th Marines,* rev. ed. (United States

Marine Corps, Historical Reference Pamphlet, Washington, D.C., 1967), p. 1.

19. Paraphrase of telegram sent American minister, Oct. 8, 1917, Office of Secretary, Confidential Correspondence, 1917-1919, File C-22-8, Box 59, GRDN/NA, RG 80; "Intervention in Cuba Under the Platt Amendment," p. 19.

20. Colonel T. C. Treadwell, brigade commander, Santiago de Cuba, to major general commandant, Jan. 31, 1919, Records of the United States Marine Corps, Record Group 127, National Archives, Washington, D.C. (hereafter cited as USMC/NA, RG 127).

21. William E. Gonzales to Colonel M. J. Shaw, Mar. 7, 1918, 337.11/584, DS/NA, RG 59.

22. Metcalf, *A History of the United States Marine Corps*, p. 336; Harry A. Ellsworth, "One Hundred Eighty Landings of United States Marines, 1800-1934," (United States Marine Corps, Historical Section, 1934, Washington, D.C.), pp. 63-64.

23. See, for example, Captain F. D. Creamer, United States Marine Corps, to military attaché, "Military Information Covering Highway From Bayamo, Oriente," Nov. 2, 1918, File 2056-39, WD/NA, RG 165; commanding officer, 71st Company, to commanding officer, Dec. 7, 1919, 837.00/1444, DS/NA, RG 59.

24. Colonel M. J. Shaw, Seventh Regiment, "Conditions at Nipe Bay, Cuba and Vicinity," May 25, 1918, File C-22-26, GRND/NA, RG 80.

25. Colonel M. J. Shaw, Seventh Regiment, to William E. Gonzales, Feb. 28, 1918, 337.11/584, DS/NA, RG 59.

26. William E. Gonzales to Colonel M. J. Shaw, Mar. 7, 1918, 337.11/584, DS/NA, RG 59.

27. Colonel M. J. Shaw, Seventh Regiment, "Conditions at Nipe Bay, Cuba and Vicinity," May 25, 1918, File C-22-26, GRND/NA, RG 80.

28. William E. Gonzales to Colonel N. H. Hall, Nov. 27, 1918, File 2056-54, WD/NA, RG 165.

29. Ibid.

30. William E. Gonzales to Colonel N. H. Hall, Nov. 27, 1918, File 2056-24, WD/NA, RG 165. In the subsequent weeks, a dispute between the Legation and the Guantánamo Naval Station over final authority over marines reached Washington. The Navy Department refused to subordinate the marine brigade to the authority of the minister in Havana. "The Commandant at Guantanamo," Secretary Daniels insisted, "is [the] senior officer present to all forces operating in Cuba, consequently as long as he is senior to the commanding officer of the Marines, these Marines are under his direction." Out of interagency discussions in Washington, however, a compromise emerged whereby the legation would pass recommendations to the secretary of state, who would then request the appropriate action from the Navy Department. See Josephus Daniels to secretary of state, Dec. 21, 1918, 837.00/1502, DS/NA, RG 59.

31. Colonel M. J. Shaw to William E. Gonzales, Feb. 28, 1918, 337.11/584, DS/NA, RG 59.

32. Andrew DeGraux, special agent, Office of the Military Attaché, "Report on Trip Throughout the Island," Aug. 30, 1918, File 2056-188, WD/NA, RG 165.

33. Ibid.

34. Lieutenant Colonel Thomas Van Natta, Jr., to Colonel M. J. Shaw, Seventh Regiment, Sept. 8, 1918, File 10546-204, WD/NA, RG 165.

35. Ibid.

36. Lieutenant Colonel William Brackett to commanding officer, Seventh Regiment, Nov. 30, 1918, File 2056-Q-73, WD/NA, RG 165.

37. Henry H. Morgan, "Conditions of Crops in Northeastern End of Cuba," Sept. 4, 1917, 837.61351/35, DS/NA, RG 59.

38. Andrew DeGraux, special agent, Office of the Military Attaché, "Report on Trip Throughout the Island to Ascertain Facts Concerning Reported State of Unrest," Aug. 30, 1919, 837.00/1573, DS/NA, RG 59.

39. Olga Cabrera, *El movimiento obrero cubano en 1920* (Havana, 1970), pp. 51-58.

40. Major Alberto Gallatin to director of Military Intelligence, Dec. 12, 1918, File 10546-204(47), DW/NA, RG 165.

41. Harold D. Clum, American consul, Santiago de Cuba, to secretary of state, Dec. 3, 1918, File (1918) 850.4, Miscellaneous Correspondence, Santiago de Cuba, FSP/NA, RG 84.

42. Major Alberto Gallatin to military staff, Jan. 19, 1919, Series 6P, Box 1, Wilson Papers.

43. William E. Gonzales to secretary of state, Mar. 9, 1919, 837.504/118, DS/NA, RG 59.

44. William E. Gonzales to secretary of state, Mar. 9, 1919, 837.504/118, DS/NA, RG 59.

45. F. L. Mayer to Frank L. Polk, Dec. 12, 1918, 837.504/107, DS/NA, RG 59.

46. Major Albert Gallatin to military staff, Dec. 4, 1918, Series 6P, Box 1, Wilson Papers.

47. William E. Gonzales to secretary of state, Mar. 9, 1919, 837.504/118, DS/NA, RG 59.

48. Headquarters, United States Marine Corps, File C-298, USMC/NA, RG 127.

49. Josephus Daniels to secretary of state, Jan. 4, 1919, 837.504/82, DS/NA, RG 59; and Frank L. Polk to American Legation, Havana, Cuba, 837.504/185, DS/NA, RG 59.

50. Colonel M. J. Shaw, Seventh Regiment, to major general commandant, "Report of Operations, 7th Regiment," Dec. 15, 1917, File 2082-111:14, secretary of Navy, General Correspondence, 1916-1926, GRDN/NA, RG 80.

51. Colonel M. J. Shaw, Seventh Regiment, to major general commandant, Oct. 23, 1917, 837.00/1437, DS/NA, RG 59.

52. Vicente Martínez, president, Association of Machinists, and Francisco Domenech, delegate, Federation of Labor, to Samuel Gompers, Oct. 21, 1917, 837.504/35, DS/NA, RG 59. Cf. Pedro Luis Padrón, "Vandalismo de 'Marines' en la ocupación de Camagüey y Oriente desde 1917 hasta 1922," *Granma,* May 21, 1969, p. 2.

53. Major Alberto Gallatin to director, Military Intelligence, January 11, 1919, File 10546-204(90), DW/NA, RG 165.

54. Frank L. Polk to American Legation, Havana, Cuba, Jan. 14, 1918, 837.504/83a, DS/NA, RG 59.

55. William E. Gonzales to secretary of state, Jan. 24, 1919, 837.504/98, DS/NA, RG 59.

56. William E. Gonzales to secretary of state, Jan. 28, 1919, 837.504/101, DS/NA, RG 59.

57. E. D. Jones, commanding officer, U.S.S. *Eagle,* to commander, American Patrol Detachment, Feb. 10, 1919, File C-22-48, GRDN/NA, RG 59.

58. Consular district of Santiago de Cuba, "Monthly Report on Economic and Political Conditions," Jan. 31, 1919, File (1919) 850, Miscellaneous Correspondence, American Consulate, Santiago de Cuba, FSP/NA, RG 84.

59. E. D. Jones, commanding officer, U.S.S. *Eagle,* to commander, American Patrol Detachment, Feb. 10, 1919, File C-22-48, GRDN/NA, RG 80.

Chapter 7: Electoral Intervention in the Plattist System, 1919-1921

1. Frank L. Polk, confidential diary, Jan. 1, 1917-Feb. 15, 1919, Drawer 88, Polk Papers.

2. Frank L. Polk to American Legation, Havana, Cuba, Jan. 15, 1919, 837.00/1504a, DS/NA, RG 59.

3. Pablo Desvernine to Rutherford Bingham, Jan. 20, 1919, 837.00/1510, DS/NA, RG 59.

4. Frank L. Polk to American Legation, Havana, Cuba, Jan. 24, 1919, 837.00/1504a (supplemental), DS/NA, RG 59.

5. William E. Gonzales to Frank L. Polk, Feb. 4, 1919, File 243, Drawer 77, Polk Papers.

6. Ibid.

7. Crowder had gained considerable prestige in Cuba and Washington for his legal work during the second intervention, resulting in the electoral code of 1908. See David A. Lockmiller, *Enoch H. Crowder: Soldier, Lawyer and Statesmen* (Columbia, Mo., 1955), pp. 109-20.

8. William E. Gonzales to secretary of state, Feb. 12, 1919, 837.00/1514, DS/NA, RG 59; Lockmiller, *Enoch H. Crowder: Soldier, Lawyer and Statesmen,* p. 219.

9. Frank L. Polk, confidential diary, Feb. 16, 1919-Mar. 31, 1919, Drawer 88, Polk Papers.

10. Ibid.

11. For the full report of Crowder's findings see Enoch H. Crowder, "Report of Major General E. H. Crowder on Investigation of Electoral Laws in Cuba," Material on Cuba, File 1240-1247, Crowder Papers.

12. *Gaceta Oficial de la República* (edición extraordinaria), Aug. 12, 1919. Cf. Fernando Ortiz, "La reforma electoral de Crowder en Cuba," *La Reforma Social,* XX (July 1921), 214-25; and Enoch H. Crowder to secretary of state, Jan. 17, 1921, William M. Connor Papers, Box 13, Alderman Library, University of Virginia, Charlottesville, Virginia.

13. Major Harold E. Stephenson, "Report on Political Conditions," n.d., Material on Cuba, File 1207, Crowder Papers.

14. Cuba, Dirección General del Censo, *Censo de la República, 1919* (Havana, 1920).

15. Orestes Ferrara, "La lucha presidencial en Cuba," *La Reforma Social,* XVII (Aug. 1920), 349.

16. Carlos Mendieta, "Adios dictadura," in Marcos Suárez, *Carlos Mendieta,* pp. 129-33; Orestes Ferrera to secretary of state, Oct. 26, 1920, 837.00/1823, DS/NA, RG

59; Orestes Ferrara, "Supervision electoral o intervención permanente," *La Reforma Social*, XIII (Mar. 1919), 201-10.

17. José Miguel Gómez to Manuel Márquez Sterling, Dec. 21, 1918, 837.00/15Q5, DS/NA, RG 59. This letter was intercepted by postal censors in Key West.

18. *Diario de la Marina*, Feb. 1, 1919, p. 1; ibid., Feb. 3, 1919, p. 1; Leon Primelles, *Crónica cubana, 1919-1922* (Havana, 1957), p. 8.

19. Enoch H. Crowder to Newton Baker, July 19, 1919, Box 9, Baker Papers.

20. William Phillips to American Legation, Havana, Cuba, Oct. 23, 1919, 837.00/1581a, DS/NA, RG 59.

21. Ibid.

22. William E. Gonzales to secretary of state, Nov. 5, 1919, 837.00/1583, DS/NA, RG 59; Primelles, *Crónica cubana, 1919-1922*, p. 32.

23. Pablo Desvernine to Enoch H. Crowder, Nov. 17, 1919, File 186, Correspondence, Crowder Papers.

24. Enoch H. Crowder, "Memorandum for Dr. Rowe," Dec. 12, 1919, File 187, Correspondence, Crowder Papers.

25. William E. Gonzales to secretary of state, Nov. 7, 1919, 837.00/1590, DS/NA, RG 59.

26. Enoch H. Crowder to Frank Steinhart, Nov. 25, 1919, File 188, Correspondence, Crowder Papers.

27. Major Albert Gallatin, military attaché, to director of Military Intelligence, Jan. 27, 1919, 837.00/1524, DS/NA, RG 59.

28. William E. Gonzales to Frank L. Polk, Feb. 4, 1919, Drawer 77, File 243, Polk Papers.

29. Frank L. Polk, confidential diary, June 1, 1919-July 21, 1919, Drawer 88, Polk Papers.

30. Colonel Paul W. Beck, military attaché, to director of Military Intelligence, File 2056-176, WD/NA, RG 165.

31. Enoch H. Crowder to Frank M. Steinhart, Apr. 16, 1920, File 226, Correspondence, Crowder Papers.

32. Riera Hernández, *Cuba politica, 1899-1955*, pp. 265, 273.

33. Boaz W. Long to Leo S. Rowe, Mar. 20, 1920, 837.00/1639, DS/NA, RG 59.

34. Bainbridge Colby to American Legation, Havana, Cuba, Mar. 25, 1920, 837.00/1626 (Supplemental), DS/NA, RG 59; Daniel M. Smith, "Bainbridge Colby and the Good Neighbor Policy, 1920-1921," *The Mississippi Valley Historical Review*, L (June 1963), 67.

35. Boaz W. Long to secretary of state, Mar. 27, 1920, 837.00/1641, DS/NA, RG 59.

36. In "Memorandum on Platt Amendment," n.d., Box 35, White Papers.

37. Bainbridge Colby to American Legation, Havana, Cuba, Mar. 30, 1920, 837.00/1629, DS/NA, RG 59.

38. Demetrio Castillo Duany to Enoch H. Crowder, May 29, 1920, File 237, Correspondence, Crowder Papers.

39. Boaz L. Long to secretary of state, Mar. 29, 1920, 837.00/1643, DS/NA, RG 59.

40. Enoch H. Crowder to Frank M. Steinhart, Apr. 28, 1920, File 227, Correspondence, Crowder Papers. See Jacinto López, "El fracaso del General Crowder en

Cuba," *La Reforma Social,* XX (June 1921), 99-112.

41. Boaz W. Long to Frank L. Polk, Mar. 19, 1920, 837.00/1636, DS/NA, RG59.

42. Bainbridge Colby to American Legation, Havana, Cuba, Mar. 25, 1920, 837.00/ 1626 (Supplemental), DS/NA, RG 59; Smith, "Bainbridge Colby and the Good Neighbor Policy, 1920-1921," p. 67.

43. "Minutes of a Conference Held in Dr. Rowe's Office," Mar. 12, 1920, 837.00/ 1649, DS/NA, RG 59.

44. Boaz W. Long to secretary of state, Mar. 23, 1920, 837.00/1653, DS/NA, RG 59.

45. Bainbridge Colby to American Legation, Havana, Cuba, Mar. 29, 1920, 837.00/ 1641, DS/NA, RG 59.

46. Boaz W. Long to secretary of state, Apr. 5, 1920, 837.00/1652, RG 59.

47. Chapman, *A History of the Cuban Republic,* p. 360. Cf. Loló de la Torriente, "El mayoral, el chino y la Liga," *Granma,* Apr. 30, 1971, pp. 101-03.

48. Mario G. Menocal to William E. Gonzales, Dec. 23, 1920, Gonzales Papers; Boaz W. Long to secretary of state, Mar. 19, 1920, 837.00/1632, DS/NA, RG 59.

49. "Memorandum on the Platt Amendment," n.d., Box 35, White Papers.

50. Major Harold E. Stephenson to Enoch H. Crowder, July 19, 1920, File 247, Correspondence, Crowder Papers.

51. The *Havana Post,* Sept. 3, 1920, p. 1, reported learning that if the Conservatives failed to block Gómez at the polls, Menocal "would not hand over to him the reins of power on May 20 and would go to the extent of provoking a revolution and hand over the Republic to the Americans." Cf. Harold D. Clum, American consul, Santiago de Cuba, to Boaz W. Long, Oct. 1, 1920, 837.00/1808, DS/NA, RG 59.

52. "Minutes of Conference Held in Dr. Rowe's Office," Mar. 12, 1920, 837.00/ 1649, DS/NA, RG 59.

53. For the reorganization contemplated by Liberal party leaders see Fernando Ortiz to Enoch H. Crowder, May 26, 1919, File 151, Correspondence, Crowder Papers.

54. Pérez, *Army Politics in Cuba, 1898-1958,* pp. 34-43; Louis A. Pérez, Jr. "The Military and Electoral Politics: The Cuban Elections of 1920," *Military Affairs,* XXXVII (Feb. 1973), 5-8; Colonel Paul W. Beck, "Office Memorandum for Information of Successor," Apr. 15, 1920, File 2056-196, WD/NA, RG 165.

55. Charles E. Seijo, "Memorandum for Major Stephenson: Political Situation in Camaguey and Santa Clara," Oct. 27, 1920, File 266, Correspondence, Crowder Papers.

56. J. F. Buck, Consul, Antilla, to Harold D. Clum, June 28, 1920, File (1920) 800, Miscellaneous Correspondence, American Consulate, Santiago de Cuba, FSP/NA, RG 84. See also Jacinto López, "El problema del sufragio en Cuba," *La Reforma Social,* XIV (May 1919), 53.

57. "Brief Synopsis of Cuba's Present Internal Politics," Oct. 1919, Material on Cuba, File 1249, Crowder Papers.

58. Leo S. Rowe to Latin American Affairs Division, June 24, 1920, 837.00/1680, DS/NA, RG 59.

59. Guillermo Fernández Mascaró to Harold D. Clum, n.d. (received August 2, 1920), 837.00/1172, DS/NA, RG 59.

60. Boaz W. Long, "Memorandum of Interview with President Menocal and Dr. Desvernine," Mar. 27, 1920, 837.00/1646, DS/NA, RG 59.

61. Boaz W. Long to secretary of state, Apr. 5, 1920, 837.00/1652, DS/NA, RG 59.

62. Alvey A. Adee to Francis White, June 4, 1920, 837.00/1664, DS/NA, RG 59.

63. Bainbridge Colby to American Legation, Havana, Cuba, July 30, 1920, 837.00/1710, DS/NA, RG 59.

64. Norman H. Davis to Woodrow Wilson, Aug. 3, 1920, Box 3B, Bainbridge Colby Papers, Library of Congress, Manuscript Division, Washington, D.C.

65. Boaz W. Long to secretary of state, Sept. 16, 1920, 837.00/1766, DS/NA, RG 59.

66. Bainbridge Colby to Woodrow Wilson, Sept. 18, 1920, Box 3B, Colby Papers.

67. Leo S. Rowe to acting secretary of state, "Appointment of Six Temporary Assistants to Report to the American Minister at Havana with Reference to the Enforcement of the Crowder Election Law in Cuba," July 7, 1920, 837.00/1719, DS/NA, RG 59.

68. "Minutes of a Conference on the Cuban Electoral Situation," July 14, 1920, 837.00/1701, DS/NA, RG 59; Munro, *Intervention and Dollar Diplomacy in the Caribbean, 1900-1921,* pp. 510-11.

69. Bainbridge Colby to Woodrow Wilson, July 28, 1920, Box 3A, Colby Papers.

70. Division of Latin American Affairs to undersecretary of state, Aug. 27, 1920, 837.00/1764, DS/NA, RG 59.

71. Norman H. Davis to Woodrow Wilson, Oct. 16, 1920, Box 198, Series 2, Wilson Papers.

72. Francis White to secretary of state, Aug. 24, 1920, 837.00/1746, DS/NA, RG 59. See also *El Mundo,* Aug. 24, 1920, p. 1.

73. Bainbridge Colby to Francis White, Aug. 25, 1920, 837.00/1737, DS/NA, RG 59.

74. Boaz W. Long to Francis White, Aug. 25, 1920, 837.00/1737, DS/NA, RG 59.

75. Charles Evans Hughes, "Memorandum," Apr. 14, 1921, Box 174, File 65, Charles Evans Hughes Papers, Library of Congress, Manuscript Division, Washington, D.C.

76. See Carlos Manuel de Céspedes, Legación de Cuba, Washington, "Memorandum de mi conversación con el señor Secretario de Estado," Oct. 5, 1920, 837.00/1918.

77. Norman H. Davis to Boaz W. Long, Oct. 20, 1920, 837.00/1822d, DS/NA, RG 59.

78. Bainbridge Colby to American Legation, Havana, Cuba, Oct. 22, 1920, 837.00/1822a, DS/NA, RG 59.

79. Norman H. Davis to American Legation, Havana, Cuba, Oct. 25, 1920, 837.00/1826a, DS/NA, RG 59.

80. Bainbridge Colby to Boaz W. Long, Oct. 27, 1920, 837.00/1826, DS/NA, RG 59.

81. Norman H. Davis to American Legation, Oct. 28, 1920, 837.00/1826, DS/NA, RG 59.

82. Major Harold E. Stephenson to Enoch H. Crowder, Oct. 15, 1920, File 263, Correspondence, Crowder Papers. For accounts of the election by one American supervisor see Herbert J. Spinden, "Shall the United States Intervene in Cuba?" *The World's Week,* XLI (March 1921), 465-83; Herbert J. Spinden, "Elecciones espurias en Cuba," *La Reforma Social,* XIX (Apr. 1921), 353-67, and Herbert J. Spinden, "America and Her Duty in Cuba," *Boston Evening Transcript,* August 7, 1923, p. 13.

83. See J. R. Campina et al. to Bainbridge Colby, 837.00/1816, DS/NA, RG 59.

84. Boaz W. Long to secretary of state, Sept. 19, 1920, 837.00/1761, DS/NA, RG 59.

85. Boaz W. Long to secretary of state, Sept. 25, 1920, 837.00/1769, DS/NA, RG 59; Munro, *Intervention and Dollar Diplomacy in the Caribbean, 1900-1921*, pp. 514-15.

86. Major N. W. Campanole to director of Military Intelligence, General Staff, "Necessity of United States Troops in Cuba to Insure Maintenance of Law and Order," Sept. 27, 1920, File 2657-Q-27(3), WD/NA, RG 165.

87. Woodrow Wilson to Norman H. Davis, Oct. 18, 1920, Series 2, Box 198, Wilson Papers; Norman H. Davis to Boaz W. Long, Oct. 20, 1920, Norman H. Davis Papers, Library of Congress, Manuscript Division, Washington, D.C.

88. Newton Baker to Woodrow Wilson, Oct. 16, 1920, Box 3B, Colby Papers.

89. Boaz W. Long to secretary of state, Nov. 5, 1920, 837.00/1870, DS/NA, RG 59.

90. Bainbridge Colby to American Legation, Havana, Cuba, Nov. 16, 1920, 837.00/ 1876, DS/NA, RG 59.

91. Norman H. Davis to Enoch H. Crowder, Dec. 21, 1920, 837.00/1952b, DS/NA, RG 59.

92. Norman H. Davis to American Legation, Havana, Cuba, Dec. 31, 1920, 837.00/ 1947a, DS/NA, RG 59; Lockmiller, *Enoch H. Crowder: Soldier, Lawyer and Statesman*, pp. 228-29.

93. Boaz W. Long to secretary of state, Jan. 3, 1921, 837.00/1949, DS/NA, RG 59.

94. After a cabinet review of the Cuban crisis in the White House, the exasperated secretary of the navy recorded in his diary that "Marines had 4 yrs ago helped Menocal in when he was not elected." Several days later, Daniels added: "Truth is we put Menocal in 4 yrs ago when he could not have been elected & he thought he could bluff it through again." Cabinet Diaries, Daniels Papers.

95. Norman H. Davis to American Legation, Havana, Cuba, Jan. 4, 1920, 837.00/ 1949, DS/NA, RG 59.

96. Boaz W. Long to Norman H. Davis, Feb. 10, 1921, Box 40, Davis Papers. For the details of the activities of Crowder in Cuba in 1921 see Dana G. Munro, *The United States and the Caribbean Republics, 1921-1933* (Princeton, 1974), pp. 16-23, and Lockmiller, *Enoch H. Crowder: Soldier, Lawyer and Statesman*, pp. 230-32.

Chapter 8: Capital, Bureaucrats, and Policy: The Economic Contours of U.S.-Cuban Relations, 1913-1921

1. In William A. Williams, "The Large Corporations and American Foreign Policy," in David Horowitz, ed., *Corporations and the Cold War* (New York, 1969), p. 85.

2. Norman H. Davis, "Wanted: A Consistent Latin American Policy," *Foreign Affairs*, IX (July 1931), 553-54. For a general discussion of Wilson and Latin America see Burton I. Kaufman, "United States Trade and Latin America: The Wilson Years," *Journal of American History*, LVIII (September 1971), 342-63.

3. John Moody, *Moody's Analysis of Investment. Public Utilities and Industrials* (New York, 1917), p. 1644.

4. Edwin Atkins, *Sixty Years in Cuba* (Cambridge, Mass., 1926), p. 342; Benjamin Allen, *A Story of the Growth of E. Atkins and Company and the Sugar Industry in Cuba* (New York, 1925), pp. 32-33.

5. Pino-Santos, *El asalto a Cuba por la oligarquia financiera yanqui*, p. 80.

6. Franklin D. Roosevelt, longhand diary, Trip to Cuba, January 21-25, 1917, Papers as assistant secretary of the navy, Roosevelt Papers.

7. Robert W. Dunn, *American Foreign Investments* (New York, 1926), pp. 121-22.

8. These included Alfred Jaretzke, vice-president, Frederick Strauss, vice-president, and W. F. Corliss, secretary.

9. Arthur D. Dean, *William Nelson Cromwell* (New York, 1957), p. 62.

10. Sullivan and Cromwell to Robert Lansing, Mar. 1, 1917, 337.11/241, DS/NA, RG 59.

11. See the correspondence between Frederick R. Coudert and Frank L. Polk, Polk Papers.

12. Joseph S. Tulchin, *The Aftermath of War* (New York, 1971), p. 92.

13. Coudert Brothers to secretary of state, Feb. 26, 1917, 337.11/188, DS/NA, RG 59.

14. Walter S. Penfield to Robert Lansing, Mar. 21, 1917, 337.11/203, DS/NA, RG 59.

15. Isidore H. Lehman to Robert Lansing, Feb. 14, 1917, 337.11/203, DS/NA, RG 59.

16. John Foster Dulles to Robert Lansing, Feb. 14, 1917, 337.11/162, DS/NA, RG 59.

17. See Richard Schermerhorn, *Schermerhorn Geneology and Chronicle* (New York, 1914).

18. Minutes of Meeting of the Council of National Defense, June 8, 1917, Box 45, Daniels Papers.

19. "Securities Held by Mr. Davis," Box 14, Norman H. Davis Papers.

20. "Securities Held by Mrs. Davis," Box 14, Norman H. Davis Papers.

21. See William M. Whitner, manager, Insurance Department, Trust Company of Cuba, to Norman H. Davis, Box 63, Davis Papers.

22. Jones, "Carolinians and Cubans: The Elliotts and Gonzales, Their Work and Their Writings," pp. 598-99.

23. Robert Lansing to William G. McAdoo, Aug. 13, 1917, 837.57/279a, and Robert Lansing to American Legation, Havana, Cuba, Sept. 8, 1917, DS/NA, RG 59. Cf. Beals, *The Crime of Cuba,* p. 366.

24. By the early 1920s, all business groups with interests in Cuba demanded some sort of definite and settled policy toward the island. See Dwight W. Morrow to Herbert Hoover, Dec. 11, 1921, Cuba-Correspondence, 1921-1922, Dwight W. Morrow Papers, Amherst College, Amherst, Massachusetts.

25. Enoch H. Crowder to O. K. Davis, July 23, 1920, File 248, Correspondence, Crowder Papers.

26. Munro, *Intervention and Dollar Diplomacy in the Caribbean, 1900-1921,* p. 511.

27. Enoch H. Crowder to Robert J. Flick, July 21, 1920, File 247, Correspondence, and Enoch H. Crowder to Frank M. Steinhart, Aug. 13, 1920, File 253, Correspondence, Crowder Papers. Cf. Enoch H. Crowder to Philander C. Knox, Oct. 2, 1920, Box 30, General Correspondence, Philander C. Knox Papers, Library of Congress, Manuscript Division, Washington, D.C.

28. Demetrio Castillo Duany, "Memorandum for Major General Crowder," Aug. 24, 1919, File 167, Correspondence, Crowder Papers.

29. Major Harold E. Stephenson to Enoch H. Crowder, Sept. 14, 1920, File 258, Correspondence, Crowder Papers.

30. Enoch H. Crowder to Harold E. Stephenson, Sept. 25, 1920, File 258, Corre-

spondence, Crowder Papers.

31. Robert Lansing to Joseph P. Tumulty, May 14, 1916, 837.00/1784, DS/NA, RG 59.

32. *New York Sun,* Mar. 10, 1917, p. 3. In this timely interview, Menocal pledged to reimburse the bondholders of the Ports Company as well as the planters whose cane was destroyed in the February revolution.

33. Enoch H. Crowder to Colonel John H. Carroll, July 21, 1920, File 248, Correspondence, Crowder Papers. "I hate to be a part of a situation that is not open," Crowder wrote, "and hate to have any ground for thinking that our State Department is being utilized by the sugar interests in putting across a presidential election." Ibid. Cf. Theodore P. Wright, Jr. "The United States Electoral Intervention in Cuba," *Inter-American Economic Affairs,* XIII (Winter 1959), 66.

34. H. C. Lakin to Norman H. Davis, June 28, 1920, Box 11, Davis Papers.

Chapter 9: The Politico-Diplomatic Contours of U.S.-Cuban Relations, 1913-1921

1. "Report of the Committee Appointed to Confer With the Government of the United States, Giving an Account of its Labor," Subject File, Cuba, Elihu Root Papers, Library of Congress, Manuscript Division, Washington, D.C.

2. As late as 1929, Root remained committed to the original narrow interpretation of the Platt Amendment. See "Conversation with Mr. Root," Nov. 19, 1929, Jessup Papers.

3. Norman H. Davis to Woodrow Wilson, July 28, 1920, Box 3A, Colby Papers.

4. Davis, "Wanted: A Consistent Latin American Policy," p. 558.

5. Bainbridge Colby to Woodrow Wilson, July 28, 1920, 837.00/1860a, DS/NA, RG 59.

6. Enoch H. Crowder, "Report of Major General Enoch H. Crowder on Investigation of Electoral Laws in Cuba," n.d., Material on Cuba, File 1247, Crowder Papers. Crowder would later insist that administrative ineptitude threatened stable government as much as insurrection. See Enoch H. Crowder to John J. Pershing, Chief of Staff, Sept. 10, 1921, Box 56, General Correspondence, 1904-1948, John J. Pershing Papers, Library of Congress, Manuscript Division, Washington, D.C.

7. Enoch H. Crowder, "Suggestions for the Information of the American Minister," n.d., Material on Cuba, File 1219, Crowder Papers.

8. Sumner Welles, "Is America Imperialistic?" *Atlantic Monthly,* CXXIV (Sept. 1924), 414. For a general discussion of Welles's policy approaches to Latin America, see Thomas M. Millington, "The Latin American Diplomacy of Sumner Welles," (Ph.D. diss., John Hopkins School of Advanced International Studies, 1966), pp. 273-86.

9. W. Williamson to secretary of state, Jan. 7, 1920, 837.00/1612, DS/NA, RG 59.

10. Jacinto López, "La intervención en Cuba," *La Reforma Social,* XIX (Feb. 1921), 110-11.

11. Orestes Ferrara to secretary of state, May 13, 1918, 837.00, DS/NA, RG 59.

12. Faustino Guerra to secretary of state, Apr. 2, 1920, 837.00/1625, DS/NA, RG 59. Cf. Roberto Méndez Peñate, Eliseo Figueroa, and Rogelio Zayas Bazán to Woodrow Wilson, Jan. 18, 1918, 837.00/1456, DS/NA, RG 59.

13. Varona had long been conscious of the perils of *personalismo* to the structure of political parties in Cuba. See Enrique José Varona, ''Nuestra 'enquete' política: respuesta del Dr. Enrique José Varona,'' *Gráfico,* III (May 9, 1914), p. 7.

14. William Phillips, *Ventures in Diplomacy* (Boston, 1952), p. 68.

Bibliography

Unpublished Materials

I. Archival Sources

National Archives. General Records of the Department of Navy. Record Group 80.
————. General Records of the Department of State. Record Group 59.
————. Naval Records Collection of the Office of Naval Records and Library. Record Group 45.
————. Records of the Adjutant General's Office. Record Group 94.
————. Records of the Foreign Service Posts of the Department of State. Record Group 84.
————. Records of the United States Marine Corps. Record Group 127.
————. Records of the War Department General and Special Staff. Record Group 165.

II. Manuscript Collections

Newton D. Baker Papers. Library of Congress, Washington, D.C.
William D. Beer Papers. Sterling Memorial Library, Yale University, New Haven, Connecticut.
Reginald R. Belknap Papers. Library of Congress, Washington, D.C.
Bainbridge Colby Papers. Library of Congress, Washington, D.C.
William M. Connor Papers. Alderman Library, University of Virginia, Charlottesville, Virginia.
Enoch H. Crowder Papers. Western Historical Manuscript Collection, University of Missouri, Columbia, Missouri.
Josephus Daniels Papers. Library of Congress, Washington, D.C.
Norman H. Davis Papers. Library of Congress, Washington, D.C.
William E. Gonzales Papers. South Caroliniana Library, University of South Carolina, Columbia, South Carolina.
Edward M. House Papers. Sterling Memorial Library, Yale University, New Haven, Connecticut.
Charles Evans Hughes Papers. Library of Congress, Washington, D.C.
Philip C. Jessup Papers. Library of Congress, Washington, D.C.
Philander C. Knox Papers. Library of Congress, Washington, D.C.
Robert Lansing Papers. Library of Congress, Washington, D.C.
Dwight Morrow Papers. Robert Frost Library, Amherst College, Amherst, Massachusetts.

John J. Pershing Papers. Library of Congress, Washington, D.C.
Frank L. Polk Papers. Sterling Memorial Library, Yale University, New Haven, Connecticut.
Franklin D. Roosevelt Papers. Franklin D. Roosevelt Library, Hyde Park, New York.
Elihu Root Papers. Library of Congress, Washington, D.C.
Hugh L. Scott Papers. Library of Congress, Washington, D.C.
Francis White Papers. National Archives, Washington, D.C.
James H. Wilson Papers. Library of Congress, Washington, D.C.
Woodrow Wilson Paper. Library of Congress, Washington, D.C.

III. Theses and Manuscripts

Cuba. Constituent Assembly. "Record of Sessions of the Constitutional Convention of the Island of Cuba." 7 vols. Bureau of Insular Affairs Library, National Archives, Washington, D.C.
Dubé, Joseph A. "The Cuban Ports Company." 1973. Copy in author's possession.
Ellsworth, Harry A. "One Hundred Eight Landings of United States Marines, 1800-1934." United States Marine Corps, Headquarters, Historical Section, Washington, D.C., 1934.
Gibean, Victor Hugo, Jr. "Relations of Cuba with the United States, 1916-1921." Ph.D. diss., University of North Carolina, 1953.
"Intervention in Cuba Under the Platt Amendment." United States Marine Corps, Headquarters, Historical Section, Washington, D.C., n.d.
Jones, Lewis Pinckney. "Carolinians and Cubans: The Elliotts and Gonzales, Their Work and Their Writings." Ph.D. diss., University of North Carolina, 1952.
Meyer, Leo J. "Relations Between the United States and Cuba from 1895 to 1917." Ph.D. diss. Clark University, 1928.
Millington, Thomas M. "The Latin American Diplomacy of Sumner Welles." Ph.D. diss., Johns Hopkins School of Advanced International Studies, 1966.

Published Materials

I. Public Documents

Cuba. *Census of the Republic of Cuba, 1919.* Havana: Maza, Arroyo y Caso, 1920.
Cuba. Dirección General del Censo. *Censo de la República de Cuba, 1907.* Washington, D.C.: GPO, 1908.
Cuba. *Gaceta Oficial de la República.*
Cuba. *Memoria de la administración del Presidente de la República de Cuba durante el período comprendido entre el 1° de julio de 1917 el 30 de junio de 1918.* Havana, 1921.
Cuba. Secretaria de Estado. *Colección legislatura. Leyes, decretos y resoluciones.* Havana, 1899-.
Cuba. Secretaria de Hacienda. Sección de Estadística. *Inmigración y movimiento de pasajeros en el año . . . 1913-1921.* Havana, 1914-1922.
Taft, William Howard, and Bacon, Robert. "Cuban Pacification: Report of William H. Taft, Secretary of War, and Robert Bacon, Assistant Secretary of State, of What

Was Done Under the Instructions of the President in Restoring Peace in Cuba,'' Appendix E, *Report of the Secretary of War, 1906*. 59th Congress, 2nd sess., House Document Number 2, Series 5105. Washington, D.C., 1906.

United States Congress. *Congressional Record.*

United States Congress. *Statutes at Large (1903-1905).*

United States Department of State. *Foreign Relations of the United States.* 1913-1921. Washington, D.C.

United States Department of War. Director of Census of Cuba. *Census of Cuba, 1899.* Washington, 1900.

II. Memoirs, Autobiographies, and Reminiscences

Atkins, Edwin. *Sixty Years in Cuba*. Cambridge, Mass.: Riverside Press, 1926.

Cabrera, Raimundo. *Mis malos tiempos*. Havana: Imp. El Siglo XX, 1920.

Casuso, Teresa. *Cuba and Castro*. Trans. Elmer Grossberg. New York: Random House, 1961.

Consuegra, Wilfredo Ibrahim. *Hechos y comentarios. La revolución de febrero de 1917 en Las Villas*. Havana: La Comercial, 1920.

Daniels, Josephus. *The Cabinet Diaries of Josephus Daniels, 1913-1921*. Lincoln: University of Nebraska Press, 1963.

Duque, Matías. *Ocios del presidio, 1917*. Havana: Imp. Avisador Comercial, 1919.

Ferrara y Merino, Orestes. *Memorias: una mirada sobre tres siglos*. Madrid: Colección Plaza Mayor, 1976.

Ferrer, Horacio. *Con el rifle al hombro*. Havana: Imp. El Siglo XX, 1950.

Gonzales, William E. *Concerning Dollar Diplomacy, Crooks and Grafters. Incidents. Paper Read by William E. Gonzales Before the Kosmos Club of Columbia, Relating Experiences While Minister to Cuba and Ambassador to Peru*. Colmbia, S.C.: n.p., 1930.

Lansing, Robert. *The War Memoirs of Robert Lansing, Secretary of State*. New York: Bobbs-Merrill, 1935.

Menéndez Roque, Vicente. *Otros días*. Havana: n.p., 1962.

Phillips, William. *Ventures in Diplomacy*. Boston: Beacon Press, 1952.

Solano Alvarez, Luis. *Mi actuación militar. Apuntes para la historia de la revolución de febrero de 1917*. Havana: Imp. El Siglo XX, 1920.

Torriente, Cosme de la. *Cuarenta años de mi vida*. Havana: Imp. El Siglo XX, 1939.

Torriente, Loló de la. *Mi casa en la tierra*. Havana: Imp. Ucar, Garcia, S.A., 1956.

III. Newspapers

El Cubano Libre
Diario de la Marina
The Havana Post
Heraldo de Cuba
London Times
La Lucha
El Mundo
New York Evening Post

New York Sun
New York Times
New York World
The State (Columbia, S.C.)
Times of Cuba

IV. Books

Allen, Benjamin. *A Story of the Growth of E. Atkins & Company and the Sugar Industry in Cuba*. New York: n.p., 1925.

Barbarrosa, Enrique. *El proceso de la República*. Havana: Imp. Militar, 1911.

Buttari Gaunard, J. *Boceto crítico histórico*. Havana: Editorial Lex, 1954.

Cabrera, Olga. *El movimiento obrero cubano en 1920*. Havana: Instituto Cubano del Libro, 1970.

Cárdenas, Raúl de. *Como funcionó la cláusula intervencionista de la Enmienda Platt*. Havana: L. Ruiz, 1948.

Chapman, Charles E. *A History of the Cuban Republic*. New York: Octagon Books, 1969.

Collazo, Enrique. *La revolución de agosto de 1906*. Havana: Imp. C. Martínez y Cía., 1907.

Cortina, José Manuel. *La reelección presidencial*. Havana: Imp. El Siglo XX, 1916.

Dean, Arthur H. *William Nelson Cromwell*. New York: n.p., 1957.

Dolz y Arango, Ricardo. *El proceso electoral de 1916*. Havana: Imp. de Ruiz y Ca., 1917.

Dunn, Robert W. *American Foreign Investments*. New York: Viking Press, 1926.

Fitzgibbon, Russell H. *Cuba and the United States 1900-1935*. New York: Russell & Russell, 1964.

Guerra y Sánchez, Ramiro. *Sugar and Society in the Caribbean: An Economic History of Cuban Agriculture*. New Haven: Yale University Press, 1964.

Guggenheim, Harry F. *The United States and Cuba*. New York: Macmillan, 1934.

Heinl, Robert Debs, Jr. *Soldiers of the Sea: The United States Marine Corps, 1775-1962*. Annapolis: U.S. Naval Institute, 1962.

Hobsbawm, Eric J. *Primitive Rebels*. New York: W. W. Norton, 1959.

Horrego Estuch, Leopoldo. *Juan Gualberto Gómez, un gran inconforme*. 2nd ed. Havana: Editorial La Milagrosa, 1954.

Jenks, Leland Hamilton. *Our Cuban Colony*. New York: Arno, 1970.

Jerez Villarreal, Juan. *Oriente (biografía de una provincia)*. Havana: Imp. El Siglo XX, 1960.

Knight, Franklin W. *Slave Society in Cuba During the Nineteenth Century*. Madison: University of Wisconsin Press, 1970.

Lockmiller, David A. *Enoch H. Crowder: Soldier, Lawyer and Statesman*. Columbia: University of Missouri Press, 1955.

Marcos Suárez, Miguel de. *Carlos Mendieta*. Havana: n.p., 1923.

Márquez Sterling, M. *Proceso histórico de la Enmienda Platt (1897-1934)*. Havana: Imp. El Siglo XX, 1934.

Martí, Carlos. *Forjando partria*. Havana: Maza y Cía., 1917.

Martínez Fraga, Pedro. *El General Menocal*. *Apuntes para su biografía*. Havana: Talleres de Editorial Tiempo, 1941.

Merino, Bernardo, and Ibarzabal, F. de. *La revolución de febrero. Datos para la historia.* 2nd ed. Havana: Librería Cervantes, 1918.

Metcalf, Clyde H. *A History of the United States Marine Corps.* New York: G. Putnam's Sons, 1939.

Moody, John. *Moody's Analysis of Investment. Public Utilities and Industrials.* New York: Moody's Investment Service, 1917.

Munro, Dana G. *Intervention and Dollar Diplomacy in the Caribbean, 1900-1921.* Princeton, N.J.: Princeton University Press, 1964.

––––––. *The United States and the Caribbean Republics, 1921-1933.* Princeton, N.J.: Princeton University Press, 1974.

Navas, José. *La convulsión de febrero.* Matanzas: Imp. y Monotypo El Escritorio, 1917.

Núñez Jiménez, Antonio. *Geografía de Cuba.* 2nd ed. Havana: Editorial Lex, 1959.

Pérez, Louis A., Jr. *Army Politics in Cuba, 1898-1958.* Pittsburgh, Pa.: University of Pittsburgh Press, 1976.

Pérez de la Riva, Francisco. *Origen y régimen de la propiedad territorial en Cuba.* Havana: Editorial Lex, 1946.

Pino-Santos, Oscar. *El asalto a Cuba por la oligarquía financiera yanqui.* Havana: Casa de las Américas, 1973.

Primelles, León. *Crónica cubana, 1915-1918.* Havana: Editorial Lex, 1955.

––––––. *Crónica cubana, 1919-1922.* Havana: Editorial Lex, 1957.

Riera Hernández, Mario. *Cuba política, 1899-1955.* Havana: Impresora Modelo, 1955.

Rodríguez Altunaga, Rafael. *El General Emilio Núñez.* Havana: Sociedad Colombista Panamericana, 1958.

Rodríguez Morejón, Gerardo. *Menocal.* Havana: Cárdenas y Cía., 1941.

Roig, Enrique. *Los acontecimientos políticos de 1917 y el problema de la amnistía.* Havana: Imp. Avisador Comercial, 1918.

Roig de Leuchsenring, Emilio. *Historia de la Enmienda Platt.* 2 vols. 2nd ed. Havana: Oficina del Historiador de la Ciudad, 1961.

Santos Fernández, Juan. *La vida rural.* Havana: n.p., 1960.

Santovenia, Emeterio. *José Miguel Gómez.* Havana: Imp. El Siglo XX, 1958.

Santovenia, Emeterio, and Shelton, Raúl M. *Cuba y su historia.* 3 vols. 3rd ed., Miami: Cuba Corporation, Inc., 1966.

Schermerhorn, Richard. *Schermerhorn Genealogy and Family Chronicle.* New York: T. A. Wright, 1914.

Smith, Daniel M. *Aftermath of War. Bainbridge Colby and Wilsonian Diplomacy, 1920-1921.* Philadelphia: American Philosophical Society, 1970.

Smith, Robert F. *The United States and Cuba: Business and Diplomacy, 1917-1960.* New Haven: College and University Press, 1960.

Strobridge, Truman R. *A Brief History of the 9th Marines.* Washington, D.C.: United States Marines, Historical Section, 1967.

Thomas, Hugh. *Cuba, The Pursuit of Freedom.* New York: Harper & Row, 1971.

Tulchin, Joseph S. *The Aftermath of War.* New York: New York University Press, 1971.

Varona José Enrique. *De la colonia a la República.* Havana: Editorial Cuba Contemporánea, 1919.

Wright, Philip G. *The Cuban Situation and Our Treaty Relations*. Washington, D.C.: The Brookings Institution, 1931.

V. Articles

Baker, George. "The Wilson Administration and Cuba, 1913-1921." *Mid-America*, XXXXVI (Jan. 1964), 48-63.

Batchelder, Robert B. "The Evolution of Cuban Land Tenure and Its Relation to Certain Agro-Economic Problems." *The Southwestern Social Science Quarterly*, XXXIII (Dec. 1952), 238-46.

Blanck, Willy de. "Wilson — Cuba." *Cuba Contemporánea*, XIX (Mar. 1919), 264-75.

Brooks, Sydney. "An English View of Cuba." *Forum*, XXXVI (Oct. 1911), 461-70.

_____. "Some Impressions of Cuba." *North American Review*, CIC (May 1914), 734-45.

Cabrera, Raimuno. "How a Corrupt and Misguided Government Retards Cuba." *New York World*, Dec. 5, 1915, p. E-1.

Carrión, Miguel. "El desenvolvimiento social de Cuba en los últimos veinte años." *Cuba Contemporánea*, XXVII (Sept. 1921), 5-27.

Céspedes, José María. "Empleo-manía." *Cuba y América*, III (Apr. 20, 1899), 6-8.

Chapman, Charles E. "New Corollaries of the Monroe Doctrine." *University of California Chronicle*, XXXIII (Apr. 1931), 161-89.

"Civil War in Cuba." *The Independent*, XIC (Feb. 26, 1917), 344.

Cortina, José Miguel. "Por la justicia, por el derecho, por la libertad." *Cuba Contemporánea*, XIV (June 1917), 89-95.

Coyula, Miguel. "Los gobiernos de Cuba: Mario G. Menocal." *Bohemia*, XXX (June 5, 1938), 44-45, 110-14.

"Cuban Government Triumphant." *The Independent*, XIC (Mar. 19, 1917), 480.

Davis, Norman H. "Wanted: A Consistent Latin American Policy." *Foreign Affairs*, IX (July 1931), 547-69.

Ferrera, Orestes. "Las elecciones de Cuba y el gobierno de Wáshington." *La Reforma Social*, XVIII (Oct. 1920), 125-31.

Ferrara, Orestes. "El gobierno de Wáshington y las elecciones en Cuba y Nicaragua." *La Reforma Social*, XIX (Jan. 1921), 28-35.

_____. "La lucha presidencial en Cuba." *La Reforma Social*, XVII (Aug. 1920), 357-60.

_____. "Los métodos coloniales de España en Cuba reproducidos por los Estados Unidos." *La Reforma Social*, XXI (Oct. 1921), 148-52.

_____. "Supervisión electoral o intervención permanente." *La Reforma Social*, XII (Mar. 1919), 201-10.

"A Gentle Hint to Cuba." *The Literary Digest*, LXVIII (Jan. 22, 1921), 14-15.

Guas, Carlos. "¿Quien ordenó el levantamiento de febrero?" *El Mundo*, June 17, 1919, p. 16.

"La guerrita de febrero de 1917." *Boletín del Archivo Nacional*, LXI (Jan.-Dec. 1962), 207-56.

Guiral Moreno, Mario. "El problema de la burocracia en Cuba." *Cuba Contemporánea*, II (Aug. 1913), 257-67.

"Gustavo Caballero: 'cadaver' por anticipado." *Granma,* Oct. 25, 1969, p. 2.

Hill, Edwin C. "Love and a Little Luck Thwarted the Cuban Rebels." *New York Sun,* V, Mar. 18, 1917, p. 3.

Hoernel, Robert B. "Sugar and Social Change in Oriente, Cuba, 1898-1946." *Journal of Latin American Studies,* VIII (Nov. 1976), 215-49.

"A Hornets' Nest in Cuba." *The Literary Digest,* LIV (Feb. 24, 1917), 455-56.

Kaufman, Burton I. "United States Trade and Latin America: The Wilson Years." *Journal of American History,* LVIII (Sept. 1971), 342-63.

Kling, Merle. "Toward a Theory of Power and Political Instability in Latin America." *Western Historical Quarterly,* IX (Mar. 1956), 21-35.

Lavedán, Enrique. "Los ladrones de tierra en Oriente." *Gráfico,* III (Feb. 7, 1914), 10.

León Waldemar. "Caicaje: batalla final de una revuelta." *Bohemia,* LIX (June 30, 1967), 100-02, 113.

López, Jacinto. "Los Estados Unidos y las naciones del Caribe." *La Reforma Social,* XVII (July 1920), 232-47.

————. "El fracaso del General Crowder en Cuba." *La Reforma Social,* XX (June 1921), 99-112.

————. "La intervención en Cuba." *La Reforma Social,* XIX (Feb. 1921), 103-16.

————. "Los pactos de Wáshington." *La Reforma Social,* XXVI (June 1923), 99-120.

————. "El problema del sufragio en Cuba." *La Reforma Social,* XIV (May 1919), 53-56.

Loret de Mola, Luis. "Sobre la guerra civil de 1917: memorandum." *Boletín del Archivo Nacional,* LX (Jan.-Dec. 1961), 179-86.

Martínez, José A. "La entrada de Cuba en la Guerra Universal." *Cuba Contemporánea,* XIV (May 1917), 5-11.

Martínez Ortiz, Rafael. "Juicio acerca de los sucesos políticos de Cuba en 1906." *Cuba Contemporánea,* XV (Oct. 1917), 118-30.

Marvin, George. "Keeping Cuba Libre." *The World's Week,* XXXIV (Sept. 1917), 553-67.

Menocal, Mario G. "Cuba's Part in the World War." *Current History,* IX (Nov. 1918), 315-18.

Meyer, Leo J. "The United States and the Cuban Revolution of 1917." *The Hispanic American Historical Review,* X (Feb. 1930), 138-66.

Ortiz, Fernando. "La crisis política cubana. Sus causas y remedios." *Revista Bimestre Cubana,* XIV (Jan.-Feb. 1919), 5-22.

Ortiz, Fernando. "La reforma electoral de Crowder en Cuba." *La Reforma Social,* XX (July 1921), 214-25.

Padrón, Pedro Luis. "El 'cambio de paquetes' de Menocal, en 1916." *Granma,* Oct. 24, 1969, p. 2.

————. "El escandaloso robo del dragado organizado por José Miguel Gómez y su asociado yanqui Norman Davis." *Granma,* Dec. 26, 1968, p. 2.

————. "La sublevación liberal de 1917." *Granma,* Oct. 25, 1969, p. 2.

————. "Vandalismo de 'Marines' en la ocupación de Camagüey y Oriente desde 1917 hasta 1922." *Granma,* May 21, 1969, p. 2.

Pardo, Suárez, Vicente. "La elección presidencial en Cuba (I)." *La Reforma Social,* VI

(Jan. 1916), 187-205.

――――. "La elección presidencial en Cuba (II)." *La Reforma Social,* VIII (Nov. 1916), 499-520.

――――. "La elección presidencial en Cuba (III)." *La Reforma Social,* IX (Dec. 1916), 104-05.

Pérez, Louis A., Jr. "The Military and Electoral Politics: The Cuban Election of 1920." *Military Affairs,* XXXVII (Feb. 1973), 5-8.

Portell Vilá, Herminio. "La Chambelona en Camagüey." *Bohemia,* LII (May 8, 1960), 12-13, 119.

――――. "La Chambelona en Las Villas." *Bohemia,* LII (May 15, 1960), 36-37, 98.

――――. "La Chambelona en Occidente." *Bohemia,* LII (May 22, 1960), 36-37, 82.

――――. "La Chambelona en Oriente." *Bohemia,* LII (Apr. 24, 1960), 12-13, 124.

――――. "La danza de los millones." *Bohemia,* LII (June 5, 1960), 44-45, 79.

Rippy, J. Fred. "British Investments in Central America, the Dominican Republic and Cuba: A Story of Meager Returns." *Inter-American Economic Affairs,* VI (Autumn 1952), 89-98.

Roig de Leuchsenring, Emilio. "La Enmienda Platt: su interpretación primitiva y sussap-licaciones posteriores." *Anuario de la Sociedad Cubana de Derecho Internacional,* V (1922), 311-62.

――――. "La ingerencia norteamericana en los asuntos interiores de Cuba." *Cuba Contemporánea,* XXX (Sept. 1922), 36-61.

Rubiera, Guillermo. "Mario García Menocal y Deop." In Vicente Báez, ed., *La enciclopedia de Cuba.* 9 vols. Madrid, 1975. Vol. IX, 125-234.

Scott, James Brown. "The Attitude of the United States Toward Political Disturbances in Cuba." *The American Journal of International Law,* XI (Apr. 1917), 419-23.

Smith, Daniel M. "Bainbridge Colby and the Good Neighbor Policy, 1920-1921." *The Mississippi Valley Historical Review,* L (June 1963), 56-78.

Spinden, Herbert J. "America and Her Duty in Cuba." *Boston Evening Transcript,* Aug. 7, 1923, p. 13.

――――. "Elecciones espurias en Cuba" *La Reforma Social,* XIX (Apr. 1921), 353-67.

――――. "Shall the United States Intervene in Cuba?" *The World's Work,* XLI (Mar. 1921), 465-83.

Torriente, Loló de la. "El mayoral, el chino y la Liga," *Granma,* Apr. 30, 1971, pp. 101, 103.

Varona, Enrique José. "Nuestra 'enquete' política: respuesta del Dr. Enrique José Varona." *Gráfico,* III (May 9, 1914), 7.

Villoldo, Julio. "Las reelecciones." *Cuba Contemporánea,* X (Mar. 1916), 237-52.

Welles, Sumner. "Is America Imperialistic?" *Atlantic Monthly,* CXXXIV (Sept. 1924), 412-23.

Williams, William Appleman. "The Large Corporations and American Foreign Policy." In David Horowitz, ed., *Corporations and the Cold War.* New York, 1969, pp. 71-104.

Wright, Theodore P., Jr. "Free Elections in the Latin American Policy of the United States." *Political Science Quarterly,* LVIII (Mar. 1959), 89-112.

――――. "United States Electoral Intervention in Cuba." *Inter-American Economic Af-*

fairs, XIII (Winter 1959), 50-71.

X [John R. Caldwell]. ''Our 'Ruthless' Action in Cuba.'' *Pearson's Magazine,* XXXVIII (July 1917), 2.

Index

Pitt Latin American Series
Cole Blasier, Editor

My Missions for Revolutionary Bolivia, 1944-1962
Victor Andrade

The Overthrow of Allende and the Politics of Chile, 1964-1976
Paul E. Sigmund

Panajachel: A Guatemalan Town in Thirty-Year Perspective
Robert E. Hinshaw

The Politics of Social Security in Brazil
James M. Malloy

Puerto Rico and the United States, 1917-1933
Truman R. Clark

Revolutionary Change in Cuba
Carmelo Mesa-Lago, Editor

Selected Latin American One-Act Plays
Francesa Colecchia and Julio Matas, Editors and Translators

Social Security in Latin America: Pressure Groups, Stratification, and Inequality
Carmelo Mesa-Lago

Society and Education in Brazil
Robert J. Havighurst and J. Roberto Moreira

The United States and Cuba: Hegemony and Dependent Development, 1800-1934
Jules Robert Benjamin